SWANSEA BOX
(1916-2010)

SWANSEA BOXERS
(1916-2010)

Jeff Burns

DINEFWR
PUBLISHERS

Published in 2011
in the United Kingdom by
Dinefwr Publishers
Rawlings Road, Llandybie
Carmarthenshire, SA18 3YD

A catalogue record for this book
is available from The British Library.

ISBN 978-1-904323-22-8

Printed in Wales by
Dinefwr Press Ltd.
Rawlings Road, Llandybie
Carmarthenshire, SA18 3YD

To my grandchildren
Chelsey, Joel and Lowri Burns

CONTENTS

FOREWORD

I first met Jeff Burns in 1975 when on duty as a nineteen-year-old policeman I visited one of Swansea's busiest bars, the Buccaneer, which was the public bar of the Dolphin Hotel. Jeff was the manager of the Buccaneer having worked his way up from his previous role as part-time doorman. Jeff was also a professional boxer who at that time was inactive due to an injury to his right hand. Jeff claimed he had broken his hand on the head of stablemate Chuck Jones during one of their intense sparring sessions at the Gwent Amateur Boxing Club which I am told were as good as any 'nobbins' fight. What impressed me most about Jeff was how much respect he commanded for a man of such diminutive stature, he stood just five feet five inches tall.

We have remained good friends ever since and met regularly at John Burns' gym from around about 2003 where we both worked out and it was always my pleasure to enjoy a good few bottles of Bud with him on a Friday night. Even after a good session around the bars of Wind Street we would both be in the gym on Saturday morning 'sweating it out', our way of getting rid of a hangover.

Jeff was approaching his sixtieth birthday, his retirement as a Regional Officer with the GMB Union was impending, and he would often ask me how he would fill his time when he finished work. I knew that Jeff had an extensive knowledge of boxing history and was very proud of the achievements of Swansea boxers. I suggested to him that he should write a book about our local pugilistic heroes. He has often cursed me as he has toiled through the archives, but I am delighted that he took up the challenge and has produced this book which will I have no doubt be greatly appreciated by all the members of this special club – boxers, trainers, managers, promoters and most importantly boxing fans.

Jeff was particularly kind to his friend, the late Neville Meade, former British heavyweight champion, who sadly passed away while this book was being written. Accompanied by his friend Jimmy Bromfield he visited Neville in Singleton Hospital shortly before he died and presented him with a transcript of a section of this book that covered the former British heavyweight champ's career; he was very pleased with what had been written about him.

In conclusion, I convey my great respect to all you Swansea boxers, including Jeff 'Bulldog' Burns, a gentleman and true friend to many. Congratulations.

Phil Lake
(Managing Director
Lakeside Securities)

INTRODUCTION

Swansea Boxers is not intended to be a record book or a directory but is written and compiled to highlight the careers of professional boxers who inhabited the City previously the Town of Swansea. The book does not portray a comprehensive history of professional boxing in Swansea but relies on computer records, newspaper archives and human memory for data, information, pictures and the personal recollections of boxers, trainers, managers, promoters, local fight fans and the families and friends of Swansea boxers, who boxed out of Swansea between the turn of the last century until the end of 2010. There may well be notable exclusions of professional boxers resident in Swansea who have not been identified in the research facilities at my disposal and because of the pressure that local fight fans had placed upon me to complete this project, exclusion is not based on any other reason.

Swansea Boxers is not exclusively about champions or even ranked contenders but attempts to study the records of the subjects of this book, it can best be described as a written profile of the career records of professional boxers domiciled in the City. Swansea has a former World WBU and WBO champion, two ex-European champions, previous Commonwealth champions, a number of past and present British and Welsh champions to boast about. In this book these champions are depicted alongside those four, six and eight round fighters who had never or not yet been acclaimed a champion but who proudly entered a professional boxing ring and were or are announced as boxing out of Swansea.

Swansea Boxers also appreciates that boxers very rarely commence their boxing careers in the professional ring but most served their 'apprenticeships' in the amateur ranks under the unpaid but dedicated coaching and mentoring of trainers of the amateur boxing clubs. Many of the subjects of this book have been the beneficiaries of the pre professional nurturing and development of their boxing skills.

Swansea Boxers have, prior to joining the paid ranks, gained considerable status by representing Great Britain at the Olympic Games, representing their respective countries at the Commonwealth Games, the ABA Championships, also in International and Representative tournaments and some have won titles at schoolboy and junior level.

Swansea Boxers notes the enthusiastic involvement of Swansea-based promoters, managers and trainers in supporting and enhancing the aspirations and achievements of the subjects of this book. The financial risks they may have to take, the matchmaking nuance, boxing knowledge, coaching and training techniques they have to acquaint themselves with, not least the many hours that are spent by the boxer's team and the various other factors that have been and are integral to the development promotion and success of Swansea boxers.

Swansea Boxers identifies and locates the various venues where Professional boxing matches have been held in the old town and now City of Swansea and also the gymnasiums where Swansea boxers trained in preparation for their contests. I have deliberately excluded the activities of pre-war and early post-war Swansea boxers in the boxing booths due to hazy memories and the lack of accurate record keeping.

Swansea Boxers pays regard to all those promoters, managers, trainers, local fight fans and of course the boxers who have through the last and in this century placed and kept Swansea on the professional boxing map.

The writer is not a historian, a researcher or an author, just an ex-professional boxer recording the proud achievements of Swansea boxers.

Jeff Burns

ACKNOWLEDGEMENTS

Swansea Boxers is the first book of its kind that chronicles the records and accomplishments of one hundred and thirty-five boxers, and it would never have been possible to research, to write, and to illustrate without the help of so many people.

First of all I must thank my friend Phil Lake who give me the idea and set me the task a little while before my retirement as a GMB Union Regional Officer.

I would like to thank another friend, Jimmy Bromfield, who has been very supportive in assisting me with my research and providing me with photographs. He can be proud of the part he has played in enhancing the careers of Swansea boxers.

Eddie Richards, Colin Breen, Rocky Reynolds, Trevor Russell, Paul Boyce, David George, Billy Wilde, John Rees, Alan Couch, Ray Morgan, Malcolm Black, Peter St John and Brian Grey have all been of considerable assistance to me in providing information and photographs about and of Swansea boxers.

I offer special thanks to the *South Wales Evening Post* for their support in offering advice and providing me with photographs that have added some spice to *Swansea Boxers*. I am also very grateful for the guidance I have received from the late David Farmer, Stuart Sprake and Colin Jones, also Emyr and Eddie at Dinefwr Press.

Much of the content of Swansea boxers has been discussed over many cups of coffee around the table at Verdi's in Mumbles. Particular thanks go to big John Davies who had voluntarily undertaken the task of reading several proofs and offering me his opinion on the legibility and interest factor of *Swansea Boxers*.

My thanks also to the authors of *Wales and its Boxers*, *Welsh Warriors* and *All in my Corner* – these books have been useful references. The following websites have been integral tools in identifying Swansea boxers and researching their records – my gratitude to *www.boxrec.com*, *www.prewarboxing.com* and *www.welshwarriors.com*.

Special thanks go to my son Jeremy who has assisted me with the enduring task of indexing and to my nephew John Pullen who has been invaluable in providing me with technological assistance. To my long suffering wife Marlene for her forbearance in playing second fiddle to Swansea boxers for three and a half years.

Finally, my thanks to all the subjects of my book, many of whom are not around today to receive the acclamation they so richly deserve. This book would not have been possible without the desire and dedication of Swansea boxers.

Jeff 'Bulldog' Burns

SWANSEA BOXERS

1916-1959

CHRIS LANGDON boxed as a professional in the bantamweight division between 1916 and 1922; his date and place of birth are not recorded. There is some discrepancy with the recording of Chris Langdon's professional boxing career between the records of *www.boxrec.com* – who have recorded four wins, six losses and two draws in twelve fights between 1916 and 1922. According to the records of *www.prewarboxing.co.uk*, compiled by Miles Templeton, Chris participated in fifty-eight fights over the same period, which is most likely.

In his first recorded contest, which was on 4th November 1916, he outpointed Frank Moody over fifteen rounds in Maesteg, his sixteen-year-old opponent from Pontypridd had won six, lost seven and drawn two, since joining the paid ranks at the age of fourteen years, when he took on the Swansea boxer. They boxed a return contest the following June, again in Maesteg, which ended in a fifteen rounds draw.

Frank Moody's career was to span over twenty-two years until he retired in 1936, having boxed one hundred and ninety-four times, of which he won one hundred and twenty, lost fifty-three and drew fifteen. Moody won the Welsh middleweight title before his nineteenth birthday and made one defence of the title before plying his trade across the Atlantic in the United States in 1923. He boxed in the States over the next three years where he was in conflict with the likes of World light heavyweight champions Harry Greb, Tiger Flowers and Maxie Rosenbloom, before returning to Wales in 1926. He became British middleweight and light heavyweight champion and in 1935 held Tommy Farr to a fifteen rounds draw for the Welsh light heavyweight title. To win and draw against a fighter of Moody's calibre (even a young Frank Moody) indicates that the Swansea boxer was a decent fighter.

He was stopped in nine rounds by Joe Symonds in Plymouth ten months later – Symonds had previously been British and World flyweight title holder until losing to the immortal mighty atom, Jimmy Wilde. Chris drew with Australian Digger Evans at the old National Sporting Club in Covent Garden before stopping Billy O'Brien in the thirteenth round in the Liverpool Stadium. He lost on points over fifteen rounds against American sailor Terry Martin before outpointing Bill Beynon from Taibach over the same distance in December 1919. Chris lost on points against Joe Symonds before outpointing Rees Brooks from Aberavon at the Liverpool Stadium the following April.

Two successive defeats against Tommy Gardner from Birmingham and a fifteen round loss on points against Seaman Jack Davies signalled the end of the road for the Swansea boxer.

Fights: 12 • Won: 4 • Lost: 6 • Draws: 2

BILLY BIDDER boxed as a professional out of Swansea in 1928 and 1929, there is no record of his date and place of birth and there is some discrepancy over his boxing record. He may have had up to twelve professional bouts, although *www.boxrec.com* had listed only three. He boxed as a lightweight and drew with Steve Curley Fay from High Wycombe on 13th October 1928 over ten rounds, beat him on points again over ten rounds one month later, and the following October lost over fifteen rounds in their third contest – all three bouts took place at the Shaftesbury Theatre in Swansea.

Fights: 3 • Won: 1 • Lost: 1 • Draws: 1

TICH MAY made his professional debut in Llanelli on Boxing Day 1928 losing on points in a six rounds featherweight contest against Swansea-born Ammanford boxer Billy Quinlan. A return fight at the Shaftesbury Hall in Swansea on 29th January of the following year resulted in Quinlan having his arm raised in victory for the second time. Miles Templeton, *www.prewarboxing.com* has recorded seventeen bouts that Tich had participated in.

Fights: 2 • Won: 0 • Lost: 2 • Draws: 0

JOHNNY MAW beat George Rodham from Notting Hill in a bantam-weight contest over six rounds at the Vale Hall in Kilburn on 19th September 1930 in his one and only professional contest. In contrast, his opponent boxed from June 1930 until May 1944, answering the bell one hundred and forty times, he won sixty-one, lost sixty-nine and drew on nine occasions.

Fights: 1 • Won: 1 • Lost: 0 • Draws: 0

ROY HITCHINGS boxed at middleweight, drawing his professional debut in a twelve round tussle against Charlie Bundy from Treherbert at the Public Hall in Aberavon on 4th October 1930. They shared the spoils in a rematch at the Shaftesbury Theatre in Swansea the following month. Three months later they met again at the Shaftesbury, this time the Swansea boxer took the decision after ten rounds. Later in his career Bundy went the distance with Bruce Woodcock and three times with Tommy Farr, but was stopped in two rounds by Swansea boxer, Jim Wilde.

Fights: 3 • Won: 1 • Lost: 0 • Draws: 2

LEN BEYNON was born in Barry on 24th April 1912. He boxed at bantamweight and featherweight, making his professional debut on 2nd November 1930. Len's last contest was on 11th November 1942. He died on 1st October 1992, aged eighty years.

Fights: 70 • Won: 43 (11 by KO) • Lost: 26 (3 by KO) • Draws: 1

TITLE FIGHTS

07-03-1931	Freddy Morgan	L	PTS	15	Swansea	vacant Welsh flyweight title
06-06-1932	Terence Morgan	W	PTS	15	Merthyr Tydfil	Welsh bantamweight title
04-11-1933	George Williams	L	PTS	15	Swansea	Welsh bantamweight title
12-05-1934	George Williams	W	PTS	15	Swansea	Welsh bantamweight title
24-11-1934	Mog Mason	L	DQ	6	Merthyr Tydfil	Welsh bantamweight title
06-02-1936	Mog Mason	W	PTS	15	Swansea	Welsh bantamweight title
08-06-1936	Stanley Jehu	W	PTS	15	Swansea	Welsh featherweight title
03-05-1937	George Williams	W	PTS	15	Swansea	Welsh featherweight title

Refer CHAPTER THREE

BRYN JONES made his professional debut at the Royal Albert Hall in London against fellow debutant Alf Parry from Liverpool on 22nd April 1931. Alf got the nod after six keenly contested rounds as you would expect between a Scouser and a Swansea Jack. Bryn's next recorded contest was almost three years later when he drew with Wal Dearing from Fulham who had won thirty-six of his previous forty-five contests, having lost only five and drawn four. Three and a half years later the Swansea boxer outpointed Bert Buxton from Norwich over ten rounds in Lowestoft. Bryn's final encounter was on 24th January 1938 when he boxed in Great Yarmouth where he outpointed Ronnie Barber from Lowestoft. It is more than likely that Bryn boxed many more contests than are recorded by *www.boxrec.com*.

Fights: 4   •   Won: 2   •   Lost: 1   •   Draws: 1

JIM WILDE was born in Swansea on 6th September 1911. He boxed at heavyweight, making his professional debut on 20th February 1932. Jim Wilde's last contest was on 21st January 1948; he died on 1st March 1991, aged seventy-nine years.

Fights: 58   •   Won: 28 (15 by KO)   •   Lost: 26 (13 by KO)   •   Draws: 4

Jim Wilde.

TITLE FIGHTS

08-06-1935	Charlie Bundy	W	PTS	15	Swansea	vacant Welsh heavyweight title
14-09-1936	Tommy Farr	L	KO	7	Swansea	Welsh heavyweight title
21-02-1938	George James	L	DQ	15	Mountain Ash	Welsh heavyweight title
24-07-1939	George James	L	TKO 11		Swansea	Welsh heavyweight title

Refer CHAPTER THREE

RONNIE JAMES was born in Swansea on 8th October 1917. He boxed at lightweight, making his professional debut on 21st January 1933. Ronnie James's last contest was on 2nd June 1947; he died on 12th June 1977, aged fifty-nine years.

Fights: 136 • Won: 114 (61 by KO) • Lost: 17 (3 by KO) • Draws: 5

TITLE FIGHTS

12-08-1944	Eric Boon	W	KO	10	Cardiff	British lightweight title
04-09-1946	Ike Williams	L	KO	9	Cardiff	World lightweight title

Refer CHAPTERS ONE and TWO

Lewis Lewis, 1933.

LEWIS LEWIS boxed as a featherweight out of Swansea – *www.box rec.com* record his professional debut as being on 20th April 1933, when he outpointed Bob Rimmer from Liverpool over ten rounds at the Liverpool Stadium, where Rimmer had been beaten the previous November by Swansea boxer Len Beynon. Lewis's next recorded fight was at the Mannesmann Hall in Swansea two years later, where he drew with Les Greenaway from Pengam, who was later defeated by Swansea boxers Ronnie James and Len Beynon. One month later the Swansea boxer outpointed Percy Enoch from Tonyrefail over ten rounds, again at the Mannesmann Hall, in his last recorded contest. Miles Templeton (*www.prewarboxing.co.uk*) has twenty-three fights recorded for Lewis Lewis.

Fights: 3 • Won: 2 • Lost: 0 • Draws: 1

BERT BEVAN made his professional debut on 29th April 1933 losing a ten rounds points decision against Herbie Nurse from Cardiff at the Judges Hall, Trealaw. Bert's next recorded contest was in Bedminster where he drew a ten round confrontation with Billy Hood, a Plymouth-born boxer, who fought out of Orlando in Florida – two months after boxing Bert he outpointed Tony Zale, who later became Middle-weight champion of the World.

Between May and November the Swansea boxer fought Dai 'Farmer' Jones from Ammanford on five successive occasions, initially winning on a five round TKO in Swansea, followed by a six rounds points win at the Mannesmann Hall, two ten round draws ensued and in their final bout Bert was knocked out in nine rounds in an eliminator for the Welsh middleweight title in Swansea. After the loss to Jones, Bert moved to Paddington and resumed his career at the Paddington Baths in Bayswater where he knocked out Londoner Fred Bloomfield in round eight. The Welsh exile boxed four more times in 1937, all in the London area, winning one with two losses and a draw.

In 1938 the Swansea boxer beat Irishman Joe Quigley on points over six rounds at Earls Court and then lost his next three contests against Charlie Parkin from Mansfield, Londoner Nat Franks and Arthur (Ginger) Sadd from Norwich who boxed two hundred and fifty times from 1929 until 1951 and fought the likes of Tommy Farr, Joe Beckett, Don Cockell, Freddie Mills and he challenged Jock McAvoy for the British and Empire middleweight title just six months after beating Bert.

Bert didn't box in 1939. He returned to the ring in March 1940 losing on a foul against Johnny Blake from Chelsea and in the penultimate bout of his career he lost on points over twelve rounds against forty-one-year-old Billy Bird from Chelsea who was engaging in his three hundred and fourteenth contest of which he had been the victor on two hundred and twenty-nine occasions. Bert ended his career on a winning note when Glaswegian Jim Hall was disqualified in the second round in front of his home fans in Glasgow.

Fights: 19   •   Won: 6 (2 by KO)   •   Lost: 9 (3 by KO)   •   Draws: 4

HARRY TAYLOR outpointed Les Greenaway from Pengam over ten rounds at Mountain Ash in his only recorded professional contest on 11th April 1934. In a career that spanned over ten years, Les boxed at the Mannesmann Hall several times, losing against Len Beynon and Ronnie James – he drew with Lewis Lewis.

Fights: 1 • Won: 1 • Lost: 0 • Draws: 0

Willie Piper.

CAROL TAYLOR boxed just once as a professional losing on points against Les Greenaway from Pengam in a ten round lightweight contest on 14th July 1934.

Fights: 1 • Won: 0 • Lost: 1
Draws: 0

DANNY THOMAS boxed at featherweight, making his professional debut on 4th May 1935. Thomas's last contest was on 17th February 1936.

Fights: 4 • Won: 0 • Lost: 4 (3 by KO)
Draws: 0
Refer CHAPTER EIGHT

WILLIE PIPER boxed at both welterweight and middleweight, making his professional debut on 26th March 1936. Willie Piper's last contest was on 10th September 1945.

Fights: 9 • Won: 2 • Lost: 5 (1 by KO)
Draws: 2

TITLE FIGHT

03-08-1936   Ivor Pickens   L   PTS   15   Swansea   Welsh welterweight title

Refer CHAPTER SIX

PINKIE JENKINS boxed at heavyweight, making his professional debut in Cardiff on Boxing Day 1936 – he stopped Archie Norman from Harrow in the sixth round. The following May, Pinkie halted South African Joe Foord in seven rounds in London. His third and last recorded contest was in Swansea on 14th December 1937 against the renowned Canadian, Larry Gains, who was engaging in his one hundred and twenty-seventh contest, spanning fourteen years, and included victories over two future world heavyweight champions, a second round knockout against Max Schmeling and a ten round decision over Italian giant Primo Carnera. It is most unlikely that Pinkie would have been matched against someone of Gains' experience in only his third professional bout. The records of *www.prewarboxing.co.uk* state that Pinkie boxed twenty times as a professional, although there are no details of his fight record.

Fights: 3   •   Won: 2 (2 by KO)   •   Lost: 1 (1 by KO)   •   Draws: 0

Pinkie Jenkins (right) sparring with amateur star Johnny Eagles.

CUSH ALLEN boxed at welterweight in his only professional bout on 24th January 1938.

Fights: 1 • Won: 1 • Lost: 0 • Draws: 0
Refer CHAPTER EIGHT

LEN DAVIES boxed at flyweight, bantamweight and featherweight, making his professional debut on 24th January 1938. Len Davies's last contest was on 19th April 1952.

Fights: 68 • Won: 39 (6 by KO) • Lost: 27 (2 by KO) • Draws: 2

TITLE FIGHTS

28-10-1949	Jackie Hughes	L	PTS	15	Abergavenny	vacant Welsh featherweight title
23-08-1950	Jackie Hughes	L	TKO	10	Porthcawl	Welsh featherweight title
03-03-1952	Selwyn Evans	L	PTS	12	Carmarthen	Welsh lightweight title

Refer CHAPTER SIX

JACK KILEY boxed at flyweight, making his professional debut on 24th January 1938. Jack's final contest was on 18th April 1947.

Fights: 10 • Won: 5 (1 by KO) • Lost: 5 (3 by KO) • Draws: 0

TITLE FIGHTS

10-07-1939	Ronnie Bishop	L	PTS	15	Gloucester	Welsh flyweight title
13-05-1940	Ronnie Bishop	W	PTS	15	Crumlin	Welsh flyweight title

Refer CHAPTER THREE

TAFFY WILLIAMS was born in Swansea on New Year's Day 1920; he boxed at middleweight, making his professional debut on 1st October 1938. Taffy Williams final contest was on 4th June 1951, he died on 1st March 1992, aged seventy-two years.

Fights: 46 • Won: 33 (16 by KO) • Lost: 10 (8 by KO) • Draws: 3

TITLE FIGHTS

04-12-1939	George Reynolds	W PTS	15	Swansea	vacant Welsh middleweight title
11-06-1946	Tommy Davies	L TKO	4	Swansea	Welsh middleweight title

Refer CHAPTER THREE

RONNY REES – boxing out of Swansea as a lightweight – made his professional debut at The Ring in Blackfriars against Alf James on 20th November 1938, inflicting the second defeat on the South African in nineteen contests, winning by TKO in the third round. The following month, Ronny reappeared at The Ring where in his only other recorded contest he outpointed ring veteran the experienced Jack Hopwood from Camden Town over eight rounds. He is recorded as having four-teen contests by *www.prewarboxing.co.uk* without details of the fights.

Fights: 2 • Won: 2 • Lost: 0 • Draws: 0

WILLIE GREY born in Swansea in 1920 boxed at flyweight and according to the record books made his professional debut in Ponty-pool, losing on points over ten rounds against Norman Lewis from Nantymoel on 13th December 1941, although there is a report of Willie outpointing Welsh champion Ronnie Bishop in 1938. Willie's next contest looked on paper to be an astonishing mismatch – he was taking on the future world flyweight and European bantamweight champion Peter Kane and not surprisingly was KO'd in five rounds at the Royal Albert Hall on 30th March 1942. Four months after the defeat to Kane, Willie appeared at the Stadium in Liverpool, suffering a five-round TKO loss against Ronnie Clayton. In 1943, the Swansea boxer fought Peter Kane twice, a glutton for punishment you might say! Willie fared better than on the first encounter – he took Kane the distance in Liverpool on 14th January, losing on points over ten rounds. On 24th February he fought Kane again, this time in London, where the fight was declared a no contest after five rounds.

In his next bout Willie tasted success stopping Jimmy Wilde in seven rounds at the St Helen's Rugby Ground in Swansea in May 1944. This

Willie Grey.

Jimmy Wilde was not the mighty atom or Swansea's heavyweight, but was a flyweight who hailed from Oxford. Topping the bill that night was fellow Swansea boxer Ronnie James who sufferd a rare defeat, losing on points over ten rounds to Arthur Danahar. The following year Willie drew with Jimmy Stubbs in Willenhall, and then dropped a ten round decision to Syd Worgan in a bill topper at the Vetch Field. The chief supporting bout on that programme was the up-and-coming Cliff Curvis who outpointed Vernon Ball in eight. Willie then went to the Blackpool Tower Circus where they let Ronnie Clayton out of his cage to knock out the Swansea boxer in two rounds.

After two inside the distance defeats at the Stadium in Liverpool in 1948, and with a troublesome and continuing hand problem, Willie decided it was time to call it a day – his final contest was on 7th November 1946, he was twenty-six years old. Willie is recorded as having twenty professional bouts by *www.prewarboxing.co.uk.*

Fights: 11 • Won: 2 (1 by KO)

Lost: 8 (5 by KO) • Draws: 1

Willie Grey vs Peter Kane.

South Wales Ex-boxers Association, including Willie Grey, Len Beynon,
Jim Wilde and Tommy Davies.

CLIFF CURVIS, born in Swansea on 19th November 1927, boxed at featherweight, lightweight and welterweight and made his professional debut on 26th August 1944; he was sixteen years of age. Cliff Curvis's last contest was on 21st March 1953; he died on 22nd April 2009, aged eighty-one years.

Fights: 54   •   Won: 42 (12 by KO)   •   Lost: 12 (4 by KO)   •   Draws: 0

TITLE FIGHTS

13-09-1950	Eddie Thomas	L	PTS	15	Swansea	British welterweight title
24-07-1952	Wally Thom	W	KO	9	Liverpool	British & Commonwealth welterweight title
08-12-1952	Gerald Dreyer	L	PTS	15	Johannes-burg	Commonwealth welterweight title
22-03-1953	Gilbert Lavoigne	L	DQ	10	Paris	European welterweight title

Refer CHAPTER TWO and CHAPTER SEVEN

Cliff Curvis.

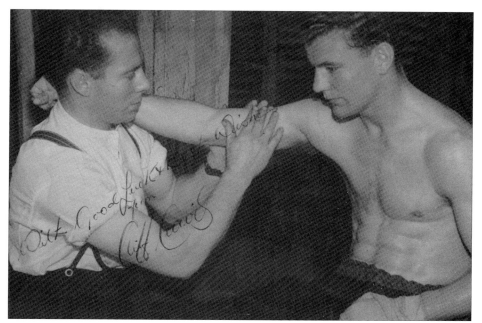

Cliff Curvis with father trainer Dai Curvis.

WILLIE JAMES was born in Swansea. The only recorded professional bout involving the Swansea welterweight was an eight rounds points defeat at the Drill Hall, Swansea, on 20th March 1945 against Dennis Chadwick from Bridlington, who was participating in his one hundred and fifty-fourth contest, one of which was a twelve round points defeat against Swansea boxer Ronnie James in 1939, also at the Drill Hall.

Fights: 1 • Won: 0 • Lost: 1 • Draws: 0
Refer CHAPTER EIGHT

CURLEY ROBERTS boxed as a featherweight and made his professional debut on 20th March 1945; he retired after his fourth contest, 13th September 1946.

Fights: 4 • Won: 0 • Lost: 3 (2 by KO) • Draws: 1
Refer CHAPTER EIGHT

ALBERT GOVIER boxed as a featherweight – his only recorded professional contest was on 29th July 1946.

Fights: 1 • Won: 0 • Lost: 1 • Draws: 0
Refer CHAPTER EIGHT

KEN MORGAN boxed as a professional for the first time on 4th June 1946 in Swansea – he was stopped in six rounds by Danny Jones from Ammanford. Morgan boxed once in 1947 against Harry Legge from Bournemouth in Watford – the bout was declared a no contest in the second round.

In 1948 he stopped Billy Parsons from Bath at Weston-Super-Mare in two rounds, lost by knockout in the sixth against Albert Bessell from Bristol, lost on points over eight rounds against Arthur Gould from Woolwich, knocked out Jackie Horseman from West Hartlepool in the sixth round and was on the wrong end of the decision against Tommy Jones from Neath at the Neath Drill Hall. The following year Ken was knocked out in the fourth round by Dai Davies from Skewen and in the sixth round by George Pook from Torquay at Newton Abbot on 25th November after which Ken decided to call time on his boxing career.

Fights: 8 • Won: 2 (2 by KO) • Lost: 6 (4 by KO) • Draws: 0

DAVE LLOYD made his professional boxing debut in the lightweight division on Boxing Day 1946; his last of twenty recorded professional bouts was on 21st September 1953.

Fights: 20 • Won: 3 • Lost: 13 (5 by KO) • Draws: 4

TITLE FIGHTS

16-02-1953	Haydn Jones	L	PTS 12	Cardiff	vacant Welsh featherweight title
04-05-1953	Haydn Jones	L	PTS 12	Rhyl	Welsh featherweight title

Refer CHAPTER SIX

KEN CURVIS boxed as a welterweight and made his professional debut on 21st April 1947, his final contest was on 21st June 1950.

Fights: 6 • Won: 4 (1 by KO) • Lost: 1 (1 by DQ) • Draws: 1

TITLE FIGHTS
21-06-1950 Allan Wilkins L DQ 6 Porthcawl vacant Welsh welterweight title

Refer CHAPTER SIX and CHAPTER SEVEN

DOUG RICHARDS was born in Swansea on New Year's Day 1923. He boxed at light heavyweight and made his professional debut on 21st April 1947. His last contest was on 15th July 1950; he retired at the age of twenty-six.

Fights: 24 • Won: 10 (1 by KO) • Lost: 14 (12 by KO) • Draws: 0

TITLE FIGHTS
26-11-1949 Dennis Powell L KO 5 Newtown Welsh light heavyweight title

Refer CHAPTER SIX

GARETH BEVAN boxed only once as a professional, losing by technical knockout in the fifth round of a bantamweight contest against Dudley Lewis of Brecon in Ammanford. Gareth became the trainer at Penyrheol Amateur Boxing Club and trained the Jones brothers: Ken, Colin and Peter, through their amateur and professional careers.

Fights: 1 • Won: 0 • Lost: 1 (1 by KO) • Draws: 0

BILLY JONES boxed at middleweight, making his professional debut on 17th February 1949; he retired after his next contest which was on 21st November 1949.

Fights: 2 • Won: 0 • Lost: 2 (1 by KO) • Draws: 0

Refer CHAPTER EIGHT

WILLIE JONES made his professional debut against fellow debutant Auber Davies at Trealaw on 10th June 1949, sharing a decision after four rounds. Willie was back in action on 2nd July when he outpointed Terry Edwards over four rounds at Onllwyn. Willie suffered his first and only defeat in his third contest against Dennis Rowley from Aberavon, losing the decision after four hard fought rounds. Rowley went on to challenge unsuccessfully for the Welsh welterweight title, before getting knocked out in one round by Dick Tiger, a Liverpool-based Nigerian who later domiciled himself in the United States and became World middleweight and light heavyweight champion.

In his next contest the Swansea boxer outpointed Jack Badland from Blaenavon in Abergavenny on 31st October – Cliff Curvis knocked out Gwyn Williams on the same bill. Willie had been a pro for six months and had won two out of four contests with one draw and one defeat.

In January of the ensuing year, Willy added to his winning tally by outpointing Harry James from Merthyr Tydfil in Abergavenny – on the same bill Eddie Thomas and Swansea boxer Billy Brain both recorded successes. Dai Hopkins, who was from Neath, was Willie's next victim, losing on points after six rounds in his home town on 6th February. Cliff Curvis and Billy Brain made it a hat-trick of wins for Swansea boxers on that bill. Willie then won the decision in a six-round contest against Arthur Thomas from Skewen; they boxed in Neath. In his final outing, he gained sweet revenge by reversing an earlier decision against unbeaten Dennis Rowley, this time over six rounds in Pontypridd on 29th July 1950.

Fights: 8 • Won: 6 • Lost: 1 • Draws: 1

BILLY BRAIN made his professional debut boxing in the middle-weight division on 16th January 1950, winning by technical knockout in the fourth round against Billy Potter from Trealaw, in Abergavenny, which seemed to be a popular venue for Swansea boxers at that time. Billy won his next fight by a second round technical knockout win over Dennis Williams at the Gwyn Hall in Neath. He followed this with a draw against Cardiff's Malcolm Innocent over six rounds in Ponty-pridd. He then returned to Abergavenny where he had made his successful debut, but this time Billy was less fortunate, he was stopped in the second round by Ray Agland who went on to win the Welsh middleweight title and ended his career with a decent record of eleven wins and two defeats. This fight took place on 13th November in what turned out to be Billy's final encounter.

Fights: 4 • Won: 2 (2 by KO) • Lost: 1 (1 by KO) • Draws: 1

JACKIE HUGHES made his professional debut as a welterweight in Ammanford on 22nd November 1948, when he was knocked out by Bryn Williams of Ystradgynlais in five rounds. He next fought in Neath on 6th February 1950, when he knocked out debutant and home town boy Harold Williams, in the 2nd round.

There are no other professional bouts listed on Jackie's boxing record, although recollections of fight fans of that era are that he boxed professionally on at least twenty occasions.

Fights: 2 • Won: 1 (1 by KO) • Lost: 1 (2 by KO) • Draws: 0

TEDDY BARROW was born in Swansea on 28th April 1934. He boxed as a middleweight and made his professional debut on 11th August 1954; he retired after his final contest which took place on 3rd September 1958. Teddy Barrow passed away in 1988; he was fifty-four years of age.

Fights: 23 • Won: 14 (2 by KO) • Lost: 9 (6 by KO) • Draws: 0

TITLE FIGHTS

16-01-1957	Freddy Cross	L	TKO	11	Cardiff	Welsh middleweight title

Refer CHAPTER SIX and CHAPTER SEVEN

LEN BARROW was born in Swansea on 31st March 1937; he boxed at welterweight and made his professional debut on 21st November 1957. He retired after his final contest on 12th May 1960 when he was twenty-three years of age.

Fights: 12   •   Won: 9 (3 by KO)   •   Lost: 3 (1 by KO)   •   Draws: 0
Refer CHAPTER SEVEN

BRIAN CURVIS was born in Swansea on 14th August 1937. He turned professional as a welterweight on 2nd June 1959, and retired after his final contest which was on 12th September 1966; he was twenty-nine years of age.

Fights: 41   •   Won: 37 (22 by KO)   •   Lost: 4 (2 by KO)   •   Draws: 0

TITLE FIGHTS

09-05-1960	George Barnes	W PTS	15	Swansea	Commonwealth welterweight title
21-11-1960	Wally Swift	W PTS	15	Nottingham	British & Commonwealth welterweight titles
08-05-1961	Wally Swift	W PTS	15	Nottingham	British & Commonwealth welterweight titles
31-10-1961	Mick Leahy	W KO	8	Wembley	British & Commonwealth welterweight titles
20-02-1962	Tony Mancini	W TKO	5	London	British & Commonwealth welterweight titles
12-02-1963	Tony Smith	W TKO	9	London	British & Commonwealth welterweight titles
28-07-1964	Johnny Cooke	W TKO	5	Porthcawl	British & Commonwealth welterweight titles
22-09-1964	Emile Griffith	L PTS	15	Wembley	World welterweight title
25-11-1964	Sammy McSpadden	W TKO	12	Cardiff	British & Commonwealth welterweight titles
25-04-1966	Jean Josselin	L RTD	14	Paris	European welterweight title

Refer CHAPTERS ONE, TWO and SEVEN

1960-1979

ALAN COUCH was born in Swansea and boxed at welterweight in his only professional bout on 28th November 1967.

Fights: 1 • Won: 0 • Lost: 1 (1 by KO) • Draws: 0
Refer CHAPTER EIGHT

BOBBY RUFFE was born in Hereford on 24th August 1948 but lived in and boxed out of Swansea. He was a useful amateur, boxing for the Gwent ABC before turning professional at middleweight and joining Glyn Davies's stable. His first professional contest was on an Eddie Richards promotion at the Cwmfelin Club, Swansea, on 24th April 1972. He lost on points over six rounds against fellow debutant Kenny Webber from Merthyr Tydfil in a hard fought middleweight contest in which Kenny always had the edge. The Swansea boxer lost his next two contests in five rounds and two rounds respectively against Arthur Winfield in Nottingham and the hard punching Paddy Doherty in Croke Park, Dublin, on a bill headed by the Muhammad Ali and Alvin Lewis spectacle. Bobby stopped Dave Nelson from Wolverhampton before losing to both Dusty Smith and Kevin McCann on points over six rounds. In his final contest, just six months after his debut, Bobby was knocked out by Londoner Mick Hussey in four rounds in Kensington.

Fights: 7 • Won: 1 (1 by KO) • Lost: 6 (3 by KO) • Draws: 0

JEFF BURNS was born in Swansea on 16th May 1948. He boxed at middleweight and made his professional debut on 8th May 1972. He

Jeff Burns.

retired after his twentieth contest on 14th September 1976; he was twenty-eight years of age.

Fights: 20 • Won: 11 (3 by KO) • Lost: 9 (7 by KO) • Draws: 0

TITLE FIGHTS

27-06-1973 Mike McCluskie L KO 8 Swansea vacant Welsh middleweight title

Refer CHAPTER SIX

CHUCK JONES was until 1972 renowned for keeping goal for St Josephs AFC and as a heavy punching light heavyweight with Gwent ABC under the mentoring of Bill Pitson, Cliff Teasdale and Terry Grey. Chuck made his professional debut on an Eddie Richards promotion at the Top Rank Suite in Swansea on 12th June 1972, not wasting any time in knocking out John Smith in the first round. At this time Smith had won six out of eleven contests; he went on to become Scottish light middleweight champion in 1980 in a career that spanned

PROGRAMME

Heavyweight—Seniors

1.—**Howell Davies**   **v.**   **Trevor Roberts**
Towy A.B.C.   Merlin's Bridge A.B.C.

Middleweight

2.—**Chuck Jones**   **v.**   **Billy Brothers**
Gwent A.B.C.   Pyle A.B.C., Welsh Rep.

Welterweight

3.—**Jeff Burns**   **v.**   **Ken Jones**
Swansea Youth, Welsh Rep.   Trostre, Welsh Rep.

or Mike McCluskie
Croeserw, Welsh Rep.

Bantamweight

4.—**Cliff Nancurvis**   **v.**   **Vincent Howells**
Gwent   Llanelli

Featherweight

5.—**John Llewellyn**   **v.**   **J. Taylor**
Merlin's Bridge   Pembroke

Juniors

6.—**Eric Daniel**   **v.**   **Kim Parry**
Gwent, Welsh Champion 1969   Croeserw

7.—**Alan Dagless**   **v.**   **Keith Davies**
Gwent   Cymmer

8.—**Gareth Ace**   **v.**   **Martin Singleton**
Gwent   Neath

9.—**J. Blackmore**   **v.**   **Ray Ismail**
Cymmer   Gwent

Other Schoolboy Contests arranged on night
Commencing 7.30 approx.

Amateur Boxing Tournament Programme, Swansea Dockers' Club, 3rd June 1969.

ten years. Chuck scored another inside the distance win when he halted Liverpudlian John Judson in two rounds in Nottingham a week later. Chuck returned to the Top Rank Suite on another Eddie Richards bill where he outpointed another scouser by the name of Pat Thompson who went on to win the Central Area light heavyweight title in a career of seventy-two contests.

The Swansea boxer will admit he hadn't prepared himself properly for his next contest, resulting in his first and only defeat as a professional boxer when he was stopped in four rounds by Vic Humphries from Kilburn on a Mike John promotion at the Glen Ballroom in Llanelli on 22nd August. The following month the Swansea boxer repeated his earlier win over Pat Thompson this time over eight rounds at the Top Rank Suite Swansea. A better conditioned Chuck Jones gained sweet revenge over Vic Humphries stopping the Kilburn boxer in seven rounds at the National Sporting Club in Piccadilly in October. The Swansea boxer travelled to Leeds for his next encounter where he earned a creditable draw against Leeds-based St. Kitts boxer, Bob Tuckett. Chuck then outscored Mancunian Terry Armstrong over eight rounds in Bradford in December.

Since his debut in June of 1972 the Swansea boxer had won six, lost one and drawn one of eight contests. On the 8th January 1973, Chuck stopped Londoner Mick O'Neill at the National Sporting Club in what was to be his last contest. He was forced to retire from boxing as he was suffering from rheumatoid arthritis. His manager, Glyn Davies, swears that Chuck Jones would have become British champion – few would argue with that opinion.

Fights: 9 • Won: 7 (4 by KO) • Lost: I (I by KO) • Draws: I

DAI DAVIES – known as Dai 'Muscles' Davies – was born in Swansea on 2nd May 1954. He boxed as an amateur for Gwent ABC and turned professional with Llanelli boxing manager Glyn Davies at the age of eighteen. He won his first professional bout outpointing Cardiff debutant Joey Deriu over six rounds at the National Sporting Club,

Piccadilly, on 13th November 1972; Joey went on to challenge for the Welsh bantamweight title.

By the end of 1973, Dai had taken part in six bouts, two at feather-weight, three at lightweight and one at welterweight. Dai won two of the six, against Deriu and Errol Francis. He lost to Martyn Galleozzie from Merthyr Tydfil (who went on to win the Welsh lightweight title), Gary Dunks (who was unbeaten in four pro starts), debutant Kevin Evans (who went on to challenge for the Midlands Area lightweight title) and Jimmy Flint. Jimmy later held the Southern Area feather-weight title and unsuccessfully challenged Pat Cowdell for the British featherweight championship.

After the Flint fight the Swansea boxer didn't don the gloves again until 26th April 1977, when he lost a six-round points decision to Sylvester Gordon, followed by a draw against Philip Morris from Cefn Hengoed, who had been outpointed over six rounds in his professional debut by Swansea boxer Frank McCord. The Morris bout took place at the Mayfair Suite in Swansea – this was Dai's first performance in front of his own supporters. A return six-round contest with Sylvester Gordon, again at the National Sporting Club, ended with the same result as in their previous encounter. Dai lost on points over six rounds against Eric Wood in Doncaster and earned a draw in a return contest in Swansea three weeks later.

He kept busy in 1978 engaging in fifteen contests, winning five, losing nine and drawing the other. One of the successes was against fellow Swansea boxer Nigel Thomas whom he beat on points at the Afan Lido over six rounds on 7th October. He ended the year on a promising note by beating Selvin Bell from Manchester and Dave Farrell from Birkenhead.

The Swansea boxer maintained his busy schedule in 1979, boxing on ten occasions, losing eight times with one draw and one solitary victory. Only once did he manage to box in Wales during that year when he lost on points over eight rounds against Pat Smythe from Gainsborough, Lincolnshire. Dai lost six rounds decisions against Mickey Baker from Worcester and Jackie Turner from Hull.

In January of 1981 Dai faced the biggest challenge of his career – he was to test the highly-touted hot prospect Lloyd Honeghan, who went on to become welterweight champion of the World; the Swansea boxer fought gallantly, but was halted in five rounds due to an eye injury. Dai didn't box again until September, facing another tough assignment against hard-hitting Robbie Robinson from Liverpool, who stopped him in three rounds. He concluded the year with three fights in nine days, all taken at short notice; he lost on points over eight rounds against Johnny Burns of Birmingham, on points over six rounds against Delroy Pearce a Tottenham-based Jamaican, who in his next outing lost on points to Swansea boxer Geoff Pegler, and was stopped in five rounds by John Lindo, another Jamaican, who was based in Bradford.

In March of 1982 Dai 'Muscles', approaching his twenty-eighth birthday, boxed in his penultimate contest, losing on points after six rounds against Iranian Sam Omidi at the Top Rank Suite in Swansea. On 26th April 1982 Dai Davies entered the pugilistic prize ring for the final time, he lost on points over six rounds against Tyrell Wilson from Newport in Cardiff. The Swansea boxer had lost thirty-five and drawn four of his forty-seven contests spanning over very nearly ten years. His tally of victories doesn't appear very impressive statistically, but Dai was always able to answer the call to fight anybody, anywhere and anytime, usually at very short notice.

Fights: 47 • Won: 8 (I by KO) • Lost: 35 (8 by KO) • Draws: 4

YOTHAM KUNDA came to the United Kingdom from his native Zambia in 1974 to commence and enhance his career as a professional boxer. He settled in Swansea and started training at Eddie's Gym in Oystermouth Road, preparing for his pro debut, which took place on 9th September 1974 when Yotham was approaching his twenty-fifth birthday.

In his first engagement at welterweight he lost on points to the unbeaten Tommy Dunn from Reading at the World Sporting Club in Mayfair. He fought Dunn, who later in his career won the Southern Area lightweight title, in a return contest a week later in Reading which was declared a no contest as both fighters were guilty of refusing to break when ordered to do so by the referee. His third pro bout, and his first taste of victory, was when he outpointed Alan Jones of Merthyr Tydfil at the Top Rank Suite Swansea, in a programme promoted by Eddie Richards. On the same bill Swansea boxer Neville Meade stopped Roger Barlow in three rounds.

Yotham boxed Jimmy Batten from Millwall at the York Hall, Bethnal Green, on 21st October, losing the decision after six rounds. Batten boxed from 1974 until 1983 and became British light middleweight champion – he defeated Swansea boxer Jeff Burns, shortly before being crowned British champion.

The Swansea boxer knocked out Eric Williams from Llandeilo at the National Sporting Club, before losing on a second round TKO to highly promising debutant Dave 'Boy' Green who won the British and European light welterweight titles and also the European welterweight title, before unsuccessfully challenging both Carlos Palomino and Sugar Ray Leonard for the World welterweight crown.

Yotham was busy in 1975, boxing thirteen times, of which he won three and lost ten. The following year, 1976, Yotham was more successful, winning three out of four, including a victory back home in Zambia where he stopped Australian Greg Badman in five rounds at Kitwe on 2nd July in what turned out to be Yotham's penultimate contest. Yotham, who had returned to Zambia, didn't fight again until 4th November 1978 when he lost his last contest to Chris Sanigar from Bristol on points over eight rounds in Lusaka.

Fights: 23 • Won: 8 (6 by KO) • Lost: 15 (4 by KO) • Draws: 0

NEVILLE MEADE was born in Montserrat on 12th September 1948. He boxed in the heavyweight division and made his professional debut on 9th September 1974 and fought for the last time on 22nd September 1983; he was thirty-five years of age.

Fights: 33 • Won: 20 (18 by KO) • Lost: 13 (9 by KO) • Draws: 0

TITLE FIGHTS

29-03-1976	Tony Blackburn	W	TKO 4	Swansea	Welsh heavyweight title
22-01-1980	David Pearce	W	TKO 2	Caerphilly	Welsh heavyweight title
01-10-1980	Winston Allen	W	TKO 2	Swansea	Welsh heavyweight title
12-10-1981	Gordon Ferris	W	KO 1	Birmingham	British heavyweight title
22-09-1983	David Pearce	L	TKO 9	Cardiff	British heavyweight title

Refer CHAPTER TWO and CHAPTER FOUR

Mike Copp.

Alan Copp.

MIKE COPP was born in Swansea on 21st August 1956 and made his professional debut at welterweight on 9th February 1976. His last fight was on 30th July 1980; he was approaching his twenty-fourth birthday.

Fights: 31 • Won: 12 (2 by KO) • Lost: 18 (5 by KO) • Draws: 1

TITLE FIGHTS

10-07-1978	Horace McKenzie	L	PTS 10	Aberavon	vacant Welsh welterweight title

Refer CHAPTER SIX and CHAPTER SEVEN

ALAN COPP was born in Swansea on 2nd July 1953 and made his professional debut on 11th August 1976 as a welterweight. He retired after his last contest on 17th April 1978. Alan sadly passed away in 1994 aged forty-one years.

Fights: 4 • Won: 3 (1 by KO) • Lost: 0 • Draws: 1
Refer CHAPTER SEVEN and CHAPTER EIGHT

COLIN BREEN was born in Swansea in 1946. He didn't start boxing until he was twenty-two years old. He had his first amateur contest in 1968 when he boxed for the Swansea Dockers ABC and later joined the Gwent ABC. Colin was Welsh ABA light middleweight champion in 1973 and represented Wales against Ireland, England, Combined Services, Midland Counties, and Northern Counties.

He made his professional debut at the Sophia Gardens in Cardiff on 11th August 1976, losing on points

Colin Breen.

over six rounds against Jamaican-born Cardiff-based boxer Bonny McKenzie. This was McKenzie's second victory in as many starts – he would go on to enter the professional ring a total of fifty-six times which would include two stoppage defeats against British, Commonwealth and European champion Tony Sibson. Colin lost two six round decisions against Al Neville of Tottenham before recording his first professional success on 2nd February 1977 outpointing experienced Cardiff boxer Tony Burnett in Swansea. Burnett was engaging in his fortieth professional contest including a recent six rounds points defeat to Colin's stablemate Jeff Burns. The Swansea boxer was again successful in his next contest, knocking out Southampton-based South

African Owen Lotriet in the second round at the Double Diamond Club in Caerphilly. In the penultimate contest of a short career, the Swansea boxer did well to take Leicester's Steve Fenton to an eight rounds decision in Bedford. This bout, which was originally scheduled for six rounds, was a real thriller – both fighters were presented with a fifty pounds bonus by former World title challenger Don Cockell. Colin boxed just once more – his final contest, an eight rounds bill topper at the Mayfair Suite, Swansea, on 11th May 1977, ended in a draw against Leicester-based Jamaican Joe Jackson, who had won eleven of his previous eighteen contests. The Swansea boxer was so disgusted with the decision that he quit boxing. His professional boxing career had spanned from August 1976 to May 1977; during that period he had boxed seven times, winning twice, four defeats and a draw – he had not been matched in any of his bouts with what you might class as a predictable win. Following his retirement Colin opened his own boxing stable with trainer Jimmy Bromfield and became a very successful boxing manager.

Fights: 7 • Won: 2 (1 by KO) • Lost: 4 • Draws: 1

COLIN JONES was born in Gorseinon on 21st March 1959 – he made his professional debut at welterweight on 3rd October 1977 and retired on 19th January 1985; he was approaching his twenty-sixth birthday.

Fights: 30 • Won: 26 (23 by KO) • Lost: 3 (1 by KO) • Draws: 1

TITLE FIGHTS

01-04-1980	Kirkland Laing	W TKO 9	Wembley	British welterweight title
12-08-1980	Peter Neal	W TKO 5	Swansea	British welterweight title
03-03-1981	Mark Harris	W TKO 9	Wembley	Commonwealth welterweight title
28-04-1981	Kirkland Laing	W TKO 9	London	British & Commonwealth welterweight titles
14-09-1982	Sakarai Ve	W KO 2	Wembley	Commonwealth welterweight title

05-11-1982	Hans-Henrik Palm	W TKO 2	Copenhagen	European welterweight title
19-03-1983	Milton McCrory	Draw 12	Reno	vacant WBC welterweight title
13-08-1983	Milton McCrory	L PTS 12	Las Vegas	vacant WBC welterweight title
19-01-1985	Donald Curry	L TKO 4	Birmingham	WBA & IBF welterweight titles

Refer CHAPTER ONE, CHAPTER TWO and CHAPTER SEVEN

KEN JONES was born in Gorseinon and boxed at light heavyweight, making his professional debut on 2nd November 1977. His last contest was on 6th October 1980.

Fights: 15 • Won: 8 • Lost: 6 (1 by KO) • Draws: 1

TITLE FIGHTS

19-03-1979	Chris Lawson	L PTS 10	Haverfordwest	Welsh light heavyweight title
12-08-1980	Chris Lawson	L PTS 10	Swansea	Welsh light heavyweight title

Refer CHAPTER FOUR and CHAPTER SEVEN

FRANK McCORD was born in Swansea on 6th August 1958; he made his professional debut at welterweight on 29th March 1977, his final contest was on 12th January 1988. He was approaching his thirtieth birthday when he retired.

Fights: 56 • Won: 20 (11 by KO) • Lost: 33 (12 by KO) • Draws: 3

TITLE FIGHTS

07-06-1982	Billy Waith	L PTS 10	Swansea	vacant Welsh welterweight title
10-12-1983	Billy Waith	L PTS 10	Swansea	Welsh welterweight title
26-03-1986	Steve Davies	L TKO 4	Swansea	vacant Welsh light middleweight title

Refer CHAPTER SIX and CHAPTER SEVEN

NIGEL THOMAS was born in Swansea in 1960. He became a protégé of the Gwent ABC before turning professional under the management of Glyn Davies at seventeen years of age. He boxed frequently in England and Wales against good class opposition and like so many other Swansea boxers accepted fights at very short notice.

Nigel made his debut in the Afan Lido on 3rd October 1977 out-pointing Phillip Morris of Cefn Hengoed over four rounds. He boxed twice more in that year, losing on a second round stoppage against Eddie Baker of Luton, who the following month was knocked out by Swansea boxer Frank McCord. His other contest was against Derek Trew from West Bromwich who won the decision after four rounds.

In 1978 Nigel touched gloves to commence thirteen ring battles of which he won seven, lost five all by decision and drew one. He beat Johnny Beauchamp, from Portsmouth, three times all on points, he was beaten twice by the useful Liverpudlian Tony Carroll and he was also outpointed over six rounds by Swansea boxer Dai Davies. After this contest Nigel joined the Colin Breen boxing stable. His drawn bout was against Roger Guest from Dudley in the West Midlands.

The Swansea boxer was just as busy in 1979, again stepping inside the ropes on fourteen occasions; his arm was raised in victory eight times, he lost on points against Roger Guest, Gary Newell from Wolverhampton, and future British and Commonwealth light middleweight champion Lloyd Hibbert from Birmingham. He was knocked out by John F. Kennedy from Draycott, drew with Roger Guest for the second time and also shared the spoils with Norman Morton from Newcastle.

1980 was a difficult year for Nigel, not yet twenty years of age coming into the year, he had won sixteen, lost eleven and drawn three of thirty contests in just twenty-seven months as a professional. He began the year with the sweet smell of success, outpointing Dillwyn Collins from Llantwit, but lost six bouts in succession in a very obvious step-up in class. He lost points decisions against Londoner Mickey Mapp, Kenny Webber from Merthyr Tydfil, Lee Hartshorn from Manchester, Dave Ward and Cliff Gilpin from Woverhampton; he was knocked out by Roy Varden from Nuneaton.

The following year he drew with Paul Murray from Birmingham and outpointed Jimmy Smith from Tottenham, who had previously lost to

Swansea boxer Frank McCord. He was outpointed over eight rounds by John F. Kennedy and was knocked out in two rounds by Liverpool star Joey Frost, who had previously knocked out Swansea boxer Jeff Aspel.

In 1992 Nigel was offered up as 'cannon fodder' for rising star Nicky Wilshire and was duly stopped in the first round at the Royal Albert Hall. Wilshire, from Bristol, became Commonwealth light middleweight champion in 1985.

Just two bouts in 1983 – the twenty-three-year-old 'veteran' lost to Mick Courtney, who had previously beaten Swansea boxer John McGlynn. Nigel was stopped in three rounds by R. W. Smith, who was unbeaten in ten bouts – he was the son of Andy Smith who had managed world title challengers Joe Bugner and Dave 'Boy' Green. R. W. Smith is now the General Secretary of the British Boxing Board of Control.

In his final outing Nigel was unceremoniously knocked out in two rounds by Robert Armstrong from Doncaster on 25th January in Stoke. The Swansea boxer was not yet twenty-four years of age and had boxed forty-five times as a professional. He had fought against good class opposition, some perhaps a little too early in his career, but Nigel could never shun a challenge.

Fights: 45 • Won: 18 (3 by KO) • Lost: 23 (7 by KO) • Draws: 4

WINSTON ALLEN was born in Cardiff on 12th November 1957. He made his professional debut on 20th April 1978 – his last fight was on 1st November 1985; he was approaching his twenty-eighth birthday.

Fights: 29 • Won: 11 (6 by KO) • Lost: 18 (5 by KO) • Draws: 0

TITLE FIGHTS

01-10-1980   Neville Meade   L   TKO   2   Swansea   Welsh heavyweight title

Refer CHAPTER SIX

Pip Coleman.
(Courtesy of *South Wales Evening Post*).

PIP COLEMAN was born in Neath on 16th April 1958; he boxed at bantamweight, making his professional debut on 4th September 1978 – he was twenty-two years old when he retired on 1st October 1980.

Fights: 14 • Won: 7 (2 by KO) • Lost: 7 (2 by KO) • Draws: 0

TITLE FIGHTS

04-10-1979	Glyn Davies	L	TKO 7	Ebbw Vale	vacant Welsh bantamweight title
01-10-1980	Glyn Davies	W	PTS 10	Swansea	Welsh bantamweight title

Refer CHAPTER FOUR

BRYN JONES, better known as Brindley, was born on 27th September 1960. He boxed in the bantamweight division, making his debut on 21st May 1979 when he lost on points over six rounds against Jimmy Bott from Liverpool, who had recently been beaten by Swansea boxer Pip Coleman. Brindley boxed five more times in that year, losing on points in three bouts, drawing one, and was stopped in three rounds by Alan Storey.

Nine fights and nine defeats in 1980, all by decision, but the highlight of the year was boxing Gary Nickels to a six round decision at the Royal Albert Hall on a bill that featured John L. Gardner, Sylvester Mittee and Cornelius Boza Edwards.

There were three losses in 1981, after sixteen defeats, one draw and never having tasted victory Brindley walked away from the square ring for the final time. Although he lost sixteen bouts he was only stopped on two occasions.

Fights: 17 • Won: 0 • Lost: 16 (2 by KO) • Draws: 1

JEFF ASPEL was born in Swansea on 30th July 1958. He started boxing at the Gwent Amateur Boxing Club. Jeff turned professional under the management of Colin Breen and trainer Jimmy Bromfield. He made his pro debut in Manchester on 17th September 1979, losing on points over six rounds to fellow debutant Wayne Barker, who had won his first eight contests before drawing against another Swansea boxer Terry Matthews. Jeff lost his next two bouts, a six rounds points decision against Londoner Micky Mapp at the Royal Albert Hall on 9th October 1979, and three weeks later in Wolverhampton he was knocked out in round four by Gary Newell who was fighting in front of his home crowd.

In his next contest Newell outpointed Swansea boxer Nigel Thomas – two months later he too was beaten by Terry Matthews. At the end of November Jeff recorded his first pro victory when he knocked out Pat Smythe in two rounds at Doncaster. Another defeat followed when he lost a six round decision in a return contest against Micky Mapp in London on 3rd December.

The Swansea boxer lost his next three bouts, all by decision, against Ian 'Kid' Murray in Stoke, Dave Sullivan over six rounds at the Double Diamond Club in Caerphilly – a popular boxing venue – and to Dave Douglas in Birmingham. Jeff earned a long-awaited victory when he

51

won a points decision over six rounds against Steve Henty at Hove in Sussex and did well when boxing at the Adelphi Hotel in Liverpool where he took Sheffield's Brian Anderson to a close decision over six rounds. Anderson later became British middleweight champion – losing to such a quality fighter was no disgrace. A week later he lost a four round 'shut out' against Cardiff's George Sutton in Reading. Seven days later the Swansea boxer stopped Stephen Ward in the third round in Birmingham. Back in action at the end of May, and in his fifth contest in thirty-four days, after flooring his opponent several times and who on one occasion was saved by the bell he lost a disputed eight round decision to Irishman Gerry Young in Belfast. He then took a three week break before losing another eight round decision to Billy Ahearne in Manchester, this was on 16th June 1980.

The Swansea boxer for the first time in his pro career went on to win two on the bounce, a six round decision over Dave Sullivan at Swindon followed by a revenge victory over Ian 'Kid' Murray at the Eisteddfod Pavilion in Gowerton on 12th August. Over the next fourteen months Jeff was beaten in each of his five contests, all inside the distance, commencing with a crushing one round stoppage against Mancunian prospect Johnny Francis.

Jeff's last fight was in Evesham on 11th November 1981 when he was knocked out in two rounds by the highly regarded Peter Stockdale. Jeff's professional record stands at just five wins in twenty-one contests, statistically unimpressive, but the sixteen defeats were mostly against boxers of good potential, bouts often taken at short notice, sometimes on the day of the fight. In the first eleven months of his career he boxed sixteen times against anyone, anywhere and never let the boxing fraternity down.

Fights: 21 • Won: 5 (2 by KO) • Lost: 16 (6 by KO) • Draws: 0

STEVE BABBS was born in Barbados on 18th June 1953. Following a long and established career in martial arts, Steve made his debut as a professional boxer on 19th March 1979, joining the Colin Breen stable, when he lost a six rounds points decision to Peter Tidgewell in his opponent's home town of Bradford, a decision he reversed over eight rounds, again in Bradford, two months later. Steve had boxed twice between the two contests with Tidgewell, losing on points against debutant Mark Bennett in Birmingham, who never fought again, and winning on a disqualification in round five against Tommy Jones in Barnsley. On 6th June he achieved his third consecutive victory when he outpointed Peter Les Reed over eight rounds in Burslem, Staffordshire. Twelve days later Steve was on the losing end of a six round points decision against six feet two-inch Yorkshireman, Liam Coleman, who was enjoying a four fight unbeaten run since turning professional – later in his career Coleman was beaten by Denis Andries and Herol Graham. The Swansea boxer ended 1979 by losing on points to Billy Keen at Evesham in Worcestershire on 17th October.

The new year got off to a bad star with four consecutive defeats, against Danny McLoughlin in Liverpool, Joe Jackson at the NSC London, Swansea boxer John O Neil in his Swansea debut and Al Stevens in Birmingham. Steve turned things around, winning his last three contests of that year with points wins over Joe Dean in Bradford, Battersea boxer Gordon Stacey at the World Sporting Club, Mayfair and Jamaican Joe Frater in Evesham.

In 1982, the year in which Steve brought the curtain down on his pro career, he suffered a points defeat against Gary Jones in Glasgow, knocked out Phil Williams from Plymouth in Swansea, drew with Eddie Vierling again in Swansea and finally scored a sensational one round knockout over Walsall prospect Cordwell Hylton on 13th December in Wolverhampton. Hylton would later in his career lose a six round decision to rising star and future World heavyweight champion John Ruiz.

Steve retired at the age of twenty-nine due to ill health after his eighteenth bout, of which he had won eight, lost nine and drawn one over a period of three years and nine months. When he retired he held a number three ranking in Britain.

Fights: 18 • Won: 8 (2 by KO) • Lost: 9 (2 by KO) • Draws: 1

STEVE CROCKER was born in Swansea on 26th February 1958. He made his professional debut as a lightweight on 26th February 1979, losing on points to Norman Morton from Newcastle in Marton, Yorkshire. Steve boxed on two more occasions, outpointing Brendan O'Donnel from Liverpool on 8th March 1979 in Bangor and Billy Rabbit from Strabane in Derry on 27th June 1979.

Fights: 3 • Won: 2 • Lost: 1 • Draws: 0

DAVID GEORGE was born in Swansea on 13th November 1959. He turned professional on 3rd October 1979, boxing at flyweight; he retired on 25th October 1989, aged thirty.

Fights: 31 • Won: 17 (2 by KO) • Lost: 12 (5 by KO) • Draws: 2

TITLE FIGHTS

| 14-09-1982 | Kelvin Smart | L | KO | 6 | Wembley | vacant British flyweight title |

Refer CHAPTER SIX and CHAPTER SEVEN

DONALD GEORGE was born in Swansea on 4th November 1957. He turned professional at featherweight on 9th December 1979 – his last fight was on 1st November 1983, three days before his twenty-sixth birthday.

Fights: 14 • Won: 8 (2 by KO) • Lost: 6 (2 by KO) • Draws: 0

TITLE FIGHTS

| 19-11-1981 | Mervyn Bennett | W | PTS | 10 | Ebbw Vale | vacant Welsh featherweight title |

Refer CHAPTER FOUR and CHAPTER SEVEN

Doug James.
(Courtesy of *South Wales Evening Post*).

DOUG JAMES was born on 31st March 1958 – his first professional contest was at middleweight on 17th September 1979 – his final bout was on 6th May 1985. He was twenty-seven years old when he retired.

Fights: 25 • Won: 13 (9 by KO) • Lost: 10 (6 by KO) • Draws: 2

TITLE FIGHTS

28-1-1983	Horace McKenzie	W TKO 9	Swansea	vacant Welsh middleweight title

Refer CHAPTER FOUR

TERRY MATTHEWS was born in Swansea on 1st May 1959. He made his professional debut at light middleweight on 10th May 1979; he boxed until 18th November 1982. Matthews was twenty-three years old when he retired from boxing.

Fights: 25 • Won: 13 (4 by KO) • Lost: 11 (6 by KO) • Draws: 1

TITLE FIGHTS

07-04-1981	Gary Pearce	L TKO 9	Newport	vacant Welsh light middleweight title

Refer CHAPTER SIX

JOHN O'NEIL was born in Liverpool on 6th November 1957 – he boxed at light heavyweight and travelled to Wolverhampton with manager Colin Breen and trainer Jimmy Bromfield for his first professional fight on 17th December 1979. The twenty-two-year-old Swansea boxer was on the wrong end of a six rounds decision against Rocky Burton from Bedworth in Warwickshire.

In 1980 he stopped debutant Lenny Remice from Blackley in the third round, drew with Paul Newman from Bognor Regis over six rounds, boxed another draw with Gordon George from Wood Green over eight rounds, he outpointed Nigel Savory from Leeds over six rounds, in a return fight stopped Paul Newman in five rounds and in another return lost on points over six rounds against Savory.

On 1st October he made his home debut, outpointing fellow Swansea boxer Steve Babbs at the Top Rank Suite in Swansea. In his final contest of the year John was stopped in the first round by Tommy Taylor from Hednesford at Wolverhampton, Taylor went on to draw with Chris Lawson, beat Johnny Nelson and he also won the Midlands area light heavyweight title.

On 10th February 1981 John was stopped by Cordwell Hylton from Walsall in the sixth round; later in his career Hylton was knocked out in one round by Swansea boxer Steve Babbs, yet went on to win the Midlands area cruiserweight title. In his final contest John O'Neil, who was just twenty-four years of age, stopped Jonjo Greene, a Manchester-based Irishman, in the sixth round in Pembroke on 8th December. John had been a professional just nine days short of two years, had fought eleven times, winning five, losing four and drawing twice.

Fights: 11 • Won: 5 (3 by KO) • Lost: 4 (2 by KO) • Draws: 2

Ray Price.
(Courtesy of *South Wales Evening Post*).

RAY PRICE was born in Swansea on 16th July 1961. He made his professional debut on 30th Apri 1979 at light welterweight and he finally ended his career at super middleweight on 10th March 1994; he was approaching his thirty-third birthday.

Fights: 38 • Won: 13 (3 by KO) • Lost: 20 (8 by KO) • Draws: 4 • No Contest: 1

TITLE FIGHTS

22-03-1982	Geoff Pegler	W	PTS	10	Swansea	vacant Welsh light welterweight title
27-05-1983	Geoff Pegler		NC	1	Swansea	Welsh light welterweight title
19-12-1983	Geoff Pegler	L	TKO	8	Swansea	Welsh light welterweight title
13-06-1984	Michael Harries	L	PTS	10	Port Talbot	Welsh light welterweight title

Refer CHAPTER FOUR

1980-1989

MICK REDDEN was born in Swansea on 21st December 1960. He made his professional debut under the management of Colin Breen as a lightweight against Terry Parkinson from Brighton at Hove in Sussex on 28th January 1980 – he was nineteen years of age, and lost on points after four rounds. Three weeks later he outpointed Neil Brown from Norwich in Mayfair; Brown had lost twice against Ray Price. His next contest was in Edgbaston against Birmingham boxer Don Aagesen; Mick retired in the first round. On the 16th June he fought Mancunian prospect Johnny Francis in Manchester, losing on points after six rounds. Francis later knocked out Swansea boxer Jeff Aspel in the first round. In his final contest, just seven months after his debut, Mick once again outpointed Neil Brown, this time over six rounds.

Fights: 5 • Won: 2 • Lost: 3 (1 by KO) • Draws: 0

ANDY THOMAS was born Andrew Bruton in Swansea on 5th March 1962. He was eighteen years old when making his professional debut at light welterweight on 30th April 1980; his final contest was on 12th April 1983.

Fights: 22 • Won: 8 (5 by KO) • Lost: 13 (5 by KO) • Draws: 1

TITLE FIGHTS

4-03-1983	Ray Hood	L	PTS	10	Queensferry	vacant Welsh lightweight title

Refer CHAPTER SIX

RICHARD WHITE was born on 3rd October 1949 – his first professional engagement was in a lightweight contest on 3rd November 1980, his second and only other contest was on 1st December 1980.

Fights: 2 • Won: 0 • Lost: 2 • Draws: 0
Refer CHAPTER EIGHT

TONY HART was born on 3rd January 1958. He made his professional debut under manager Colin Breen in a super middleweight contest at the Pennar Palladium, Pembroke, on 8th December 1981 against fellow debutant Noel Blair from Slough, losing on points after four rounds. Blair was later halted by Swansea boxer Valentino Maccarinelli.

Tony then outpointed Roy Wada from Shrewsbury over six rounds at Evesham on 13th October 1982. Five days later Tony was stopped in the fourth round by Tony (T.P.) Jenkins from Brentford in what was to be his final appearance in a professional boxing ring.

Fights: 3 • Won: 1 • Lost: 2 (1 by KO) • Draws: 0

PETER JONES was born in Gorseinon Swansea on 16th June 1961. He made his professional debut on 3rd September 1981 in a bantamweight contest – his final contest was on 20th April 1983.

Fights: 7 • Won: 5 (2 by KO) • Lost: 2 • Draws: 0
Refer CHAPTER SEVEN

STEVE KANE was born in Swansea on 19th September 1963. He lost on points over 4 rounds against Alan Thomas in front of his opponent's home crowd in Bristol on 4th December 1981. This was Steve's one and only professional contest.

Fights: 1 • Won: 0 • Lost: 1 • Draws: 0
Refer CHAPTER EIGHT

GEOFF PEGLER was born in Swansea on 18th January 1959. He boxed professionally for the first time on 3rd September 1981 at light welterweight. He retired after his last contest which was on 14th March 1986.

Fights: 32 • Won: 12 (5 by KO) • Lost: 18 (4 by KO) • Draws: 1 • No Contest: 1

TITLE FIGHTS

22-03-1982	Ray Price	L PTS	10	Swansea	vacant Welsh light welterweight title
27-05-1983	Ray Price	NC	1	Swansea	Welsh light welterweight title
19-12-1983	Ray Price	W TKO	8	Swansea	Welsh light welterweight title
14-03-1986	Rocky Feliciello	W TKO	7	Rhyl	vacant Welsh welterweight title

Refer CHAPTER FOUR

DAI WILLIAMS was born in Swansea and made his professional debut in Glasgow on 14th September 1981 against Glaswegian Eddie Glencross – he was disqualified in round two. In December he outpointed Steve Reilly from Newport over six rounds at the Ebbw Vale Leisure Centre, but didn't box again until 27th October 1983 when he was outpointed over six rounds by George Bailey from Bradford – Bailey had previously been stopped in three rounds by Swansea boxer Robert Dickie and outpointed over six rounds by another Swansea boxer, Dave George. Dai did well to earn a draw in his next contest against Graham 'Kid' Clarke from Cardiff, who coming into this bout was unbeaten in five.

Dai seemed determined to make up for lost time; he travelled to Glasgow to win on points after six rounds against Ghanaian Gabriel Kipley on 21st November. He then took on Irish debutant Roy Webb and was knocked out in the second round in Belfast the following January. Webb notched up quite an impressive record, winning fifteen, ten by knockout and losing just two. One of those defeats was against Swansea boxer Peter Harries who knocked the Irishman out in the eighth round.

Dai took another spell away from the ring, returning on 28th February 1985, when he lost on points against Rocky Lawlor from Birmingham over eight rounds in Wolverhampton – three months later Rocky won the vacant Scottish bantamweight title. In October the Swansea boxer was stopped in two rounds by John Hyland from Liverpool, who later in his career unsuccessfully challenged Billy Hardy for the British bantamweight title. In his final ring engagement Dai was again stopped in two rounds by London-based Jamaican Little Currie in Cardiff on 30th November.

The ring career of Dai Williams spanned over four years. He boxed only nine times, winning three, losing five and drawing the other.

Fights: 9 • Won: 3 • Lost: 5 (3 by KO) • Draws: 1

MICHAEL HARRIES was born in Swansea on 14th August 1964. He made his professional debut in a light welterweight contest on 18th November 1982. His final contest was at light middleweight on 26th May 1989 when he was approaching his twenty-fifth birthday.

Fights: 35 • Won: 23 (3 by KO) • Lost: 11 (3 by KO) • Draws: 1

TITLE FIGHTS

13-06-1984	Ray Price	W PTS 10	Port Talbot	vacant Welsh light welterweight title
25-10-1986	Tony McKenzie	L KO 10	Stevenage	British light welterweight title
03-02-1988	Gary Cooper	L PTS 12	Wembley	vacant British light middleweight title
01-03-1989	Kevin Hayde	W PTS 10	Cardiff	vacant Welsh light middleweight title
26-05-1989	Troy Waters	L TKO 8	Ettalong, NSW	Commonwealth light middleweight title

Refer CHAPTER FIVE, CHAPTER SIX and CHAPTER SEVEN

VALO MACCARINELLI was born in Swansea on 16th October 1959 – he boxed as a professional at welter and light middleweight. His professional career commenced on 27th April 1982 and ended on 12th April 1983.

Fights: 8 • Won: 3 (1 by KO) • Lost: 4 (3 by KO) • Draws: 1

Refer CHAPTER SEVEN

JOHN McGLYNN was born in Swansea on 1st November 1964. He boxed professionally at light middleweight from 7th June 1982 at seventeen years of age until 30th September 1991.

Fights: 19 • Won: 12 (6 by KO) • Lost: 7 (7 by KO) • Draws: 0

TITLE FIGHTS

17-02-1984	Rocky Feliciello	L	TKO 8	Rhyl	vacant Welsh light middleweight title
18-11-1986	Steve Davies	L	TKO 3	Swansea	Welsh light middleweight title

Refer CHAPTER SIX

JOHN DAVIES was born in Swansea on 10th September 1964. He boxed at welterweight, making his professional debut on October 1982, and boxed for the last time on 11th March 1992.

Fights: 17 • Won: 14 (10 by KO) • Lost: 2 • Draws: 1

TITLE FIGHTS

26-04-1990	Kelvin Mortimer	W	TKO 2	Merthyr Tydfil	vacant Welsh welterweight title
15-10-1991	Andy Till	L	PTS 12	Dudley	WBC International light middleweight title

Refer CHAPTER FIVE

John Davies.
(Courtesy of *South Wales Evening Post*).

PETER HARRIES was born in Swansea on 23rd August 1962. He boxed at featherweight in his first professional contest on 28th February 1983 – his final bout was on 6th July 1996 – he was approaching his thirty-fourth birthday.

Fights: 33 • Won: 16 (5 by KO) • Lost: 15 (3 by KO) • Draws: 2

TITLE FIGHTS

18-11-1986	Kelvin Smart	W PTS 10	Swansea	vacant Welsh featherweight title
24-02-1988	Kevin Taylor	W PTS 12	Port Talbot	vacant British featherweight title
18-05-1988	Paul Hodkinson	L TKO 9	Port Talbot	British featherweight title
06-09-1989	Paul Hodkinson	L TKO 9	Port Talbot	European and British featherweight title
18-07-1991	Steve Robinson	L PTS 10	Cardiff	Welsh featherweight title
20-05-1994	Nigel Haddock	W PTS 10	Neath	vacant Welsh featherweight title
27-08-1994	Wilson Docherty	L PTS 12	Cardiff	WBB featherweight title

Refer CHAPTER TWO, CHAPTER FIVE and CHAPTER SEVEN

ROBERT DICKIE was born in Carmarthen on 23rd June 1964. He made his professional debut on 12th March 1983 at bantamweight and his final bout was on 10th November 1993.

Fights: 28 • Won: 22 (15 by KO) • Lost: 4 (4 by KO) • Draws: 2

TITLE FIGHTS

25-02-1985	John Sharkey	W TKO 2	Glasgow	vacant Scottish featherweight title	
09-04-1986	John Feeney	W PTS 12	London	vacant British featherweight title	
30-07-1986	Steve Sims	W KO 5	Ebbw Vale	British featherweight title	
29-10-1986	John Feeney	W PTS 12	Ebbw Vale	British featherweight title	
31-08-1988	Hengky Gun	W TKO 5	Stoke	WBC International super featherweight title	
31-08-1988	Kamel Bou-Ali	L TKO 6	Stoke	WBC International super featherweight title	
05-03-1991	Kevin Pritchard	W TKO 8	Cardiff	British super featherweight title	
30-04-1991	Sugar Gibiluru	L TKO 9	Stockport	British super featherweight title	

Refer CHAPTER TWO

NEIL CROCKER was born in Swansea on 3rd February 1961. His first professional bout took place 8th September 1983 at middleweight; his final contest was on 8th December 1984.

Fights: 7 • Won: 2 (1 by KO) • Lost: 5 (2 by KO) • Draws: 0

Refer CHAPTER SEVEN

CHRIS JACOBS was born in Llanelli on 28th April 1961. He made his debut in the professional boxing ring under the management of Colin Breen in a heavyweight contest on 13th June 1984; his last fight was on 29th October 1991. He was thirty years old when he retired.

Fights: 19 • Won: 8 (3 by KO) • Lost: 10 (4 by KO) • Draws: 1

TITLE FIGHTS

25-09-1985	Andrew Gerrard	W PTS 10	Newport	vacant Welsh heavyweight title
08-06-1989	Andrew Gerrard	W PTS 10	Cardiff	Welsh heavyweight title

Refer CHAPTER FIVE

KEITH PARRY was born in Swansea on 27th October 1963. He boxed professionally as a lightweight between 12th October 1985 and 22nd March 1989.

Fights: 15 • Won: 10 (7 by KO) • Lost: 5 (1 by KO) • Draws: 0

TITLE FIGHTS

30-07-1986	Andy Williams	L PTS 10	Ebbw Vale	Welsh lightweight title
28-10-1987	Andy Williams	W TKO 8	Swansea	Welsh lightweight title

Refer CHAPTER FIVE

YOUNG DOHERTY was born Pat Doherty in Swansea on 4th January 1966. He boxed at super featherweight, making his debut on 31st July 1985 – his only other contest was on 26th March 1986.

Fights: 2 • Won: 2 • Lost: 0 • Draws: 0
Refer CHAPTER EIGHT

FLOYD HAVARD was born in Swansea on 16th October 1965. He boxed professionally at super featherweight between 30th November 1985 and the same date in 1996; he was thirty-one years old when he retired.

Fights: 36 • Won: 34 (21 by KO) • Lost: 2 (2 by KO) • Draws: 0

TITLE FIGHTS

18-05-1988	Pat Cowdell	W TKO 8	Port Talbot	British super featherweight title
06-09-1989	John Doherty	L TKO 11	Port Talbot	British super featherweight title

22-01-1994	John John Molina	L	RTD	6	Cardiff	IBF super featherweight title
23-03-1994	Neil Haddock	W	TKO	10	Cardiff	British super featherweight title
13-12-1994	Dave McHale	W	TKO	10	Ilford	British super featherweight title
05-05-1995	Michael Armstrong	W	KO	9	Swansea	British super featherweight title

Refer CHAPTER ONE and CHAPTER TWO

GEOFF SILLITOE was born in Swansea on 22nd January 1964. He boxed professionally in the featherweight division from 30th July 1986 until 15th April 1987. He was stopped in two rounds by fellow Swansea boxer Paul Parry in his first professional bout at Ebbw Vale Leisure Centre. Geoff was knocked out in five rounds by Mark Champney of Bournemouth before he beat Rick Dimmock, who was making his professional debut, on points in Maidenhead. A first round knockout defeat by Gary De Roux from Peterborough, who in 1991 became British featherweight champion, followed by two successive losses against Mark Bates from Essex signalled the end of the line for the Swansea boxer.

Fights: 6 • Won: 1 • Lost: 5 (4 by KO) • Draws: 0

DEAN LYNCH was born in Swansea on 21st November 1964 and made his professional debut on 18th September 1986 as a super bantamweight his final contest was on 11th May 1994, six months before his thirtieth birthday.

Fights: 20 • Won: 6 (1 by KO) • Lost: 14 (5 by KO) • Draws: 0
Refer CHAPTER SIX

CARL PARRY was born in Swansea on 6th August 1967; he made his professional debut as a featherweight on 18th November 1986. His last contest was on 29th April 1989.

Fights: 10 • Won: 5 (1 by KO) • Lost: 4 (1 by KO) • Draws: 1
Refer CHAPTER SEVEN

PAUL PARRY was born in Swansea on 20th March 1966. He boxed at featherweight making his professional debut on 26th March 1986; he retired after his second bout which was on 30th July 1986.

Fights: 2 • Won: 1 (1 by KO) • Lost: 1 • Draws: 0
Refer CHAPTER SEVEN

ROCKY REYNOLDS was born in Swansea on 13th July 1968. He was eighteen years of age when he fought Danny St Clair, who was also making his professional debut in Southend on 16th September 1986. Rocky stopped the Londoner in the first round. His arrival into the paid ranks followed a sixty-bout amateur career representing the Swansea Dockers ABC. Rocky was unsuccessful in three attempts at winning a Welsh ABA title but did win an international vest when he won his bout in an international tournament against Germany.

Following his debut he was back in action three weeks later against debutant Kesem Clayton from Coventry in Birmingham. Clayton proved to be a much tougher opponent, and took the decision after six hard fought rounds. In his third contest he made his home debut outpointing Johnny Stone from Gloucester in a middleweight contest over six rounds. Also featuring on this bill were Swansea boxers Peter Harries, John McGlynn, Dean Lynch, Carl Parry and Kevin Roper.

Rocky, who was managed by Alan Davies and trained by the late Nigel Page, concluded his first year as a professional with a loss over six rounds against Nigel Fairbairn in Peterborough, where Nigel hailed from.

Rocky boxed three times in 1987, losing to Roy Horn from Maidenhead in Bethnal Green, outpointing Kevin Hayde from Cardiff in Newport and also outscoring Michael Justin a Nottingham-based Santa Lucian in Weston-Super-Mare. Rocky had now joined Colin Breen's stable and was being coached by Jimmy Bromfield.

In 1988 the Swansea boxer won five out of seven contests all on points over six rounds. He outpointed Tony Baker from London, who had previously beaten Swansea boxer Neil Crocker. He beat Stan King, a London-based Jamaican in Southend, Swansea boxer Mark Hibbs at the Afan Lido, Jimmy McDonagh from Hastings in Southend, and Geoff Sharp, again in Southend, where Rocky was a big favourite. He

Rocky Reynolds.

was defeated by Londoner Tony Collins, brother of George Collins, who later boxed in Swansea against American Russell Mitchell and eventually went on to win the WBC International light middleweight title. The Swansea boxer took this fight with just a couple of hours notice, and he had just completed a heavy gym workout before accepting the challenge. Rocky's other defeat was against Cyril Jackson from Wrexham who stopped him in six rounds at the Afan Lido, his only stoppage loss.

Rocky retired with damaged hands which rendered him inactive for four and a half years. Returning to the ring on 10th April 1993, still only twenty-four years old, he lost a hotly disputed six round points decision against Karl Mumford from Hengoed in Swansea, before travelling to Randers in Denmark for his final engagement on 11th June 1993. He give a very good account of himself, flooring his opponent in the fifth round, before losing on a split points decision against Swede Roland 'Tiger' Ericsson.

Fights: 16 • Won: 9 (1 by KO) • Lost: 7 (1 by KO) • Draws: 0

KEVIN ROPER was born in Swansea on 24th November 1964. His professional record doesn't appear too impressive statistically, having won only four of seventeen contests. Eleven out of his twelve defeats ended inside the scheduled distance, but Kevin was the stereotype 'journeyman' – his motto being 'have gloves will travel'.

The Swansea boxer was renowned for answering the call to fight anyone, anywhere, at minimum notice, provided of course the money was right. There were many other Swansea boxers always ready to take fights at short notice, but few were as financially astute as Kevin. He boxed only once in Swansea, against Paul Hanlon from Birmingham, winning by technical knockout in the fifth round and in his other 'home' contest at the Afan Lido in Aberavon he was the 'sacrificial lamb' for debutant and hot prospect Cardiff's Nicky Piper. The Swansea boxer was knocked out in the second round of what turned out to be his penultimate ring hostility in September 1989.

Kevin's professional debut was against Andy Wright from Tooting, who in 1991 won the Southern area super middleweight title. The fight took place at the Civic Hall, Wimbledon, the Swansea boxer was knocked out in the second round.

Kevin was never discouraged by a loss or the manner of his defeat. In his fourth contest he was stopped by future World champion Nigel Benn after just 30 seconds of the first round, in Basildon in March 1887, after which he took some time out before returning in December to fight Derek Myers. In April of the following year he beat the cagey and very experienced Cardiff boxer, Winston Burnett, who was participating in his ninety-first contest.

The Swansea boxer was not adverse to foreign currency and ventured overseas on a number of occasions. His first continental journey took him to Copenhagen where he was stopped in round one by Terje Sveen a twenty-seven-year-old Norwegian who was unbeaten in seven contests. He boxed Italian Mauro Galvano, unbeaten in twelve bouts in Toscana, Italy, Kevin retired in the fifth round. Galvano later became WBC super middleweight champion before losing the title to Nigel Benn. On another excursion to Italy he was stopped by Luigi Gaudiano, who subsequently held the Italian cruiserweight. He also fought in Belfast against Irishman Sam Storey, who in his next contest became British super middleweight champion.

In his final contest on 6th December 1989, twenty-five-year-old Kevin was stopped in round one by Darren Westover from Ilford at Wembley.

Fights: 17 • Won: 4 (2 by KO) • Lost: 12 (11 by KO) • Draws: 1

NEIL BURDER was born in Gorseinon on 29th July 1962. He made his professional debut on 23rd June 1987 at light heavyweight. He retired after his second contest which was on 28th September in the same year.

Fights: 2 • Won: 1 (1 by KO) • Lost: 1 • Draws: 0
Refer CHAPTER SEVEN

DAVID HAYCOCK was born in Swansea on 30th September 1964 – he boxed professionally at cruiserweight between 15th November 1988 and 21st March 1991.

Fights: 5 • Won: 0 • Lost: 5 (5 by KO) • Draws: 0
Refer CHAPTER EIGHT

MARK HIBBS was born in Aberdare but lived in and boxed out of Swansea, making his professional debut in Manchester on St David's Day 1988; he was two weeks short of his twenty-first birthday and was stopped in three rounds by Paul Hendrick. Seven weeks later he out-pointed London-based Moroccan Rocky Boukriss in Bethnal Green over six rounds. In his final contest on 18th May, just eleven weeks after his debut, he lost on points over six rounds against Swansea boxer Rocky Reynolds.

Fights: 3 • Won: 1 • Lost: 2 (1 by KO) • Draws: 0

*Enzo Maccarinelli and Nigel Page before competing
in the Kilvey Hill 'Concrete Run'.*

NIGEL PAGE was born in Swansea on 20th April 1961. He was five feet eight inches tall and boxed at lightweight, making his professional debut in Bordeaux on 7th October 1988 when he stopped Frenchman Cecilio Ramirez in the first round.

Before boxing for cash, Nigel was highly regarded as an amateur – friend and stablemate Rocky Reynolds recalls that Nigel won four Welsh ABA titles and represented Wales on numerous occasions and also remembers Barry McGuigan publicly acknowledging that the narrow points decision he was awarded in a contest with Nigel could have gone either way. On 12th December Nigel boxed against Vernon McGriff from Buffalo, New York, and having dominated the early action the Swansea boxer retired in his corner at the end of round four complaining of muscle cramps due to the cold temperature in the hall.

After a brilliant amateur career the Swansea boxer was refused a professional licence by the British Boxing Board of Control, but was passed medically fit to obtain a licence in Belgium. Nigel died tragically in an industrial accident. Both Jimmy Bromfield and Colin Breen agreed that Nigel Page was probably the best fighter to have stepped into their gym.

Fights: 2 • Won: 1 (1 by KO) • Lost: 1 (1 by KO) • Draws: 0

ERIC GEORGE was born in Swansea on 19th August 1968. He turned professional in 1989, making his debut on his twenty-first birthday, boxing at flyweight – his final contest was on 7th December 1991.

Fights: 9 • Won: 2 • Lost: 4 (4 by KO) • Draws: 3
Refer CHAPTER SEVEN

CHRIS COUGHLAN was born in Swansea on 21st May 1963; he turned professional under the management of Colin Breen, making his debut in Southend on 3rd October 1989, when referee Larry O'Connell stopped the fight in the first round in favour of his opponent, Paddington-based Algerian Ahcene Chemali, who was also making his debut.

Chris weighed in twenty pounds lighter for his next fight, but lost in the second round against John Foreman from Birmingham. 1990 began well for the Swansea boxer. Travelling to Bristol, he beat Mark Langley from Torquay on points over six rounds. Chris lost his other five bouts in the year – four on points over six rounds and a fourth round stoppage due to swollen eyes against Art Stacey from Leeds in Southend.

The Swansea boxer lost on points over six rounds against Phil Soundy at the Royal Albert Hall and then travelled to Denmark for the second contest of 1991, where he was stopped in three rounds by the scourge of British boxers – Dane, Niels H. Madsen – who fought eight times in his professional career, all against British opponents, and retired undefeated. A third round knockout victory over Nick Howard from Hengoed in Merthyr Tydfil interrupted his sequence of defeats which continued through his next six fights, ending with a one round knockout defeat against the 'Brighton Rock', Scott Welsh, who became

British and Commonwealth heavyweight champion before unsuccess-fully challenging Henry Akinwande for the WBO heavyweight title. After the defeat against Welsh, Chris retired from the ring at thirty years of age.

Fights: 17 • Won: 2 (1 by KO) • Lost: 15 (7 by KO) • Draws: 0

DAI JENKINS was born in Swansea on 20th December 1965. He was nearly twenty-four years of age when he fought Ross Hale on the 16th November 1989 at Weston-Super-Mare in a light welterweight con-test, losing on points over six rounds. Ross later became British and Commonwealth light welterweight champion, stopping Swansea boxer Andy Robins on his route to the title.

His first success came in his third contest when he outpointed Jimi Reynolds from Birmingham over six rounds – after this loss Reynolds won nine contests before his next defeat.

The biggest name that the Swansea boxer fought was a boxer who became British, Commonwealth, European and IBO light welterweight champion – Billy Schwer from Luton – who knocked out another Swansea boxer, Andy Robins, three months after beating Dai.

Jenkins never boxed in Swansea; he only boxed in Wales on two occasions, losing a six rounds decision against Newport's Vaughan Carnegie in Cardiff, a decision Dai reversed eighteen days later in Bristol, and he beat Dean Bramhald from Doncaster on points over six rounds at the Afan Lido in Dean's one hundred and seventh ring encounter.

On 4th June, six weeks after beating Bramhald, the Swansea boxer took on Bernard Paul, known as the 'Punching Postman', who was from Mauritius and based in London. Later in his career Paul became Commonwealth light welterweight champion (he was knocked out in four rounds by Ricky Hatton en route). Bernard stopped Dai in the first round at the York Hall in Bethnal Green, after which the Swansea boxer – approaching his twenty-sixth birthday – called time on his box-ing career.

Fights: 18 • Won: 7 (2 by KO) • Lost: 11 (3 by KO) • Draws: 0

Paul Lynch.
(Courtesy of *South Wales Evening Post*).

PAUL LYNCH was born in Swansea on 27th December 1966. He boxed at light middleweight and made his professional debut on 23rd October 1989 – he bowed out of boxing after his last encounter on 24th March 1995, he was twenty-eight years old.

Fights: 15 • Won: 9 (5 by KO) • Lost: 6 (3 by KO) • Draws: 0
Refer CHAPTER SEVEN

MICK MORGAN was born in Swansea on 26th July 1962. He made his professional debut on 12th April 1989 in a super middleweight contest – his only other fight was on 20th December.

Fights: 2 • Won: 0 • Lost: 2 (2 by KO) • Draws: 0
Refer CHAPTER EIGHT

1990-2010

Ceri Farrell.
(Courtesy of *South Wales Evening Post*).

CERI FARRELL was born in Swansea on 27th October 1967. As an amateur he boxed for the Gwent ABC, trained by Terry Grey. He lost his first professional bout – a points defeat after six rounds – against Craig Hyder on 14th May 1990 at the Winter Gardens in Cleethorpes.

In his first year as a pro he was managed by former Swansea boxer Mike Copp. He took part in six contests, winning on a second round stoppage against Paul Diver in Stafford on 5th December, he drew over six rounds against Mercurio Ciaramitaro in Italy two weeks later – to draw with an Italian in Italy has got to be as good as a win. He lost his other four engagements in that year, including two six rounds decisions against the promising Tim Yeates.

The Swansea boxer lost another six rounds decision to Ammanford boxer Kevin Jenkins in his first bout of 1991. Following his tussle with Ceri, Kevin lost a ten round decision against rising star Robbie Regan for the vacant Welsh flyweight title.

The Swansea boxer lost his next three contests before outpointing Andrew Bloomer over six rounds in Merthyr Tydfil in November 1991 and again in Cardiff sixteen days later. In his last fight of the year Ceri was stopped in four rounds by John Green in Manchester. When the

Swansea boxer fought Green his opponent had won eleven of thirteen starts, winning the Central area bantamweight crown and outpointing another Swansea boxer, Dave George.

Between January 1992 and October 1994 Ceri fought seven times, firstly against Ystradgynlais boxer Miguel Matthews, who throughout his career participated in more than one hundred contests, Alan Ley, Peter Judson, Michael Aldis twice, this opponent went on to become British and Commonwealth super bantamweight champion, Neil Swain and Marcus McCabe without recording a win. Ceri Farrell called it a day after the McCabe fight.

Fights: 20 • Won: 3 (1 by KO) • Lost: 16 (7 by KO) • Draws: 1

JOHN KAIGHIN was born in Brecon on 26th August 1967 and started boxing at the RAOB Club in Swansea, coached by the late Ray Sillitoe. John boxed for Wales against the Army in his fourth amateur contest in December 1989. He lost on a disqualification in the 1990 Welsh ABA championships and subsequently turned professional with boxing manager and coach, former Swansea boxer Mike Copp.

He made his professional boxing debut on 17th September 1990 shortly after his twenty-third birthday – he fought at the City Hall in Cardiff losing on points after six rounds against Carlos Christie from Birmingham in a light heavyweight contest. Later in his career Christie fought and lost to some notable boxers including Ray Close, Nicky Piper, Glen Cattley and Joe Calzaghe. John lost his next three contests all by decision over six rounds before chalking up his first win as a pro when he outpointed Tony Wellington from Deptford over six rounds in Oldham on 15th November. In his last bout of 1990 John was knocked out in three by the very useful Nick Manners from Leeds, who later in his career became Central Area light heavyweight champion and was another fighter who suffered a stoppage defeat at the fists of Joe Calzaghe.

In 1991 John kept himself busy boxing fifteen times, winning six, losing six and drawing three. He fought twice in Swansea, losing on points to Robert Peel from Llan-dovery – fellow Swansea boxers Russell Washer and Ceri Farrell both won their bouts on this bill. On 15th May he reversed the decision against Robert Peel – Swansea boxer Mark Verikios stop-ped Lee Farrell from Pontypool on the same bill. John rounded off 1991 with a first round victory over Keith Inglis from Tunbridge Wells at the Royal Albert Hall. Top of the bill that night was American Gerald McLelland who stopped John 'The Beast' Mugabe in the first round.

Swansea boxer John Kaighin awaiting the decision at the end of a contest with cornermen Mike Copp and Mark Verikios.

Frank Bruno also won in one round, fortunately there were three eight round contests that went the distance, otherwise it might have been a very early night for the fight fans!

1992 didn't start too well for the Swansea boxer with eight suc-cessive defeats before earning a draw with the previously unbeaten Joey Peters at the Royal Albert Hall, where he always seemed to do well. Peters from Southampton only boxed once more after clashing with John – he retired undefeated with eight wins and the one draw. The Swansea boxer ended 1992 with much improved form and a hat-trick of wins. His overall record to date was ten wins, nineteen losses and four draws.

1993 was a bad year for John, losing all his ten bouts, followed by a stoppage defeat against Shaun Cummins from Leicester in 1994, a useful middleweight who later challenged Neville Brown for the British title.

In 1995 he knocked out Kevin Burton, nicknamed the Rock, in one round at Stoke and in the following year, 1996, John lost on points over four rounds against Tim Redman from Dolgellau. In his final bout on 26th September 1997, one month after his thirtieth birthday, Swansea boxer John Kaighin shared the spoils in a four rounder against

Tim Brown who was also from Dolgellau at the Rugby Ground Port Talbot. After seven years as a pro John hung up his gloves with a career record of eleven wins, thirty-one losses and five draws.

Fights: 47 • Won: 11 (6 by KO) • Lost: 31 (10 by KO) • Draws: 5

ANDY ROBINS was born in Swansea on 15th January 1966. He was twenty-four years old when he became a professional boxer, managed by Mike Copp, and made his debut in Southend against Londoner Tony Gibbs – Andy lost on points after six rounds. The Swansea boxer lost his next four fights against Mark Dinnadge from London on points over six rounds, against future British and Commonwealth champion Ross Hale from Bristol, who stopped him in four rounds, against Colin Sinnott from Preston on points over six rounds and Wayne Windle from Sheffield on points, also over six rounds. Wayne became Central area lightweight champion in 1991 and light welter-weight champion in 1997.

In his last engagement of 1990 Andy upset the formbook by stopping Caerphilly's Lyn Davies in the second round at the Royal Albert Hall on 12th December. Lyn had won his four previous contests all inside two rounds. Andy, still looking for his first win, must have appeared as 'cannon fodder' for the Caerphilly boxer, who never boxed again after this shock defeat.

In his first encounter of 1991 Andy was up against Dean Holligan from West Ham, unbeaten in three contests – the Swansea boxer was stopped in four rounds. With just one win in seven outings, the matches weren't getting any easier – his next opponent was Billy Schwer from Luton, a hot prospect, unbeaten in six starts. Schwer went on to become British, Commonwealth and European lightweight champion and was also crowned IBO welterweight champion. He knocked out Andy in the second round, after which the Swansea boxer decided to end his career as a professional boxer.

Fights: 8 • Won: 1 (1 by KO) • Lost: 7 (3 by KO) • Draws: 0

RUSSELL WASHER made his professional debut boxing at middle-weight on 15th September 1990. He was thirty-five years old when he boxed for the last time on 27th October 1995.

Fights: 46 • Won: 9 (5 by KO) • Lost: 36 (10 by KO) • Draws: 1

TITLE FIGHTS

11-05-1992	Carlo Calarusso	L	TKO 5	Llanelli	Welsh light middleweight title

Refer CHAPTER SIX

DEAN ALLEN was born in Swansea on 3rd August 1967. He boxed at light heavyweight and made his professional debut under manager Mike Copp on 24th January 1991, losing a six rounds points decision to Max McCracken at Brierley Hill in the West Midlands. McCracken was having his second contest, having previously beaten Swansea boxer John Kaighin on points over six rounds.

Dean's next bout was in April 1991 when he outpointed Paul Hanlon over six rounds at the Afan Lido. Hanlon had been beaten by Swansea boxer Kevin Roper in his pro debut. Two-and-a-half years after losing to Dean the Birmingham boxer was to end his career as a first round victim to a debutant by the name of Joe Calzaghe.

The Swansea boxer followed up with another win by stopping Terry Johnson in two rounds at Liverpool; Johnson had previously been stopped in two rounds by John Kaighin. After these two successes Dean didn't box again until September 1992 when he was matched with Phil Soundy at the York Hall, Bethnal Green. Phil held a respect-able record of fourteen wins in seventeen fights and proved to be to strong an opponent to take on after a ten month lay-off. Dean was stopped in four rounds.

Ten months wouldn't be a long time out of the ring for a champion-ship boxer who is boxing over a twelve rounds, but a six or eight round fighter needs to be boxing far more regularly. Dean decided the Soundry bout was to be his last.

Fights: 4 • Won: 2 (1 by KO) • Lost: 2 (1 by KO) • Draws: 0

NIGEL BURDER was born in Swansea and boxed at welterweight between 11th April 1991 and 11th May 1992.

Fights: 3 • Won: 0 • Lost: 3 (3 by KO) • Draws: 0

Refer CHAPTER SEVEN and CHAPTER EIGHT

Lee Crocker.
(Courtesy of *South Wales Evening Post*).

LEE CROCKER was born in Swansea on 9th May 1969 – he boxed at light middleweight. His first professional contest was on 31st January 1991, his last bout took place on 31st May 1996, he was twenty-seven years old.

Fights: 21 • Won: 8 (5 by KO) • Lost: 12 (11 by KO) • Draws: 1

Refer CHAPTER SEVEN

CARL HOOK was born in Swansea on 21st November 1969. He boxed at lightweight, making his professional debut on 18th July

1991. He retired at the age of twenty-three after his last contest which was on 27th January 1993.

Fights: 13 • Won: 4 (I by KO) • Lost: 9 (I by KO) • Draws: 0

TITLE FIGHTS

27-01-1993 Mervyn Bennett L PTS 10 Cardiff vacant Welsh lightweight title

Refer CHAPTER SIX

JULIAN JOHNSON was born in Swansea on 4th April 1967. He boxed in Cardiff on 20th November 1991 when he drew after six rounds with Nigel Rafferty from Wolverhampton, marking his entry into the paid ranks at the age of twenty-four. He was managed by Colin Breen. Rafferty went on to win the Midlands cruiserweight title in 1995 – five years later he was stopped by Enzo Maccarinelli in three rounds in Swansea.

Julian boxed at middleweight and started 1992 with another share of the spoils, drawing after six rounds against Paul McCarthy from Southampton, who was very experienced, having boxed thirty-three times as a pro in which time he had won the Southern area super middleweight title and had also lost in three rounds to Nicky Piper. Julian travelled to St. Leonards in Sussex for his third professional encounter, where he fought Johnny Uphill from Hastings, who found that boxing Julian was all uphill – getting knocked out in round three. Julian lost his next two bouts on six rounds points decisions against Nicky Wadman from Brighton in Cardiff and Andy Manning from Warrington in Llanelli.

On 25th November Julian stopped Eddie Knight from Ashford in two rounds in Mayfair, a popular haunt for Swansea boxers and, in what turned out to be his final contest, he outpointed John McNeil from Bristol over six rounds in Swansea, on a bill that was topped by Nicky Piper.

Fights: 7 • Won: 3 (2 by KO) • Lost: 2 • Draws: 2

Chris Coughlan, Kevin Simmons and Julian Johnson (Front)
sign up with manager Colin Breen and trainer Ray Price.

DARREN LINEY was born in Swansea. He boxed only once at light middleweight on 28th May 1991.

Fights: 1 • Won: 1 • Lost: 0 • Draws: 0
Refer CHAPTER EIGHT

CHRIS MYLAN was born in Swansea on 6th November 1972. He made his professional debut in Dunstable on 26th September 1991, losing on points over six rounds against Paul Ryan from Hackney. Three weeks later he drew with Mark O'Callaghan from Tunbridge Wells after six rounds in Burton on Trent. He then lost to Howard Clarke from Warley in the West Midlands at Dudley on 15th October. This was Clarke's first contest in a career that would span sixteen years and one hundred and nine fights – among his opponents would be Wayne Alexander, Gary Lockett, Ryan Rhodes and Fernando Vargas, who he challenged for the IBF light middleweight title. Three weeks later Chris knocked out debutant Nigel Burder from Gorseinon at the Rhydycar Leisure Centre in Merthyr Tydfil. He fought in Birmingham in December, winning on points over eight rounds against Darren Morris, who was boxing in his home city.

In his final contest the decision went against him in an eight round encounter against unbeaten Steve McGovern from the Isle of Wight. Chris Mylan had boxed professionally for just eighty-two days.

Fights: 6 • Won: 2 • Lost: 3 • Draws: 1

KEVIN SIMMONS was born in Swansea on 8th November 1968. He boxed at super featherweight, making his professional debut under the management of Colin Breen in Cardiff on 22nd January 1992, when he was outpointed over six rounds by Jason Lepre of Portsmouth. Kevin didn't box again until 22nd September 1993 when in his final contest he was stopped in two rounds by Paul Webster at Bethnal Green.

Fights: 2 • Won: 0 • Lost: 2 (1 by KO) • Draws: 0

MARK VERIKIOS was born in Swansea on 31st October 1965. He made his professional boxing debut in a welterweight contest on 15th May 1991 and retired on 12th November 1992.

Fights: 5 • Won: 5 • Lost: 0 • Draws: 0
Refer CHAPTER EIGHT

JASON McNEILL was born in Bristol on 12th August 1971 but turned professional when living and boxing out of Swansea, making his debut in Burton on Trent on 23rd October 1991 when he was outpointed in a six rounds super middleweight contest by fellow debutant Marc Pain at Burton on Trent. He boxed twice more in 1991, suffering another six rounds defeat on points against Tony Colclough from Birmingham. In his third and final contest of the year Jason tasted victory, winning the decision after six rounds against Marc McBiane of Skegness. Jason continued boxing until 1994. He retired after being stopped in the fifth round by Swedish-based Albanian, Louis Morina. In his three year career he had boxed sixteen times, but fought only once in Swansea, losing a six rounds points decision against fellow Swansea boxer Julian Johnson on 10th April 1993.

Fights: 16 • Won: 2 • Lost: 14 (8 by KO) • Draws: 0

PHIL CULLEN was born in Swansea on 4th February 1972. He only boxed once as a professional on 25th March 1992.

Fights: 1 • Won: 0 • Lost: 1 (1 by KO) • Draws: 0
Refer CHAPTER EIGHT

PAUL DAVIES was born in Swansea on 18th October 1968. He boxed once as a professional in a light welterweight contest on 30th March 1993.

Fights: 1 • Won: 0 • Lost: 1 • Draws: 0
Refer CHAPTER EIGHT

DARREN PULLMAN was born in Swansea on 11th January 1974 – he participated in one professional bout on 10th April 1993.

Fights: 1 • Won: 0 • Lost: 0 • Draws: 1
Refer CHAPTER EIGHT

Mark Hughes.
(Courtesy of *South Wales Evening Post*).

MARK HUGHES was born in Swansea on 8th July 1971. He boxed professionally in the flyweight division between 21st September 1994 and 25th October 1995.

Fights: 5 • Won: 4 • Lost: 0 • Draws: 1
Refer CHAPTER EIGHT

MARC SMITH was born in London – nicknamed 'too cute'. A resident of Swansea, he turned professional with local manager and boxing promoter Paul Boyce and made his professional debut at the Glyn Clydach Hotel on 20th May 1994 when he drew with fellow debutant Andrew Smith from Bedworth in Warwickshire. The south-paw lightweight won three, drew one and lost six contests with Paul before transferring allegiance to Midlands manager/promoter Ron Gray.

On 27th May 1997 and again on 31st October 1997 he lost on points over four rounds against Jason Cook from Maesteg. Cook later became European and IBO lightweight champion.

Marc continued boxing without many successes until March 2000 when he boxed a three round no contest against Gary Steadman in Bethnal Green. The Swansea boxer had won eight and lost forty-two and drawn one going into this bout, but would turn up anywhere any time for a fight with a minimum amount of notice. After the Steadman bout Marc didn't box again until 11th December 2009 when he resurrected his career in Spain. He retired in round four against Spanish-based Argentine, Emiliano Casal.

Fights: 52 • Won: 8 (2 by KO) • Lost: 43 (10 by KO) • Draws: 1

CLIVE SWEETLAND was born in Swansea on 23rd January 1967. He participated in his only professional boxing contest on 12th April 1995 in a welterweight contest in Llanelli. He was knocked out in the second round by Tom Welsh from Holyhead who was also making his debut in the paid ranks.

Fights: 1 • Won: 0 • Lost: 1 • Draws: 0

ROSS McCORD was born in Swansea on 31st August 1977. He made his professional debut as a twenty-year-old in the welterweight division on 2nd December 1997 and boxed on until 15th September 2002.

Fights: 15 • Won: 6 (3 by KO) • Lost: 8 (6 by KO) • Draws: 1

TITLE FIGHTS

15-09-2002	Keith Jones	L	TKO	4	Swansea	Vacant Welsh welterweight title

Refer CHAPTER SIX and CHAPTER SEVEN

DARREN WILLIAMS was born in Swansea on 17th July 1975 – he boxed at light middleweight, making his professional debut on mid summer's day 1997; his last encounter was on 24th April 2002.

Fights: 11 • Won: 8 (1 by KO) • Lost: 2 • Draws: 1
Refer CHAPTER SEVEN

Jason Williams.

JASON WILLIAMS was born in Swansea on 11th July 1974. He boxed at light middleweight, making his professional debut on 19th April 1997. His final bout was on 1st May 2004 when he was approaching his thirtieth birthday.

Fights: 25 • Won: 15 (6 by KO) • Lost: 10 (6 by KO) • Draws: 0

TITLE FIGHTS

24-09-1999	Michael Smyth	L	TKO	3	Merthyr Tydfil	vacant Welsh welterweight title
23-02-2003	Keith Jones	W	PTS	10	Aberystwyth	Welsh welterweight title

Refer CHAPTER FIVE and CHAPTER SEVEN

ENZO MACCARINELLI was born in Swansea on 20th August 1980. Boxing at cruiserweight, he made his professional debut on 2nd October 1999 and was still active on 31st December 2010.

Fights: 37 • Won: 32 (25 by KO) • Lost: 5 (5 by KO) • Draws: 0

TITLE FIGHTS

28-06-2003	Bruce Scott	W TKO 4	Cardiff	WBU cruiserweight title
13-09-2003	Andrei Karsten	W KO 1	Newport	WBU cruiserweight title
06-12-2003	Earl Morais	W KO 1	Cardiff	WBU cruiserweight title
21-02-2004	Garry Delaney	W TKO 8	Cardiff	WBU cruiserweight title
03-07-2004	Ismail Abdoul	W PTS 12	Newport	WBU cruiserweight title
03-09-2004	Jesper Kristiansen	W KO 3	Newport	WBU cruiserweight title
21-01-2005	Rich LaMontagne	W TKO 4	Bridgend	WBU cruiserweight title
04-06-2005	Roman Bugaj	W TKO 1	Manchester	WBU cruiserweight title
26-11-2005	Marco Heinichen	W KO 1	Rome	WBU cruiserweight title
04-03-2006	Mark Hobson	W PTS 12	Manchester	WBU cruiserweight title
08-07-2006	Marcelo Fabian Dominguez	W TKO 9	Cardiff	Interim WBO cruiserweight title
14-10-2006	Mark Hobson	W TKO 1	Manchester	WBO cruiserweight title
07-04-2007	Bobby Gunn	W TKO 1	Cardiff	WBO cruiserweight title
21-07-2007	Wayne Braithwaite	W PTS 12	Cardiff	WBO cruiserweight title
13-11-2007	Mohamed Azzaoui	W TKO 4	Cardiff	WBO cruiserweight title
08-03-2008	David Haye	L TKO 2	London	WBA, WBC, WBO cruiserweight titles
14-03-2009	Ola Afolabi	L TKO 9	Manchester	Interim WBO cruiserweight titles
18-07-2009	Denis Lebedev	L TKO 3	Manchester	WBO inter-continental cruiserweight title
27-04-2010	Alexander Kotlobay	W TKO 1	St Petersburg	vacant European cruiserweight title
18-09-2010	Alexander Frenkel	L KO 7	Manchester	European cruiserweight title

Refer CHAPTER ONE and CHAPTER SEVEN

DALEBOY REES was born in Swansea on 6th July 1975. He boxed at light welterweight, managed by Paul Boyce and trained by Jimmy Bromfield, making his professional debut on 15th September 2002 outpointing Greg Edwards from Hereford over four rounds at the Swansea Leisure Centre. In 2003 he boxed four times, commencing with a stoppage win over Joel Viney from Blackpool in Aberdare, the bout ended in round five. He outpointed Pavel Potopko from Belarus in Bridgend and Henry Jones from Pembroke at the Manor Park Hotel in Clydach, both over four rounds, before losing the decision and his unbeaten tally after four rounds against Buster Dennis at the Brangwyn Hall in Swansea.

In 2004 Daleboy lost by technical knockout against Henry Castle from Salisbury at the York Hall, Bethnal Green. He hung up his gloves after dropping a six rounds decision to Michael Graydon in Bristol on 1st October 2004.

Fights: 7 • Won: 4 (1 by KO) • Lost: 3 (1 by KO) • Draws: 0

CERI HALL was born in Swansea on 25th March 1980 and made his debut as a professional boxer on 15th September 2002. He retired from boxing in June 2007.

Fights: 17 • Won: 10 (3 by KO) • Lost: 5 • Draws: 2

TITLE FIGHTS

| 02-03-2007 | Stuart Green | W | TKO | 9 | Neath | British Boxing Board of Control Celtic light welterweight title |
| 23-02-2003 | Stuart Phillips | L | PTS | 10 | Neath | BBB of C Celtic light welterweight title |

Refer CHAPTER FIVE

CHRIS BROPHY was born in Preston, Lancashire, on 28th January 1979, but resides in and boxes out of Swansea, thus qualifying as a Swansea boxer. He turned professional and made his debut on 29th October 2003 at the age of twenty-four going on twenty-five at the salubrious Equinox Nightclub in Leicester Square. Unfortunately, Chris didn't have such a good night at the Equinox, losing on a technical knockout in five rounds to Aidan Mooney from Newcastle. Chris won his second bout, his first of only two fights, on 'home soil' – he out-scored Casey Brooks from Birmingham over six rounds at the Brangwyn Hall on 30th November 2003. The Swansea boxer lost four and drew one of his next five contests and then outpointed Tommy Marshall over six rounds in Plymouth, their second meeting at this venue, having boxed a six round draw the previous April.

Chris failed to win any of his next ten contests between 21st November 2004 when he was stopped in one round by Jay Morris from the Isle of Wight at Bracknell, and on the 18th March 2007 when he drew with Chris Long at the Marriot Hotel in Bristol. Chris lost his next three bouts to Patrick Doherty in London, Louis Byrne in Bristol, and to Swansea boxer James Lilley at the Brangwyn Hall, Swansea, on 27th October. Chris Brophy's last winning contest was on 2nd December 2007. In 2008 he fought and lost seven times. He lost his three bouts in 2009 and in 2010 he lost four times but earned a draw after four rounds with debutant John Brennan from Slough at the York Hall, Bethnal Green. In six years as a professional, Chris has entered the ring forty-nine times, winning on only three occasions, with forty-three defeats and three draws. Chris continues to answer the call to box anywhere at any time against anybody.

Fights: 49 • Won: 3 • Lost: 43 (17 by KO) • Draws: 3

DAMIAN OWEN was born in Swansea on 7th May 1985 – boxing at lightweight he made his professional debut on 1st October 2004. He was still active on 31st December 2009.

Fights: 13 • Won: 11 (5 by KO) • Lost: 2 (1 by KO) • Draws: 0

TITLE FIGHTS

02-03-2007	Dean Phillips	W KO 4	Neath	vacant Welsh lightweight title

Refer CHAPTER FIVE and CHAPTER SEVEN

RICKY OWEN was born in Swansea on 5th May 1985. He made his debut on 5th November 2004, and is still active at featherweight.

Fights: 13 • Won: 13 (4 by KO) • Lost: 0 • Draws: 0
Refer CHAPTER EIGHT

GARETH PERKINS was born in Swansea on 17th December 1982. He made his professional debut at welterweight on 29th February 2004 – his only other contest was on 17th January 2006.

Fights: 2 • Won: 1 • Lost: 0 • Draws: 1
Refer CHAPTER EIGHT

DARREN MORGAN was born in Swansea on 26th October 1976. Appropriately known as 'The Beast from Bonymaen', he has to date boxed ten times as a professional, winning his first five fights and losing the next five. He was twenty-four years old when he made his debut at the Bridgend Leisure Centre on 21st January 2005; he stopped Brighton-based Gambian Ebrima Secka in the first round.

In June he stopped experienced trial horse Dave Clarke from Dover again in the first round. Clarke had also been stopped by Swansea boxer Enzo Maccarinelli in October 2002. He outpointed Tony Booth, who was engaging bout number one hundred and thirteen, at the Cardiff International Arena.

In 2006 he beat Radcliffe Green, a London-based Jamaican, in three rounds and outpointed Wolverhampton-based Hungarian Istvan Kecsces at Newport Leisure Centre. In his final bout of 2006 he lost on points to Irishman Martin Rogan in Belfast.

In 2008 Rogan won the Prizefighter heavyweight competition and in 2009 beat Matt Skelton to annex the Commonwealth heavyweight title. Darren fought just once in 2007 losing the decision after four rounds against Finchley-based Zimbabwean Derek Chisora, who is due to fight WBC heavyweight champion Vladimir Klitschko for his crown in 2011. His losing run continued in 2008 when he lost on points over eight rounds against Sam Sexton at the York Hall – sixteen months later Sexton won the Commonwealth heavyweight title, beating defending champion Martin Rogan.

The Swansea boxer entered a Prizefighter tournament at the York Hall losing on points after four rounds against David Dolan from Sunderland. In a similar tournament held in Newcastle he lost a quarter final bout on points over four rounds against Lee Swaby from Doncaster on 12th September.

Fights: 10 • Won: 5 (3 by KO) • Lost: 5 • Draws: 0

JAMES LILLEY was born on 14th November 1968. He got his professional career off to a dream start by stopping trial horse Anthony Christopher from Aberystwyth in the first round of a welterweight contest at the Brangwyn Hall in Swansea on 8th October 2006. James participated in three more contests in 2006, losing decisions to Darren Hamilton from Bristol and Chris Goodwin from Chester at Stoke. Both of these opponents hold respectable records. Hamilton is currently unbeaten in five contests, but hasn't fought since December 2007; Goodwin has won eleven, lost one and drawn one. In his last bout of 2007 James inflicted defeat number eighteen on fellow Swansea boxer Chris Brophy, winning on points after four rounds at the Brangwyn Hall in October.

On Leap Year's day, 29th February 2008, James lost the decision after six rounds against Ben Wakeham from Torquay at the Guildhall in Plymouth. His next bout was nearer to home – he fought at the Afan Lido in March, when he beat Russell Pearce from Welshpool. The Swansea boxer didn't box again until June 2009 when he outpointed Rocky Chakir a Bristol-based Turkish boxer at the Newport Leisure Centre on a bill that included a clash between two Swansea boxers, James Todd and Adam Farrell.

Fights: 7 • Won: 4 (1 by KO) • Lost: 3 • Draws: 0

LEON OWEN was born in Mountain Ash but resided in and boxed out of Swansea He made his professional debut as a super middle-weight when he stopped another debutant, Scotsman Greg Baxter, in the first round at Dagenham on 26th February 2006. Leon was stopped in the second round by George Katsimpas from Cheddar, outpointed Jay Jerome from Birmingham in Bristol and outpointed David Pearson from Middlesborough at the Brangwyn Hall Swansea to conclude his opening campaign.

In 2007 he dropped a four round decision against Dunfermline's Gordon Brennan in Motherwell, and in his final contest lost on points over six rounds against Shon Davies from Llanelli at the Brangwyn Hall in Swansea on 21st October 2007.

Fights: 6 • Won: 3 (1 by KO) • Lost: 3 (1 by KO) • Draws: 0

CRAIG DYER was born on 23rd August 1986. He first entered a professional boxing ring shortly after his twenty-first birthday on 21st September 2007. He is still active up to December 2010.

Fights: 15 • Won: 0 • Lost: 15 (1 by KO) • Draws: 0
Refer CHAPTER EIGHT

ADAM FARRELL was born in Swansea on 8th June 1986. He made his debut as a professional boxer on 13th March 2009 and is still active in the light welterweight division.

Fights: 2 • Won: 0 • Lost: 2 (1 by KO) • Draws: 0
Refer CHAPTER EIGHT

JAMES TODD was born in Swansea on 4th March 1988. In his first professional contest he drew with Andrew Cummings over four rounds at the Thistle Hotel in Bristol on 14th December 2008 – both the Swansea boxer and Cummings, who hails from Bristol, were making their professional debuts. James began his 2009 campaign with a victory on points over six rounds at the Rhydycar Leisure Centre in Merthyr Tydfil against veteran trial horse Jason Nesbitt from Birmingham. The Swansea boxer acquitted himself well, winning every round against his seasoned opponent who was participating in his ninety-second professional contest. This triumph was followed by another success, outpointing fellow Swansea boxer Adam Farrell, again dominating the fight by winning every round at the Newport Leisure Centre.

James then joined a training regime in the United States and boxed debutant Dean Peters Jr. from the state of Wisconsin – he lost the decision and his unbeaten tally after four rounds, in Milwaukee. In his final bout of the year he somewhat speculatively challenged Mohammed Kayango from Uganda for the vacant World Boxing Foundation Intercontinental welterweight title. He was stopped in three rounds in St Pauls, Minnesota. Coming into this fight Kayongo, who was resident in St Pauls, had won fourteen, lost two and drawn one of seventeen contests, eleven of those wins coming inside the scheduled distance.

Fights: 5 • Won: 2 • Lost: 2 (1 by KO) • Draws: 1

TOBIAS WEBB was born in Swansea on 25th August 1988. He made his professional debut at super middleweight on 14th March 2009.

Fights: 5 • Won: 4 • Lost: 0 • Draws: 1
Refer CHAPTER SEVEN and CHAPTER EIGHT

JOE SMITH was born on 29th January 1981. He made his debut as a professional boxer on 22nd May 2010, losing on points in a six round welterweight contest against fellow debutant Lee Bennett from Burnley. The Swansea boxer climbed back into the ring on 2nd July in Doncaster against Steven Swinburn of Lincoln when he was stopped in two rounds. Twenty-three-year-old Liverpudlian Terry Needham, a southpaw, made a successful debut by halting Joe, who still looking for his first win, dropping him with a right uppercut before the referee stopped the fight in the third round.

Fights: 3 • Won: 0 • Lost: 3 (2 by KO) • Draws: 0

IANTO JENKINS made his professional debut in a four rounds light heavyweight contest at the King's Hall in Belfast on 15th December 2010, losing the decision after four rounds against Brian Cusack, who was a thirty-two-year-old Irishman who had won his two other contests as a professional.

Fights: 1 • Won: 0 • Lost: 1 • Draws: 0

Chapter One

IN SEARCH OF THE ULTIMATE PRIZE

Welsh sports fans were filled with jubilation and optimistic expectation – it was the 7th of April 2007, the Welsh rugby team had just seen off the Gaelic challenge to win the Grand Slam at Croke Park in Dublin. In just a few hours time Swansea boxer **Enzo Maccarinelli** World Boxing Organisation cruiserweight champion would be defending that title and challenging David Haye for his World Boxing Association and World Boxing Council titles at the 02 Arena in Greenwich. Enzo's journey to his assault on the titles had been carefully piloted by promoter Frank Warren.

This was the big one, the fight that the Swansea boxer had worked so hard for since making his professional debut in October 1999 when he outpointed Paul Bonson over four rounds at the International Arena in Cardiff. This was the culmination of all those hours of blood and sweat in the gym each evening when his mates were out having good times, those miles and miles of early morning roadwork, when it would have been so very easy to have hidden under the blankets.

In spite of all the hard work and sacrifice it had not been all plain sailing for Enzo – in his fourth professional fight, after three comfortable and impressive wins, his world tumbled down around him. He was sensationally knocked out in the third round by Lee Swaby who was not expected to trouble the Swansea boxer. Enzo's fans witnessed the humiliation at the Swansea Leisure Centre. But all credit to the Swansea boxer and his camp as they put the pieces back together and steered their way to the fight he had dreamed of, where he hoped all his aspirations would be realised.

The comeback began six months after the Swaby setback when Enzo cautiously outpointed experienced Chris Woolas. The Swansea boxer showed that he had lost none of his determination and was regaining confidence by winning all three contests inside the distance in 2001, testimony to his tremendous power, knocking out Darren Ashton from Stoke in the first round, Eamon Glennon from Blackpool in the second and stopped Kevin Barrett in two rounds at the Wembley Conference Centre on a bill topped by Ricky Hatton.

In the ensuing year, 2002, the Swansea boxer stopped London-based Zimbabwean James Gilbert in two rounds, achieved two victories over the experienced Tony Booth from Hull and completed the year's campaign with a second round stoppage victory over Blackpool's Dave Clarke.

Enzo's rehabilitation continued to flourish in 2003; a repeated victory against Paul Bonson on points over four rounds and a first round stoppage win over Ukrainian Valeri Semiskur culminated in a challenge for the vacant World Boxing Union cruiserweight against London-based Jamaican Bruce Scott who had won twenty-five, losing only six. Enzo was approaching his twenty-third birthday with thirteen wins and one loss on his record. The bout took place at the International Arena in Cardiff on 28th June 2003 and started sensationally with the Swansea boxer on the canvas in the first round. He quickly recovered to floor his opponent in the fourth round when the referee stopped the contest proclaiming Enzo as WBU champion. He successfully defended the title seven times, scoring two first round knockout wins in title defences against Estonian Andret Karsten, who had won fifteen out of seventeen, and another decent fighter, South African Earl Morais, rounding off a very successful year.

Enzo was now in top gear. He stopped Gary Delaney from West Ham in eight rounds, got the full twelve rounds and a points win under his belt against tough Belgian Ismael Abdoul, who later in his career took David Haye and Marco Huck the full distance. In his last bout of 2004 the Swansea boxer successfully defended the WBU title for the fifth time by knocking out Danish cruiserweight Jesper Kristiansen in three rounds at the Newport Leisure Centre.

Enzo Maccarinelli.

Three stoppage wins in 2005 against American Rich LaMontagne who was beaten in four rounds and never boxed again, Polish boxer Roman Bugaj was stopped in the first round and also retired from boxing, German boxer Marco Heinichen was knocked out in the first round in front of a Roman audience in Enzo's twenty-second win in twenty-three fights. The Swansea boxer was made to 'earn his corn' next time out, winning a hard earned but unanimous decision against Mark Hobson over twelve rounds. The win earned Enzo a match with WBO champion Johnny Nelson from Sheffield in a unification title fight. Nelson was sidelined due to injury consequently Enzo was matched with tough Argentine and South American heavyweight champion, Marcelo Fabian Dominguez, who had lost only six times in forty-six contests and had never been stopped. He had previously taken Johnny Nelson and the Russian giant Nikolay Valuev the scheduled distance losing points decisions. The Swansea boxer achieved his greatest triumph to date by stopping the tough Argentine gladiator in the ninth round at the Millennium Stadium, topping a fifteen fight programme featuring Danny Williams versus Matt Skelton and rising stars Kevin Mitchell, Amir Kahn and Nathan Cleverly.

Johnny Nelson announced his retirement, and accordingly Enzo was declared WBO champion after an impressive first round stoppage of Mark Hobson. Unable to display the resilience he had shown in the first encounter he had the resistance knocked out of him from heavy body shots.

The Swansea boxer continued to impress in making progress towards a crack at the WBA and WBC titles which seemed to be changing hands on a regular basis. He stopped American Bobby Gunn in the first round, outpointed highly ranked New York-based Wayne Braithwaite from Guyana over twelve rounds and overpowered New Zealand-based Algerian Mohamed Azzaoui, who was previously unbeaten in twenty-four contests, stopping him in the fourth round.

Enzo on his way to beating unbeaten challenger Mohamed Azzaoui at the Millennium Stadium.

The only obstacle left in his way was hard-punching David Haye a confident swaggering fighter from Bermondsey who was nicknamed the 'Hayemaker'. Enzo at this time was twenty-six years of age. Haye, two months younger, had been a professional boxer since December

2002 and had won twenty fights, nineteen inside the distance. He had lost just one fight by a technical knockout in the fifth round against the International Boxing Organisation champion Carl Thompson, who was best remembered for his two epic battles with Chris Eubank, winning on both occasions in defence of his WBO title. Haye had been European cruiserweight champion since knocking out Ukrainian holder of the title Alexander Gurov in December 2005. He won the WBA and WBC titles in November 2007 when he sensationally stopped the defending champion, Frenchman Jean Marc Mormeck, in the seventh round after being on the canvas himself in round four.

Was this the hour when Enzo would become the beneficiary of the dedicated mentoring and the lifestyle disciplines imposed on him by his father Mario? Was this the time when he would reap the reward for the many rounds of tortuous and tiring sparring with the invincible Joe Calzaghe in the Spartan, almost primeval surroundings of Enzo Calzaghe's gym in Newbridge?

The atmosphere in the arena was electrifying as both boxers entered the ring. Haye looked cool and confident, Enzo looked nervous and tense. This was the moment when two of the heaviest punchers in the cruiserweight division would pit their wits, their skill and their might against each other – this was the long awaited showdown.

As the bell sounded for the opening round Enzo began well attempting to reach Haye with fast left jabs. It was as expected a tentative, cagey and close first round. The Swansea boxer started the second round with some promise, catching his opponent with a couple of hefty hooks to the body, but was repeatedly getting caught with overhand right hand counter punches, the third of which put him on the canvas. He quickly, perhaps too quickly, got to his feet but was in no condition to defend himself, his numbed brain had momentarily lost control of his legs when the referee had no alternative but to stop the fight. Enzo and his band of followers were absolutely gutted – all the hard work, the meticulous preparation blown away inside two rounds.

However, the accomplishment of David Haye in becoming the WBA heavyweight champion by defeating the Russian giant Nikolay

Valuev put Enzo's challenge into perspective. David Haye was a steep mountain to climb.

Enzo returned to the ring on 6th December to rebuild his career for the second time. He boxed Matthew Ellis from Blackpool who had won twenty of twenty-six contests since turning professional in February 1996. Referee Dave Parris stopped the fight in the second round – Ellis had been punched into a condition whereby he was unable to defend himself.

The Swansea boxer was then matched with Ola Afolabi who was born in London and based in California – he had lost only once in seventeen contests, the bout was billed as the interim WBO cruiser-weight title and took place in Manchester. In round nine Enzo seemed to be running out of steam and ideas against his unorthodox opponent and appeared in trouble when referee Terry O'Connor came to his rescue.

Determined to resurrect his career the Swansea boxer ambitiously and adventurously took on unbeaten Denis Lebedev, a dangerous southpaw from Checkov in Russia, who had stopped twelve of his seventeen opponents – certainly not the ideal opponent when coming back from an inside the distance defeat. The Russian retained his unbeaten record and won the vacant WBO intercontinental cruiser-weight title by stopping Enzo, who was totally lacking in confidence, in round three.

It seemed there was nothing left for Enzo, nowhere to turn; after three inside the distance defeats in his last four contests all the Swansea boxer had left was sheer determination to regain his status in the World cruiserweight rankings. The rebuilding programme was underway marked by two one round victories against Hungarians Kristian Jaksi and Zoltan Czekus.

Earlier than expected the Swansea boxer was offered a tilt at the vacant European cruiserweight title against the promising Russian Alexander Kotlobay who had won eighteen out of twenty with one draw. The bout took place in St Petersburgh on 27th April 2010. Most of the boxing pundits believed the Russian would benefit from home advantage, but the Swansea boxer had other ideas, sensationally stopping the Russian in round one to become only the second Swansea boxer to win a European title.

Enzo made his first defence of the title on Frank Warren's 'Magnificent Seven' show in Manchester on 18th September 2010. He was matched with the unbeaten twenty-five-year-old German-based Ukrainian, Alexander Frenkel, who had halted eighteen of his twenty-three opponents. Going into round seven the challenger appeared to be losing belief in himself; the Swansea boxer had cautiously built up a lead but was caught with a right hand that sent him crashing to the canvas. He bravely beat the count and the referee allowed the fight to continue. The defending champion was a sitting target for the German's continuing onslaught – he was down for the second time when the referee stopped the contest, Frenkel was European champion, Enzo's career was once again at the crossroads, the only Swansea boxer to hold any version of a World title.

Can he resurrect his career yet again?

Some sixty-two years before, in September 1946, **Ronnie James** from Bonymaen had challenged Ike Williams from Trenton, New Jersey, for the National Boxing Association (NBA) World lightweight title at Ninian Park, Cardiff. Ronnie, who was twenty-nine years of age, was in his fourteenth year as a professional boxer, he had won one hundred and twelve bouts against fifteen losses and five draws. His title challenge was promoted by Jack Solomons who had lured the champion from America to defend his title in Cardiff. Williams had been World champion since April of the previous year when he'd stopped the Mexican Juan Zurita in the second round in Mexico City; this would be his second defence of the title. Coming into this fight the American, only twenty-three years of age, had been victorious seventy-five times in his professional career against nine losses and four draws. The Swansea boxer's chance of victory was enhanced by rumours that the champion was struggling to make the weight. He was reported to be one pound and six ounces over the championship limit of nine stones and nine pounds one hour before the official weigh in. Nevertheless, Ike Williams tipped the scales four ounces inside.

Ronnie James.

An estimated forty thousand turned up for the fight which had been threatened by a torrential and persistent downpour. Mr Solomons, whose recording of the attendance was a little more conservative at twenty-six thousand, ensured that everything was alright on the night as the rainfall subsided.

The Swansea boxer, although giving of his best, was no match for the champion who was showing no signs of weakening from his efforts to 'make the weight' and was 'doubling up' the challenger with his famed 'bolo' punch to the body. Ronnie James showed great courage surviving six knockdowns before being 'counted out' in the ninth round. He became the first Swansea boxer to fail in search of the ultimate prize.

Brian Curvis.

It would be eighteen years on before another Swansea boxer would make a World title challenge on another Jack Solomons promotion on this occasion at the Empire Pool, Wembley, in September 1964. **Brian Curvis** who was born Nancurvis, from Peter Street, Waun Wen, was managed and trained by his brother Cliff, assisted by Dickie Dobbs. The Swansea boxer was the current British and Empire welterweight champion and had won two Lonsdale belts, he was twenty-seven years of age had won all but one of his thirty-one contests, his one defeat a cut eye stoppage against Guy Sumlin from Mobile, Alabama.

Brother Cliff didn't plan an easy return to the ring for Brian. After the Sumlin setback his next fight was to be against the highly ranked and very experienced Ralph Dupas from New Orleans, Louisiana, at the Empire Pool, Wembley, in what was without doubt Brian's finest performance to date. The American was floored in the first round by a terrific left hook and only his great experience enabled him to survive the round. He was disqualified in the sixth for persistent holding which was all he could do to keep the relentless Swansea boxer at bay. The victory and indeed the manner of victory made the Americans take notice and realise that the Swansea boxer had all the credentials of a genuine title contender.

Next on Brian's agenda was an eagerly awaited rematch with Guy Sumlin – the Swansea boxer avenged his sole defeat by winning a well earned comfortable ten rounds points decision.

The Swansea boxer was now among the leading contenders in the *Ring* magazine World ratings but was still considered to be a few scraps away from a world title shot. He was kept busy building his reputation and maintaining his boxing fitness with a successful defence of his British and Commonwealth titles against Tony Smith and wins over Frenchman Maurice Auzel and Sugar Cliff from the Bahamas.

Brian was approaching his twenty-seventh birthday and he was nudging closer and closer to a shot at the world title. In what was considered to be a 'warm up' the Swansea boxer locked horns with the British, Commonwealth and European lightweight champion, the 'Dartford Destroyer', Dave Charnley. They fought a tremendous battle of two southpaws over ten rounds at the Empire Pool. Referee Jack Hart declared Brian Curvis the winner by what must have been the narrowest of margins. In another 'warm up' Brian defended his British and Empire titles stopping Johnny Cooke in five rounds.

Brian Curvis floors Ralph Dupas in the first round of their World title eliminator.
(Courtesy of *South Wales Evening Post*).

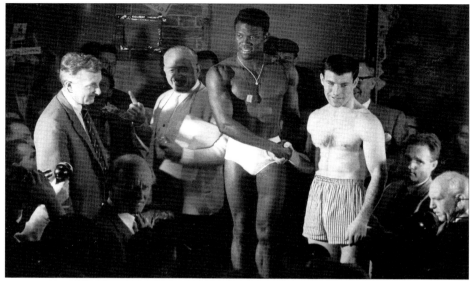

22nd September 1964 – World welterweight champion Emile Griffith shakes hands with his challenger Brian Curvis at the weigh-in prior to his title defence at the Empire Pool Wembley.

Contracts were signed, the stage was set, Brian Curvis was to challenge Emile Griffith for the World welterweight championship at the Empire Pool, Wembley, on 24th September 1964. Griffith, a milliner by trade, from the Virgin Islands, USA, was twenty-six years of age, just a few months younger than Brian. He had been a professional boxer since June 1958, was managed by Gil Clancy and had fought forty-six times, winning forty-one and had lost five.

Emile was making the second defence of the title he had regained from Cuban gladiator Luis Rodriguez in June of 1963. The champion first won the World welterweight title in April 1961 when he KO'd the defending champion Benny Paret, who like Rodriguez was from Cuba. In a return bout six months later Paret regained the title winning a split decision after fifteen hotly contested rounds. They fought for a third time in March 1962 at Madison Square Garden in New York. There was a lot of needle, a tirade of insults were exchanged preceding a genuine grudge match. Griffith regained the title when referee Ruby Goldstein stopped the contest in the twelfth round, the Cuban was not responding to a two-fisted onslaught from the Virgin Islander; Benny slipped into a coma in the ring and tragically died several days later from injuries sustained in the fight.

Griffith made two successful defences after the Paret tragedy before losing the title for a second time against Rodriguez. As referred to earlier he regained the title from Luis and successfully defended the title against him before the defence against Brian.

The Swansea boxer fought his heart out in trying to match the skill, speed, strength and ring craft of a superb champion, but with little success. Brian rose to his feet after being decked in the sixth, tenth and thirteenth rounds, gallantly making the champion fight to the final bell to retain his title on a fifteen rounds decision. Brian became the second Swansea boxer to fail in his quest for the ultimate prize.

Colin Jones.

Colin Jones from Gorseinon was one of four fighting brothers, Ken and Peter boxed professionally, while Terry was a useful amateur. Colin boxed for Penyrheol Boxing Club, his father was the secretary. Gareth 'Gus' Bevan his trainer was with the Swansea boxer throughout his professional career. He won a host of schoolboy, junior and senior titles including two Amateur Boxing Association titles and represented Great Britain at the 1976 Olympic Games in Montreal when only seventeen years of age. He had turned professional in October 1977 when just eighteen years of age, under the management of former British welterweight champion Eddie Thomas from Merthyr Tydfil who had already managed two world champions, Howard Winstone and Ken Buchanan, and he was confident that Colin would become his third.

In his debut contest he stopped fellow Swansea boxer Mike Copp in the fifth round at the Afan Lido. In March 1983 Colin, the reigning British, Commonwealth and European champion, was to challenge the unbeaten Milton McCrory from Detroit, Michigan, for the vacant WBC title. The Swansea boxer was twenty-four years of age and had won twenty-four of twenty-five professional contests, his one defeat a pretty harsh disqualification for a low blow against Curtis Ramsey. The twenty-one-year-old American, nicknamed 'The Ice Man', was unbeaten in twenty contests, seventeen wins inside the scheduled distance.

When the fight was announced McCrory was rated a seven to one hotshot to lift the title vacated by Sugar Ray Leonard who had retired, temporarily as it turned out, he returned to campaign in the middle-weight division. The odds shortened to three to one closer to the fight but there was no doubt this match presented an onerous task for the hard-punching Welshman.

At the end of twelve severely contested rounds in the burning desert sun of Reno, Nevada, the fair skinned Welshman had given a very good account of himself against the tall rangy negro, and many at ringside thought he had done more than enough to win the fight and so did one of the judges scoring Colin the winner by one hundred and sixteen to one hundred and thirteen; one judge called it even at one hundred and fifteen to one hundred and fifteen, the third judge give the nod to McCrory one hundred and sixteen to one hundred and fourteen – the result was a draw and the championship was still vacant. President of the WBC Jose Sulamain immediately ordered a rematch which was arranged for the Dunes Hotel, Las Vegas, for 13th August.

The return encounter was probably more exciting as the initiative switched from one to another as the fight progressed. In the first round Colin was dumped on the seat of his pants from a left uppercut.

He recovered from the early shock and staggered the American several times during the contest, many in the crowd expected to see Colin crowned as champion having seemingly done enough to earn the decision. One of the judges certainly saw it that way scoring one hundred and fourteen to one hundred and thirteen in Colin's favour, but the other two judges held different opinions voting for McCrory one hundred and fifteen to one hundred and eleven and one hundred and fifteen to one hundred and fourteen. The American was declared the winner and the new WBC champion by a very slender margin, and he wasn't going to be lured into an early title defence against Colin Jones!

There's an old saying 'three times for a Welshman', and the third time for Colin Jones was against the 'Lone Star Cobra' Don Curry from Fort Worth, Texas, who was the WBA champion. Curry boasted an unbeaten tariff after winning all his twenty contests, fifteen inside the scheduled distance. He won the vacant WBA title in February 1993 by unanimous decision after fifteen rounds against South Korean Jun-Suk Hwang. The Texan had made four successful defences of the title beating Roger Stafford by TKO in the first, outpointing Marlon Starling after fifteen rounds, halting Elio Diaz in eight rounds and knocking out Nino La Rocca in Monaco in round six. The challenge for the WBA title was to take place at the National Exhibition Centre (NEC) in Birmingham on January 1985. Many Welshmen made the journey up the M5 in the hope that Colin would be crowned World welterweight champion, a title many boxing followers believed he richly deserved.

Curry took control of the fight from the first bell as Colin got off to his customary slow start – it usually took Colin, a very patient boxer, a few rounds to move up the gears. The WBA champion put the Swansea boxer under early pressure and when Colin sustained a nasty gash across the bridge of his nose the referee, Ismael Fernandez, had little alternative but to halt the contest and declare Curry the winner in round four.

Colin retired from the ring after the WBA title challenge with an impressive record of twenty-six wins, all but three inside the distance and one draw. He was undoubtedly one of the best welterweights to come from these shores and many boxing pundits regard him as being very unfortunate never to have won the ultimate prize.

Floyd Havard.

When **Floyd Havard** from Clydach challenged John John Molina from Puerto Rico for the IBF super featherweight title he had lost his British title and his unbeaten record when he retired in the eleventh round against challenger John Doherty at the Afan Lido in September 1989.

After that defeat the twenty-four-year-old didn't box for eighteen months but won five straight over the next three years and was quite unexpectedly offered a shot at Molina's title. He had been a professional boxer since November 1985 a month past his twentieth birthday, coming into the Molina fight and had won twenty-six with just the one defeat. The IBF champion John John Molina was seven months older than Floyd, had turned professional three months later in February 1986. He won the WBO super featherweight title when he outpointed fellow countryman Juan Laporte over twelve rounds in San Juan in April 1989 and became the IBF champion six months later stopping Californian Tony Lopez in the tenth round. He made one successful defence before losing to Lopez in a return fight. He later regained the vacant IBF title when he beat Jackie Gunguluza in South Africa.

The fight with Floyd was Molina's fifth defence, he had won thirty-three fights with three losses when he stepped into the ring with the Swansea boxer. Floyd did his best but was no match for Molina – the champion had won every round before the Swansea boxer's corner retired him after the sixth round due to facial cuts. Losing to a boxer of Molina's calibre was no disgrace, the champion made two successful defences of his title before challenging Oscar De La Hoya for the WBO lightweight title.

Floyd regained the British title just nine weeks after the Molina fight. In spite of a determined and ambitious effort the Swansea boxer failed to win the ultimate prize.

Five Swansea boxers have attempted to win the ultimate prize and become the undisputed champion of the world. Enzo Maccarinelli held two versions, the WBU and the WBO titles. Colin Jones came so very close in two fights with Milton McCrory and was extremely unlucky not to be crowned champion. Both Brian Curvis and Ronnie James made gallant efforts but were up against great champions in Emile Griffith and Ike Williams. Floyd Havard, a very capable boxer, was perhaps a little out of his depth when making a brave challenge against John John Molina, a very good champion. The Swansea boxing fraternity hold these five boxers in very high esteem, as Swansea boxers they have earned great respect. The Swansea boxing fraternity is still looking forward to the day when a Swansea boxer has his arm raised in victory as the undisputed champion of the world, the ultimate prize.

Chapter Two

SWANSEA'S BRITISH CHAMPIONS

On 12th August 1944 **Ronnie James** became the first Swansea boxer to win a British title when he knocked out defending champion Eric Boon from Charteris in Cambridgeshire in the tenth round at the Cardiff Arms Park. Ronnie was at this time approaching his twenty-seventh birthday and had been a professional boxer for eleven years since stopping Sid Williams in round two at the Mannesman Hall, Swansea, on 21st January 1933. This would be his one hundred and twenty-second contest, of which he had won on one hundred and three occasions, he'd lost thirteen and drawn five. Boon, twenty-five years old, had been a professional since January 1935 – when he had just turned fifteen years of age his duel with Ronnie would be his ninety-third contest, seventy-nine were victories with eight losses and five draws.

Ronnie 'Rennie' James was born in Swansea on 18th October 1917, the son of an amateur boxer. Apart from his very obvious pugilistic potential Ronnie was also a very talented musician and as a child won a number of competitions, playing a variety of instruments. However, his first love was boxing, his ambition was to be a professional boxer, an ambition he fulfilled when he was just fifteen years of age.

By the end of 1935, and only eighteen years of age, the Swansea boxer was unbeaten in fifty-two fights, winning on forty-eight occasions and drawing four times. He had twice beaten fellow Swansea boxer Len Beynon winning twelve round decisions at the Vetch Field and at the Mannesman Hall and had drawn with former British Empire bantam-weight champion Dick Corbett. The Swansea boxer suffered his first defeat in 1936, he was disqualified in the sixth round against Dave Crowley who went on to become British lightweight champion. Shortly afterwards he lost for the second time, but was not disgraced when losing on points after twelve rounds against the reigning World bantamweight champion Baltazar Sangchilli of Spain at the Liverpool Stadium.

He also suffered a shock defeat against Billy Charlton from Gateshead, but he did chalk up thirteen wins and drew with Dick Corbett for the second time.

On 27th June 1938, twenty-year-old Ronnie James was to fight former World featherweight champion, the 'Cincinnati Express', Freddie Miller, over twelve rounds at the Mannesmann Hall. This was to be Miller's two hundred and thirty-seventh bout, he had won two hundred and four, lost twenty-four and drawn eight. Miller, twenty-seven years old from Cincinnati, Ohio, had won the World featherweight title by outpointing Tommy Paul in January 1933 and made thirteen successful defences before losing a fifteen rounds decision to Petey Sarron in March 1936.

The Swansea boxer was giving the former World champion a torrid time smashing right hand counter punches under Miller's heart. In round eight Miller crashed to the canvas having succumbed to a right hand punch to the ribs, and according to Roland Deakin's account of the fight in his book *Welsh Warriors*: 'hadn't a hope of beating the count.' The referee inexplicably halted the count and disqualified Ronnie for punching low, robbing him of a sensational victory.

The Swansea boxer enlisted into the Army during the war years but managed to maintain a reasonable level of ring activity. Between 1940 and 1943 Ronnie boxed twenty times, winning eighteen, losing twice against Lefty Satan Flynn from Belize in London and at the St Helen's Rugby Ground in Swansea.

In 1944, having lost two decisions against Arthur Danahar – once for the British Army welterweight title – Ronnie was offered a shot at the British lightweight title held by Eric Boon who had been British lightweight champion since 15th December 1938 when he knocked out the reigning title holder Dave Crowley in the thirteenth round. He knocked out Arthur Danahar in his first defence in round fourteen and won the Lonsdale belt by repeating his success over Dave Crowley again by knockout, this time in the seventh round.

In the pre-fight build up it was rumoured that the champion was struggling to make the lightweight limit of nine stone and nine pounds, but the Swansea boxer was leaving nothing to chance, he entered the ring looking in absolutely superb condition. In the early rounds there was little to choose between champion and challenger as both boxers were getting the measure of each other. Ronnie opened up in the third dropping the champion for a count of nine, exciting the predominantly Welsh audience. The boxer from Bonymaen took control of the fight, flooring Boon twelve times before knocking out his opponent in the tenth round.

Ronnie never defended the title but was still British champion when he challenged Ike Williams for the World lightweight title on a wet September evening in 1946.

Ronnie was never quite the same boxer after his brave attempt to win the World title and retired after losing to the up-and-coming Swansea boxer Cliff Curvis, when just a shadow of his former self, and was outgunned and stopped in the seventh round at St Helen's Rugby Ground in Swansea on 2nd June 1947. He had boxed one hundred and thirty-seven times, winning one hundred and fourteen losing eighteen and drawing five.

After his retirement, Ronnie James migrated to Australia, but visited Swansea in 1976 and notably called on Eddie's Gym where he was reunited with Cliff Curvis and offered words of encouragement to the stable of Swansea boxers as he watched them train. Ironically, Ronnie passed on shortly after his visit. He will be remembered as one of Wales all time greats.

On 24th July 1952 twenty-four-year-old **Cliff Curvis** became British and Commonwealth welterweight champion when he knocked out Wally Thom in the ninth round at The Stadium in Liverpool. Thom had won the titles from Eddie Thomas from Merthyr Tydfil at Harringay Arena after winning a final eliminator against Cliff on a ninth round disqualification the previous July.

Cliff was born Cliff Nancurvis at the Nancurvis family home in Peter Street, Waun Wen, on 19th November 1927. He had made his professional debut on 26th August 1944, just sixteen years of age – he knocked out Bryn Collins in the second round in Brynamman and was entering the prize ring for the fifty-second time when challenging Thom from Birkenhead for the title.

He was just nineteen years of age when he fought the experienced 'Aldgate Tiger' Al Phillips in an eliminator for the British featherweight title. A weakened Cliff, reported as having 'outgrown' the featherweight division and having difficulties making the nine stone weight limit, was knocked out in the second round; it was his last fight in this weight division.

Undeterred by this setback the Swansea boxer returned to winning ways with wins over Johnny Russell and fellow Swansea boxer Ronnie James. In his next outing Cliff lost on a TKO to Harry Hughes in a final eliminator for the British lightweight title, in what was a terrific but bloody battle in which the Welshman was badly cut.

He then went through a sticky period in his career, certainly by his standards, losing three of his next nine contests, but he did win an eliminator for the British welterweight title with a twelve rounds victory on points over Gwyn Williams in Abergavenny, avenging an earlier knockout defeat.

Cliff, now twenty-three years of age, was coming into contention for a British title challenge against reigning champion Eddie Thomas from Merthyr Tydfil. Before his title shot the Swansea boxer engaged in a 'warm up' against the brilliant Frenchman, Charles Humez. He was handicapped by a badly cut eye but fought gamely losing on points to Humez, which was no disgrace, as Charles went on to become European welterweight and middleweight champion – he also challenged Randolph Turpin for the European version of the World middleweight crown.

Undaunted by the defeat against Humez, Cliff mounted a strong challenge against Eddie Thomas at the St Helen's Rugby Ground, but was on the wrong side of a fifteen round decision. Eddie went on to make an unsuccessful challenge for the European welterweight title against none other than Charles Humez. After retiring from boxing Eddie Thomas became a successful boxing manager, steering Howard Winstone and Ken Buchanan to World titles and almost made it a hat-trick when Swansea boxer Colin Jones came within a hair's breadth of becoming World champion on two occasions.

Cliff took a deserved six month break after his title challenge, returning to the ring in March 1951 to earn a ten round decision win against Stan Reypens at Earls Court, followed by a second round knockout win against Scottish champion Billy Ratray in an eliminator for the British welterweight title.

He then boxed Wally Thom in a final eliminator for the welterweight title, still held by Eddie Thomas. The fight took place in Liverpool where referee Peter Muir disqualified the Swansea boxer in very controversial circumstances. Although behind on points going into round nine Cliff had the champion in trouble, bombarding him with an array of lefts and rights, when there was a clash of heads after which Cliff was warned for butting. Cliff crashed a left hook on Thom's jaw before the referee had given the order to box.

The Swansea boxer won two of his next three contests – he beat Emmanuel Clavel in Porthcawl, drew with Kay Kalio in Neath and won on a disqualification against Danny 'Bang-Bang' Womber from Chicago. This fight was held at the Sophia Gardens in Cardiff and ended sensationally and controversially – the bell sounded for the end of round four with Cliff well ahead on points, but the American kept on punching, claiming he'd not heard the bell. The referee ignored his pleas and disqualified him.

In his fifty-second professional contest Cliff became the second Swansea boxer to be crowned British champion and he also won the Commonwealth title with a ninth round knockout victory against Wally Thom. Cliff gained sweet revenge for the earlier disqualification defeat with a superb performance, dominating the contest from the first round.

Cliff was back in the ring within a month of winning the title, winning a close fight on points over ten rounds in a return fight with Danny Womber in Porthcawl.

Cliff defended his Commonwealth title against Gerald Dreyer in Johannesburg, losing the fight and his title on points over fifteen rounds. The defending champion had floored his South African challenger with a stunning left hook in the sixth round. It was reported that Dreyer had been on the canvas for sixteen seconds when rising at the count of nine. The Swansea boxer had broken his hand when landing the punch but fought on gallantly for the remaining nine rounds, but was adjudged to have lost on points.

Having lost his Commonwealth title Cliff was lined up for a European title challenge against Frenchman Gilbert Lavoigne in Paris. The Frenchman was floored in the second round, after which he clung on to Cliff for dear life. The rest of the fight was just clinching and mauling, but according to the Belgian referee it was the Swansea boxer who was the perpetrator and as a consequence he was disqualified in round nine. This was to be Cliff's last contest. He retired rather than accept a derisory purse offer to defend his British title. He was twenty-five years of age, his professional career had spanned over nine years, he'd boxed fifty-four times winning on forty-two occasions. Cliff Curvis passed away on 22nd April 2009 aged eighty-one years.

The Vetch Field was the home of Swansea Town Football Club who at the end of the 1959-60 season had finished up in seventh position in Division Two, now known as the Championship, of the Football League under the management of Trevor Morris. Players included in the Swans squad at that time were skipper Mel Nurse, Len Allchurch, Peter Davies, Johnny King, Colin Webster, Brian Hughes, Alan Sanders, Reg Davies, Roy Saunders, Brayley Reynolds, Graham Williams and Ken Morgan. On 9th May 1960, just at the end of the soccer season, Swansea welterweight **Brian Curvis**, who was unbeaten in thirteen professional contests since making his debut at the Empire Pool, Wembley, where he stopped Harry Haydock in the second round just eleven months earlier, was to challenge experienced and rugged Australian George Barnes for the Commonwealth welterweight championship in the open air at the Vetch Field.

Brian's close friend Ray Morgan of Mumbles, who was at the fight, recalls the Swansea boxer dominating from the first round with superior hand speed and a faster tempo against the tough, durable, experienced Aussie warrior and was fully deserving of the decision after fifteen rounds. Supporting contests on this bill included Merthyr Tydfil featherweight prospect Howard Winstone who stopped George Carroll in four rounds.

Brian was born into a boxing family with father Dai coaching Brian and elder brothers Cliff and Ken in the rudiments of boxing. The Swansea boxer was a formidable amateur who although born in Wales of Welsh parentage won a bronze medal for England in the 1958 Commonwealth Games at Cardiff as Army, Inter Services and ABA champion.

Brian was managed by his brother Cliff who was ably assisted by ex-Swansea rugby player Dickie Dobbs, honing Brian into tip top condition. Inside the distance wins over Emile Vlaemynck in the third, which was chief supporting bout to the infamous 'Porthbrawl' between Dick Richardson and Brian London, and Johnny Gorman in the ninth

Brian Curvis with manager Cliff and trainer Dickie Dobbs after beating Wally Swift to become British welterweight champion.

preceded a British and Commonwealth title showdown with the then British champion, Nottingham's Wally Swift. The fight took place in Wally's home town where the Swansea boxer won a hard fought but comfortable fifteen rounds decision against the cagey British champion.

Brian was back in the ring soon after his championship success stopping Italian Rino Borra in four rounds and then outpointing Spanish champion Luis Folledo over ten rounds.

Six months after their first encounter, Brian and Wally Swift engaged in a return confrontation, again in Nottingham, with the Swansea boxer emerging triumphant, winning the decision after fifteen rounds.

On 31st October 1961, less than twelve months after winning the British title, the Swansea boxer became the proud holder of a Lonsdale belt with a stunning eighth round knockout over tough Irishman Mick Leahy at the Wembley Empire Pool. The victory over Leahy was no mean achievement as the Irishman went on to become British middleweight champion by knocking out George Aldridge in the first round, took European middleweight champion and Olympic legend Laszlo Papp of Hungary the full fifteen rounds and also went the distance with Italian Nino Benvenuti who at that time was unbeaten in fifty-two fights and went on to become undisputed middleweight champion of the world. Leahy also won a decision over the ageing all time great Sugar Ray Robinson.

Brian stopped Londoner Tony Mancini in the fifth round in his third defence of the British title and had chalked up twenty-three wins in as many contests, fifteen inside the distance.

His next defence of his titles followed the career defining fights twice versus Guy Sumlin and Ralph Dupas, against Tony Smith from Liverpool who had previously beaten Swansea boxer Len Barrow. Brian halted Smith in the ninth round at the Royal Albert Hall. Following victories over Frenchman Maurice Auzel, Sugar Cliff and Dave Charnley he won his second Lonsdale belt outright by stopping Johnny Cooke in the fifth round before his world title challenge against Emile Griffith.

Following the Griffith defeat the Swansea boxer returned to the ring in January 1965 under the management of Arthur Boggis who was also

Brian Curvis training on Swansea beach with trainers
Dickie Dobbs (right) and brother Cliff (left).

the manager of Dave Charnley. He won a decision against Hawaiian Vince Shomo over ten rounds.

He kept himself busy engaging in eight contests before his retirement which was announced after his last fight when he stopped Des Rea in the eighth round in Carmarthen in September 1966, one month after his twenty-ninth birthday. Brian beat Mexican Gaspar Ortega, lost a decision to Willie Ludick in South Africa and stopped American Isaac Logart in six rounds before making his sixth defence of the British title and his seventh of the Commonwealth belt. He halted Sammy McSpadden in the twelfth round at the Sophia Gardens in Cardiff on 25th November 1965, which happened to be the same night that Muhammad Ali knocked out Sonny Liston with the 'anchor punch' in their infamous return fight in Lewiston, Maine. A fourth round stoppage win over Cuban Jose Stable and a points win over ten rounds against Tito Marshall, both at the Royal Albert Hall, led him to his penultimate contest.

He challenged Frenchman Jean Josselin for the vacant European welterweight title in the Palais des Sports in Paris. Brian was approaching his twenty-ninth birthday and was clearly past his best. He fought gallantly, but was forced to retire in the fourteenth round.

After the Des Rea contest in Carmarthen the Swansea boxer called time on a fabulous career spanning over seven years – he had boxed forty-one times, winning all but four. He had won two Lonsdale belts, successfully defended his Commonwealth title seven times, retired undefeated as British and Commonwealth champion and had challenged for the World and European titles.

It was the end of 1979 that **Colin Jones** from Gorseinon had lived up to all that was expected of him, making steady progress in the professional ranks. He had engaged in twelve professional contests, including an eliminator for the British welterweight title. He was unbeaten, with nine of his twelve victories ending inside the distance. Colin was capable of knocking out opponents with either hand.

The year ahead was a big one for the Swansea boxer. He stopped the experienced Billy Waith from Cardiff in the sixth round. There weren't many boxers around who were capable of halting the Cardiff veteran who was participating in his seventy-second contest – he had unsuccessfully challenged Luton's Henry Rhiney for the British welterweight title losing on points after fifteen rounds.

Colin was facing an onerous task in his next contest – he was to challenge the brilliant and undefeated Kirkland Laing for his British welterweight title which he won by stopping Henry Rhiney in the tenth round ten months earlier in Birmingham.

The title challenge was to take place at the Wembley Conference Centre on 1st April 1980. What a match! Laing, the brilliant boxer, eighteen wins and one draw in a career of nineteen fights, and Colin Jones the two-fisted knockout puncher, unbeaten in thirteen contests. The Jamaican-born Laing was twenty-six years old and also a former ABA champion. He was managed by the renowned and recently deceased Terry Lawless. From round one the defending champion moved around the ring confidently peppering the challenger with left jabs but he was always on the back foot. The Swansea boxer had little success in the early rounds, hands held high, trying to cut off the corners of the ring as the champion danced around. In round three the Swansea boxer did make some progress, catching his opponent with a solid right hand, smashing the gumshield from his mouth. Laing kept up his good work evading Colin's bombs and stepping up the pace with a variety of his own repertoire of fast accurate punches; he was building up a significant points lead and the bookmakers were gaining in confidence that they had laid the correct odds. As the fight progressed, it was noticeable that Colin was edging closer and closer and in round seven he achieved some success in trapping the champion, forcing him to stand toe to toe, resulting in Laing sustaining a bad cut inside his mouth. In the ninth round the Jamaican appeared to be regaining control of the fight when Colin tagged him with a solid right hand punch. Again the gumshield flew out of his mouth, he was trapped and Colin bombarded him with a fusillade of punches forcing referee Roland Dakin to intervene, rescuing Laing from any further punishment. The deposed champion went into hysteria – he couldn't believe that after being a fair way out in front that the Swansea boxer had taken his title from him.

The newly-crowned British champion hastily returned to the ring demolishing Richard House by knockout in the first round. Four months after winning the title, Colin made a voluntary defence of the British title against Peter Neal at the Eisteddfod Pavilion in Gowerton, a bout in which the challenger survived until the fifth round.

Inside the distance wins against Clement Tshinga and Horace McKenzie were followed by a contest with Guyanan Mark Harris for the Commonwealth title. In all fairness to the unheralded Harris, he offered the Swansea boxer some stiff resistance before the referee came to his rescue in the ninth round.

His next contest was a return encounter with Kirkland Laing, who was determined not to get suckered again. The former champion must have thought he was experiencing déjà vous as Colin came from behind to halt Laing in round nine. Less than eighteen months after his second defeat against Colin, Kirkland Laing achieved what the

Red Corner		Blue Corner
1	P. DAVIES (Llandaff A.B.C.) (Welsh Representative)	**BANTAMWEIGHT** v.	C. NAN CURVIS (Pen-y-Rheol A.B.C.)
2	C. DAVIES (Llandaff A.B.C.) (W.A.B.A. Jnr. Champion. Welsh Rep.)	**FEATHERWEIGHT** v.	K. HALL (Pen-y-Rheol A.B.C.) (W.A.B.A. Jnr. Champion)
3	S. LEWIS (Llandaff A.B.C.) (W.A.B.A. 1972 Champion. Welsh Rep.)	**LIGHTWEIGHT** v.	G. WATTS (Trostre A.B.C.) (W.A.B.A. Jnr. Champion)
4	E. McKENZIE (Prince of Wales A.B.C.) (Welsh Representative)	**WELTERWEIGHT** v.	B. BAIRD (Sam Lewis A.B.C.)
5	B. PRICE (Prince of Wales A.B.C.)	v.	B. JOHNSON (Trostre A.B.C.)
6	H. WILLIAMS (Sam Lewis A.B.C.)	**LIGHT MIDDLEWEIGHT** v.	S. BATEMAN (Pembroke A.B.C.)
7	J. HOWELLS (Sam Lewis A.B.C.)	**MIDDLEWEIGHT** v.	C. BREEN (Gwent A.B.C.) (Welsh Representative)
8	A. BLACKBURN (Rhondda A.B.C.)	**LIGHT HEAVYWEIGHT** v.	A. ROBERTS (Cymmer Afan A.B.C.) (1971/1972 W.A.B.A. Champion. Welsh Rep. 1971/1972 A.B.A. Finalist)
9	A. REARDON (Prince of Wales A.B.C.)	v.	M. BOAST (Croeserw A.B.C.)
		Junior Contests	
10	H. McKENZIE (Prince of Wales A.B.C.) (W.A.B.A. Schoolboy Champion)	v.	G. DAVIES (Towy A.B.C.) (W.A.B.A. Jnr. Champion)
11	I. HAMID (Prince of Wales A.B.C.)	v.	D. QUINLAN (Amman Valley A.B.C.)
12	L. LAWLESS (Rhondda A.B.C.)	v.	M. COPP (Gwent A.B.C.) (W.A.B.A. Jnr. Champion. A.B.A. Jnr. Finalist)
		Schoolboy Contests	
13	H. TANNER (Swansea Docks A.B.C.)	v.	S. GRIFFITHS (Gwent A.B.C.)
14	B. DALLING (Swansea Docks A.B.C.) (W.A.B.A. Schoolboy Representative)	v.	C. JONES (Pen-y-Rheol A.B.C.) (W.A.B.A. Schoolboy Champion)

From humble beginnings – Colin Jones, the last name on the bill in an amateur tournament at the Penlan Social Club, 17th January 1973.

Ring magazine awarded as the 'Upset of the Year' when he outpointed the great Roberto Duran over ten rounds in Detroit, Michigan. Laing had inflicted upon Duran only his fourth defeat in seventy-eight starts and went on to regain the British title after Colin's retirement; he also became European champion. The magnitude of Colin's achievement in beating Laing on any occasion, let alone twice, should not be underestimated.

Next time out the British and Commonwealth champion tasted defeat for the first time, albeit on a disqualification clouded in controversy against American Curtis Ramsey – referee Adrian Morgan's decision didn't go down well with a hostile and partisan crowd inside the Sophia Gardens in Cardiff.

Colin returned to his winning ways with four inside the distance victories, including a successful European title challenge. He became the first Swansea boxer to win a European title when he halted Danish holder Hans Henrik Palm in two rounds in Copenhagen on Guy

Fawkes night 1982, the challenger let off his own fireworks! The Swansea boxer engaging in World title activity and the proud owner of a Lonsdale belt did not make any further defences of his titles. He retired as undefeated British, Commonwealth and European champion after his unsuccessful attempt to wrest the WBA welterweight title from Don Curry.

On 12th October 1981 Welsh heavyweight champion **Neville J. Meade** challenged British heavyweight champion Gordon Ferris for his title at the Aston Villa Leisure Centre. Ferris from Enniskillen in Northern Ireland had won the title vacated by John L. Gardner when he outpointed Billy Aird over fifteen rounds in Birmingham in March. His title defence against Neville would be his twenty-second professional bout, he'd won seventeen and lost four and was expected to win comfortably against the thirty-three-year-old Swansea boxer.

Neville was born on the Caribbean Island of Montserrat on 12th September 1948, and with his family he settled in England in 1961. He joined the Royal Air Force and boxed as a heavyweight for the service. In 1973 he was the losing finalist in the ABA championships; the following year he won the ABA title and representing England won the Commonwealth Games heavyweight boxing gold medal.

After his Commonwealth Games success a number of promoters and managers were tempting him to join the professional ranks. He decided to leave his home base in Darlington and settle in Swansea, where he signed up with Swansea boxing promoter and local businessman Eddie Richards. He began training for his first professional contest at Eddie's Gym in Oystermouth Road.

Neville made his professional debut at the World Sporting Club in Mayfair, London, on 9th September 1974, three days before his twenty-sixth birthday, where he lost on points after six rounds against Tony Mikulski from Portsmouth, who entered the ring with a record of seven fights unbeaten.

Neville was back in the ring on 14th October to savour his first victory when stopping Roger Barlow of Coventry in the third round at the Top Rank Suite in Swansea.

Big Nev participated in and won a two thousand pounds heavy-weight competition at the World Sporting Club, stopping his quarter final and semi-final opponents Geoff Hepplestone and Les McGowan in the first round; he then outpointed Harold James in the final over four rounds, collecting the prize money. In his final contest of 1974 the Swansea boxer stopped Leicester's Eddie Fenton in five rounds.

In his first year in the paid ranks he had won five, four of those successes inside the distance and lost just once. The Swansea boxer commenced his 1975 campaign with two successive defeats. He was stopped in four rounds by the experienced ex-paratrooper from Doncaster, Richard Dunn. Shortly after beating Neville, Dunn became British, Commonwealth and European heavyweight champion, before unsuccessfully challenging Muhammad Ali for his World heavyweight crown. Neville was stopped by Tony Moore in six rounds in April at the Royal Albert Hall and drew with the same opponent over six rounds in Hammersmith, two months later. The former airman won his next five contests, stopping Lloyd Walford, Derek Simpkin and John Depledge, he turned the tables on old adversary Tony Moore winning on points over eight rounds and he sensationally stopped previously unbeaten French prospect Lucien Rodriguez in the third round in Paris. Rodriguez progressed to become European heavy-weight champion and took World heavyweight champion Larry Holmes the full twelve rounds in a World title challenge in 1983.

After losing on points to Spanish-based Argentine heavyweight Alfredo Evangelista, who unsuccessfully challenged both Muhammad Ali and Larry Holmes for the World heavyweight championship, Neville stopped Tony Blackburn from Tonyrefail in the fourth round to become Welsh heavyweight champion.

After stopping Garfield McEwan from Birmingham in nine rounds he fought unbeaten Londoner Denton Ruddock on a programme promoted by Eddie Richards at the Sophia Gardens in Cardiff that also featured Michael Copp, Alan Copp and Colin Breen who were making their professional debuts, also Jeff Burns who was on the comeback trail after two years out of the ring with hand problems.

The contest with Ruddock was billed as an eliminator for the British heavyweight title. Neville's preparations for the fight had not gone well, troubled by an injury to his right knee, which became a decisive factor after the early rounds with the Swansea boxer running out of steam and getting stopped in round seven. Two months later he was halted by rising London star, John L. Gardner, who was unbeaten in twenty-one fights and later became British, Commonwealth and European champion.

After two successive inside the distance losses, Neville began to ask himself questions about his future in the ring, but provided the perfect answer when he stopped Norwegian Bjorn Rudi in Oslo who had won all but two of seventeen previous contests. Three weeks later he lost a disputed ten rounds decision against Belgian Jean-Pierre Coopman in his home town of West Vlaanderen. Earlier in the year the Belgian was knocked out in five rounds in a World title challenge against Muhammad Ali. Three months after beating Neville, Coopman became European champion.

The Swansea boxer continued on his travels. His next excursion was to South Africa where he was halted in four rounds by Kallie Knoetze who included on his list of victims one time World heavyweight championship prospect and 'great white hope' American Duane Bobick.

Back on British soil Neville tackled Bruce Grandham who had scored three successive victories over British heavyweights. The Welsh champion, who had won thirteen, lost eight and drawn one stopped the American in the third round. In a rematch with Grandham the following March Neville was knocked out in the third round and in his only other fight in 1978 he was stopped in five rounds by Yorkshire's Paul Sykes.

It appeared that Neville's career had veered off the rails, and in his only contest of 1979 he was beaten on a four rounds technical knock-out by unbeaten Belgian Albert Syben in Brussels.

The Swansea boxer was determined to steer his hopes and aspirations back on course, and the new decade brought a change of fortune. He seemed much more comfortable 'weighing in' around sixteen and a half to seventeen stones, punching with tremendous power when he successfully defended his Welsh heavyweight title, stopping Newport's David Pearce in the second round. He trimmed down to sixteen stones and three pounds but lost none of his power when stopping fellow Swansea boxer Winston Allen in the second defence of his Welsh title. There was a lot of 'needle' in the build up to this fight which took place at the Swansea Leisure Centre on 1st October.

A rejuvenated Neville was preparing for his fights with a renewed enthusiasm under the guidance and supervision of his new team, Colin Breen and Jimmy Bromfield. He had captured impressive form, winning two British championship eliminators, stopping Stan McDermott in five rounds and Terry Mintus in three, earning him his title shot against Ferris.

Neville started cautiously concentrating on 'slipping' the champion's long left lead. As the opening round was drawing to a close the Swansea boxer detonated a right hand counter punch that exploded on the Irishman's jaw – he lay motionless on the canvas – Neville J. Meade was the first and only Swansea boxer to be crowned British heavyweight champion. His handlers Colin and Jimmy were delirious with joy, delight and pleasant surprise at the outcome. At thirty-three years of age and against the odds he had sensationally knocked out the champion Gordon Ferris in two minutes and forty-five seconds of the first round.

Neville J. Meade with Jimmy Bromfield and Colin Breen after knocking out Gordon Ferris to become Swansea's only British heavyweight champion.

*Neville J. Meade,
British heavyweight champion.*

*Neville Meade showing off his Lonsdale Belt to the landlord of
The Cockett Inn, Len Smith, with trainer Jimmy Bromfield.*

After his British title victory Neville caught the attention of London boxing manager, the late Terry Lawless, and was lured into his camp in London. Just a month after his title success he lost on points over ten rounds against American Leroy Boone at the Royal Albert Hall.

In his only contest of 1982 the Swansea boxer knocked out Rick Kellor from Iowa, USA, in the sixth round at the Birmingham NEC. Neville, who was now thirty-five years old had been inactive for eighteen months and yet to defend the British title that he had held for nearly two years. His first challenger would be former victim David Pearce who had earned his right to a title challenge by knocking out Gordon Ferris, who seemed allergic to Welsh opponents. The contest would be held at St David's Hall, Cardiff, on 22nd September1983 and would be the last British title fight scheduled for fifteen rounds.

The ageing and ring rusty champion was no match for his youthful and aggressive challenger who set a pace that Neville could no longer match, his sharp punching and alert reflexes had deserted him, the referee came to his rescue in round nine.

Neville J. Meade never boxed again but he had joined an elite group of Welsh boxers to win the British heavyweight title from Tommy Farr, Jack Petersen, Johnny Williams and Joe Erskine who had preceded him, and David Pearce and Scott Gammer who became champions after Neville's reign.

In a career that began in 1974 and ended nine years later Neville had won twenty fights, eighteen of those successes were inside the distance, he was beaten on thirteen occasions and drew once. Although born in the Caribbean and raised in England he became very much a part of Swansea and the city became very much a part of him. He lived in, trained in and boxed out of Swansea, he was proud to be a Swansea boxer and the Swansea boxing fraternity were proud of him. Neville Meade passed away on 13th March 2010, he was sixty-one years old.

Two months short of his twenty-second birthday, Carmarthen-born **Robert Dickie** who was entering his fourth year as a professional boxer was to challenge former British bantamweight champion John Feeney for the British featherweight title vacated by Barry McGuigan.

Robert Dickie.

The championship contest was scheduled to take place in London on 9th April 1986 and would be Robert's sixteenth professional bout – to date he'd won twelve, drawn two and lost one. Feeney had been a professional since 1977, he had held the British bantamweight title on two occasions and had challenged unsuccessfully for the Commonwealth and European titles. Robert, who had hailed from Cross Hands, first gained recognition as an eighteen-year-old amateur when he reached the ABA semi-finals, putting up a very good show before losing on points against Ray Gilbody.

He turned professional in 1983, moving up from bantam to featherweight. He took up residence in Swansea and was managed by Colin Breen, and trained by Jimmy Bromfield at Colin's Gym in Treboeth, Swansea.

Robert was nineteen years of age when he outpointed Merthyr-based Liverpudlian Billy Hough in Swindon on 12th March 1983, to make his mark as a professional boxer. He won his next two contests inside the distance, before having to share the verdict with Danny

Flynn at the St Andrews Sporting Club in Glasgow. In a return fight in October the Swansea boxer was stopped in the fifth round due to a cut eye, again at the St Andrews Sporting Club for the Scottish feather-weight title. Robert was eligible to challenge for this title through parentage.

Robert, undeterred by the setback, boxed four times in 1984, winning on each occasion, two wins by TKO, one by disqualification and an eight rounds points decision against Dave Pratt from Leicester in Nottingham on 14th May – Pratt had previously beaten Swansea boxer Peter Harries.

The Swansea boxer was now approaching his twenty-first birthday – he had won eight out of ten, six wins by the short route, lost once and drawn the other. On 25th February 1985 he knocked out John Sharkey in the second round at the St Andrews Sporting Club to become the Scottish featherweight champion. After stopping John Mahoney in three rounds in Solihull, Robert scored a sensational one round victory over the highly regarded, unbeaten but disrespectful Mark Reefer who boxed out of Bethnal Green. Reefer went on to win the Commonwealth super featherweight title, but he was never quite the same after losing to the Swansea boxer, who was beginning to become noticed and respected in the higher echelons of the British boxing fraternity.

Following a stoppage win in his next contest the Scottish champion fought in Western Cape, South Africa, where having floored his opponent three times obtained a commendable ten round draw against Frank Khonkhobe who became South African featherweight champion soon after this contest.

Robert lived up to the expectations of his manager, his trainer and his enthusiastic fan base in Swansea and Cross Hands by comfortably outpointing Feeney over the twelve round championship limit in a match which pitted youth against experience. The Swansea boxer defended his newly-won title by knocking out Steve Sims of Newport in five rounds at the Ebbw Vale Leisure Centre.

Robert won a Lonsdale belt in just six months when he repeated his earlier victory over John Feeney at the end of October in Ebbw Vale.

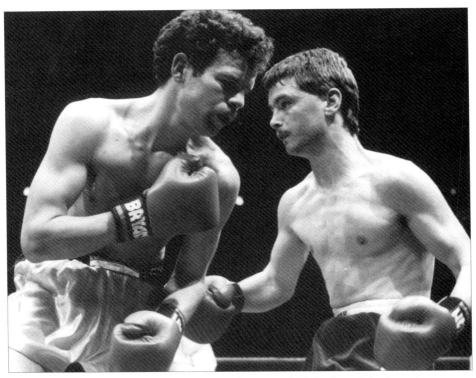

Robert Dickie outguns John Feeney to become British featherweight champion.

*Swansea boxers Robert Dickie, Geoff Pegler and Ray Price introduced into
the ring before a Welsh title fight.*

In March 1987 the British champion, driving home the day before he was due to resume training in preparation for his next contest, crashed his car, sustaining serious injuries; it was feared he may never walk again. Robert, in recovering from his injuries, showed the same determination and courage that were all too prevalent in his ring appearances.

Amazingly, he was back in the ring in October, winning on a second round disqualification against Rocky Lawlor. After outpointing American trial horse Arwel Campbell over eight rounds in his first contest of 1988 he stopped Indonesian Hengky Gun to become the WBC International super featherweight champion.

In his first defence of the title the Swansea boxer suffered his second defeat in twenty-two contests against the Milan-based Tunisian, Kamel Bou-Ali. Ahead on points going into the sixth round Robert sustained a badly cut eye and the fight was stopped in the challenger's favour. Bou-Ali went on to become the WBO super featherweight champion.

After the loss of the WBC International crown which was in August 1988 Robert didn't box again until 22nd November 1989, when he stopped Sheffield's Gary Maxwell in eight rounds, followed by an eight rounds points victory in Swansea against ex-Midlands featherweight champion Colin Lynch.

The Swansea boxer began the new decade in impressive form, forcing the Canadian featherweight champion Barrington Francis to retire in the tenth round with a dislocated jawbone. Francis won the Commonwealth featherweight title in his next bout and later became the World Boxing Federation title holder. Robert boxed again on 5th March 1991 – he became British super featherweight champion when he stopped defending champion Kevin Pritchard in eight rounds at the National Sporting Centre in Cardiff. His reign as champion lasted just fifty-five days – he was stopped in nine rounds in his first defence against underdog Sugar Gibiluru from Liverpool.

The Swansea boxer didn't enter the ring again for two and a half years and it was evident that the writing was on the wall for Robert when he was stopped in two rounds by Phil Founds from Hereford, celebrating only his third win in eight starts at the Ystrad Mynach Leisure Centre in November 1993.

Robert Dickie was twenty-nine years of age, his career had spanned over ten years, he had drawn two and lost four of twenty-eight contests. He had held the Scottish featherweight title, British feather and super featherweight titles had become WBC International champion and was the proud owner of a Lonsdale belt. After his last defeat the Swansea boxer realised his best days were behind him and wisely never boxed again. Sadly, Robert Dickie died suddenly and unexpectedly on 28th October 2010 at just forty-six years of age.

The date was 24th February 1988. Swansea boxer **Peter Harries**, twenty-five years old, winner of twelve professional contests, with five defeats and two draws, was to challenge Central area featherweight champion Kevin Taylor from Rochdale, who had won all but two of thirteen professional bouts, for the vacant British featherweight title.

Peter's title chance was just reward for a run of good form, six consecutive victories including a successful Welsh title challenge against former British flyweight champion Kelvin Smart from Caerphilly. His last contest was a close, somewhat controversial, ten rounds defeat on points against Antoine Montero, a Spaniard domiciled in Grenoble, France. Montero had won twenty-four with just two losses and one draw, he had held the European flyweight title, had challenged unsuccessfully for the WBA and WBC flyweight titles before touching gloves with Peter. After his victory over the Swansea boxer Montero won the European bantamweight title by knocking out Ray Gilbody in the first round.

Peter, the elder of two boxing brothers, started boxing with his brother Michael under the guidance of their boxing-mad father, the late Gordon Harries. After a successful amateur career he turned professional with local boxing manager and ex-Swansea boxer Colin Breen and trainer Jimmy Bromfield. He made his professional debut in August 1983, three weeks before his twenty-first birthday, losing a six rounds points decision against Dave Pratt in Birmingham. He drew his second fight in Aberdeen but was victorious in his next three contests and rounding off the year he beat Kevin Howard on points over eight rounds at the Dolphin Hotel. Ray Price and Geoff Pegler fought for

134

Peter Harries on his way to beating Kevin Taylor to become British featherweight champion.

the Welsh light welterweight title on this bill, which also featured Peter's younger brother Michael, and Swansea boxers Neil Crocker and John McGlynn.

Peter commenced his 1984 campaign inside the bantamweight limit of eight stones and six pounds, he drew with Ivor 'The Engine' Jones from Holyhead at the York Hall, Bethnal Green. The Swansea boxer returned to the York Hall in March where he halted Johnny Dorey in the sixth round before losing a ten round decision in the Bahamas against local boxer Ray Minus, who later in his career won the Commonwealth bantamweight title and challenged in vain for the WBO and IBF titles. Another defeat followed when Peter lost a points decision over eight rounds against former Central area bantam and featherweight champion John Farrell.

The following March Peter opened his 1985 account at the Midland Sporting Club, where he and his brother were very popular. He outpointed Kid Sumalia over eight rounds before losing a close ten rounds points decision against former British bantamweight champion John Feeney prior to fighting Montero in France.

After the Montero contest the Swansea boxer beat Steve Pollard in three rounds, halted Irishman Ray Webb in Belfast, won the Welsh title off Smart, stopped Albert Parr in Newport, gained revenge over John Farrell in a twelve round title eliminator and prior to his British title challenge stopped Ray Williams in the second round in Cardiff.

His title challenge took place at the Afan Lido, where Peter battled through despite sustaining cuts around the eyes to outpoint Taylor and become the British featherweight champion – a title that had been held by many accomplished boxers including Jim Driscoll, Ted 'Kid' Lewis, Nel Tarleton, Howard Winstone, Barry McGuigan and had been vacated by Swansea boxer Robert Dickie.

In defence of his newly-won title Peter could not have met a tougher opponent than his challenger, highly fancied rising star from Liverpool, Paul Hodkinson, who was unbeaten in eleven contests with ten wins and a draw against Panamanian Tomas Arguelles in Panama City. Three months later the 'Scouser' knocked out Arguelles in the sixth round in Belfast. Peter defended his title with gallant defiance but was outgunned by his younger challenger and was stopped in the twelfth and last round at the Afan Lido on 18th May 1988. This was the Swansea boxer's sixth defeat in twenty contests. On the same night Swansea boxer Floyd Havard won the British bantamweight title beating Pat Cowdell.

After losing his British title Peter took a long break, a year and four months, before attempting to regain the title and capture the European crown from Hodkinson who had kept himself busy by stopping Kevin Taylor in two rounds. The British champion stopped American Johnny 'Showboat' Carter in one round and won the vacant European title by halting French hopeful Raymond Armand in Belfast.

The twenty-seven-year-old Swansea boxer was not short of courage, but it was the champion that possessed all the other attributes, halting his game challenger in the ninth round, on a Frank Warren promotion at the Afan Lido. Hodkinson, managed by Barney Eastwood, realised his potential by winning the WBC featherweight championship and making three successful defences of the title.

Peter's next ring appearance was in April 1991, heralding a welcome return to winning ways when successful in an eight rounds points decision against former Midlands featherweight champion Colin Lynch. He then challenged future European and WBO featherweight champion Steve Robinson for his Welsh featherweight title in Cardiff, losing the decision after ten rounds in July.

The Swansea boxer was inactive until the following July when he travelled to Marseilles to box the unbeaten Stephane Haccone. The Frenchman, engaging in his twenty-second contest, retained his unbeaten record, which he was to lose four months later against Steve Robinson, by outscoring Peter over eight rounds. Peter's only other engagement in 1992 was an eight rounds points defeat against Paul Harvey, a useful featherweight from Islington, who had previously held the Commonwealth super featherweight title.

Almost a year to the day since his last contest the Swansea boxer lost on points against Jonjo Irwin over eight rounds at Mayfair. Irwin later became British and Commonwealth champion.

In 1994 Peter scored a welcome victory when he outpointed Llanelli boxer Nigel Haddock over ten rounds for the vacant Welsh featherweight title. He fought Wilson Docherty in Cardiff for the WBB featherweight title, losing on points over twelve rounds, a decision he reversed over ten rounds the following April. He was stopped in three rounds in South Africa by former IBF super bantamweight champion Welcome Nicita.

In May 1995 the Swansea boxer lost on points over eight rounds against IBO super featherweight champion Jimmy Bredal from Denmark in Copenhagen. In his final contest Peter lost on points over six rounds against South African Cassius Baloyi who became IBO and IBF super featherweight champion.

Peter was now thirty-four years old, he'd been a professional boxer for thirteen years and although beaten fifteen times in thirty-three contests, ten of those defeats were in his last thirteen bouts and against good quality opposition. Peter Harries can proudly rub shoulders with Brian and Cliff Curvis, Robert Dickie, Floyd Havard, Ronnie James, Colin Jones and Neville Meade, Swansea boxers who had become British champions.

Floyd Havard, a twenty-two-year-old southpaw, was preparing for what on paper appeared to be the toughest fight of his career to date. His opponent in his nineteenth professional contest would be the defending British super featherweight champion from Smethwick, former European champion and world title challenger Pat Cowdell. The British champion who was approaching his thirty-fifth birthday, had previously held the British and European featherweight titles and had unsuccessfully challenged Salvador Sanchez and the hard-hitting Ghanaian, Azumah Nelson, both for the WBC featherweight championship. Cowdell had won thirty-six out of forty-one contests since turning professional in 1977, and his defence of the title would be at the Afan Lido in May 1988.

The Swansea boxer had been a very useful amateur before joining the paid ranks in November 1985, one month after his twentieth birthday. He had won a National Schools title in 1980 and was just nineteen years old when he became ABA featherweight champion in 1985.

He made his professional debut at the Star Leisure Centre in Cardiff where he stopped Dean Bramhald in the third round, and in his next contest Floyd give an indication of his pedigree when he outpointed Sugar Gibiliru by a wide margin over six rounds on referee Dave Parris' scorecard. Gibiliru later won the British super featherweight title when he stopped defending champion, Swansea boxer Robert Dickie.

Floyd's challenge for Cowdell's title ended in the eighth round – his thirteenth inside the distance win in nineteen contests. The contest took place at the Afan Lido on 18th May 1988. The champion deployed all his skills and experience in a vain attempt to repel the persistent attacks of the youthful and determined challenger. The Swansea boxer was crowned champion after the fight was stopped in round eight. Cowdell announced his retirement after the fight, marking the end of a fabulous career.

Floyd surprisingly lost the title in his first defence against former champion John Doherty from Bradford, who won by TKO in the eleventh round in September 1989, and didn't fight again until March 1991.

He racked up five straight wins before challenging John John Molina for the World title. Remarkably, the Swansea boxer was back in the ring just two months after the loss against Molina, regaining the British title by beating reigning champion Neil Haddock from Llanelli, referee Roy Francis stopped the fight in round ten. Floyd successfully defended the title against unbeaten Dave McHale, stopping the Scotsman in ten rounds and knocked out former champion Michael Armstrong in the ninth round at the Brangwyn Hall, Swansea, on 5th May 1995.

Floyd ended his career following a run of eight successive victories since losing to Molina, his last contest was on 30th November 1996 one month after his thirty-first birthday when he stopped Carl Allen from Wolverhampton in the third round at the Rhondda Leisure Centre in Tylorstown. He was the fourth Swansea boxer to win a Lonsdale belt and boasted a career record of thirty-four wins and just two defeats.

Chapter Three

WELSH CHAMPIONS, 1932-1951

On 6th June 1932 **Len Beynon** outpointed Terrence Morgan of Newport at Merthyr Tydfil to become the bantamweight champion of Wales, the first Swansea boxer to win a Welsh title. Len was born in Barry on 24th April 1912 but lived in, trained and boxed out of Swansea and became a big player within the Swansea boxing fraternity.

Len Beynon's first recorded contest was on 2nd November 1930 at the Ring, Blackfriars, in London, where he outpointed Ronnie Summerton from Birmingham over fifteen rounds. This was an excellent

Len Beynon (right) with fellow Swansea boxer Willie Piper.

debut win for the Swansea boxer, his opponent had been a professional for two years and held a very respectable record, winning six on the bounce before clashing with Len. Just four months later in his fourth professional contest the Swansea boxer lost on points over fifteen rounds against Freddy Morgan from Gilfach Goch in an attempt to win the Welsh flyweight title.

Len lost four of his next five contests. After beating ex-British fly-weight champion Bert Kirby he lost to Dave Crowley who later became British lightweight champion. He was beaten by Young Perez who had only been defeated four times in sixty-one bouts and was the reigning National Boxing Association World flyweight champion when he touched gloves with Len. He was also defeated by Frenchman Eugene Huatt, who had challenged Panama Al Brown for the World bantamweight title five months earlier.

The Swansea boxer's final contest before winning the Welsh title was against Scotsman Jackie Brown who had won fifty-five out of seventy contests and was the reigning British and European flyweight champion – he went on to become World flyweight champion. He beat Len on points over fifteen rounds in Manchester.

After winning the Welsh title the Swansea boxer won his next four bouts including a fifteen rounds points decision against Dave Crowley, his winning run culminated in an eliminator for the British bantam-weight title against former British and Empire champion Dick Corbett in Swansea on 11th November 1933. Corbett was victorious and went on to regain both titles five months later.

Len lost and regained his Welsh bantamweight crown in two hard fifteen round contests against George Williams, sandwiched between these two encounters was an excellent twelve rounds points victory against Mancunian Johnny King who turned professional in 1926 when he was just fourteen years of age. King had won the British and Empire titles before his twentieth birthday, losing them two months before his encounter with Len. King had also challenged Panama Al Brown for the World bantamweight title the previous July.

After regaining the Welsh title Len embarked on a series of contests with Johnny King, losing on points twice within a month in Manchester. The Swansea boxer met King for the fourth time, losing on a TKO in the sixth round – this fight was held in Swansea on 8th July 1935 and was the first time Len had lost inside the distance.

The Swansea boxer was still only twenty-three years of age, he'd boxed twenty-eight times, winning fourteen, losing the other half against top quality opposition and usually of much greater experience. His next contest was at the Vetch Field in Swansea on 5th September against fellow Swansea boxer Ronnie James who was unbeaten in forty-six contests. Ronnie retained his tariff of wins by earning the decision over twelve rounds. In a return encounter on October 31st at the Mannesmann Hall, James again got the nod after twelve keenly contested rounds.

Len won his next six contests including a Welsh featherweight title success outpointing Stan Jehu over fifteen rounds in Swansea; he also outpointed Cuban flyweight champion Rafael Valdez at the Vetch Field. In his next fight Len was knocked out for the first and only time in his career by hard punching Jimmy Lester from Dagenham. On 30th November former World flyweight champion Jackie Brown again beat Len by winning the decision after fifteen rounds in a final eliminator for the British bantamweight title, after which he hit a winning streak of nine straight wins including a victory over Dick Corbett.

On 12th May 1938 the Swansea boxer took former World featherweight champion Freddie Miller the scheduled distance of twelve rounds, losing on points at the Mannesmann Hall.

The next big moment in his career was on 13th March 1939 when he stopped Johnny King in the seventh round. He will probably be best remembered for his epic battles with the former British bantamweight champion and World title challenger, having clashed five times, losing two on points and one inside the distance. He beat King once on points and did have the satisfaction of stopping King on the other occasion.

After his final dispute with King, Len boxed on for three and a half years winning ten and drawing one of seventeen contests including notable wins over Dick Corbett and Benny Caplan. Len Beynon boxed

Len Beynon (left) with promoter Syd Wignall.

for the last time on 11th November 1942, the end of a twelve-year career that many Swansea fight fans felt could have achieved so much more. He had entered the professional ring seventy times, winning on forty-three occasions, losing twenty-six times and sharing the decision once. Len had fought and beaten top class fighters many boxing pundits believed he had the ability to become at least British champion but it was not to be. Len Beynon passed away on 10th January 1992.

The name Jimmy Wilde is legendary in the history of Swansea boxers perhaps because one of the greatest if not the greatest of boxers to come out of Wales the 'Tylorstown Terror' was his namesake or maybe because of the famous names on 'Big Jim's' record, the likes of Tommy Farr, Jack London, Buddy Baer and Freddie Mills. Jim Wilde was the only Swansea boxer to have held the Welsh heavyweight title until Neville Meade arrived on the scene nearly forty years later.

Jim Wilde was crowned Welsh heavyweight champion when he outpointed Charlie Bundy on points over fifteen rounds in Swansea on 8th June 1935, to win the title vacated by Jack Petersen. He was approaching his twenty-fourth birthday when he became champion and had won thirteen of twenty-one contests, seven inside the distance, lost seven and drawn one. His opponent from Treherbert had won twenty-one, lost twenty-one, including a second round defeat against Jim in 1933, he had drawn six.

Jim made his professional debut on 20th February 1932 drawing with fellow debutant Eddie Evans after ten rounds in Swansea. In his fifth contest he lost on points to Tommy Farr, the scheduled distance and venue of the fight is not recorded. Farr from Tonypandy, a Welsh boxing legend, became the challenger in the first title defence of World heavyweight champion Joe Louis in 1937. American boxing pundits gave the Welshman little chance of lasting a few rounds with the 'Brown Bomber', but he fought with valour and pride and gained the respect of the stateside boxing fraternity and indeed the champion who was forced to rely on the decision of the referee Arthur Donovan and the two judges after fifteen hard fought rounds.

Two months after being crowned Welsh heavyweight champion Jim Wilde boxed in a memorable contest at the Vetch Field, snatching victory from the jaws of defeat by stopping the Egyptian prince, Salah el Din, in the sixth round, after trailing on points.

On 18th May 1936 the Swansea boxer fought a creditable twelve round draw in defence of his Welsh title against Tommy Farr in Swansea. Four months later and again in Swansea, Farr ended Jim's reign as champion winning by a knockout in the seventh round, he had been Welsh champion for fifteen months.

Jim's son, Billy, recalls Tommy Farr stating that one of the hardest punches he'd ever taken was from Jim Wilde. This was Jim's twenty-ninth contest of which he'd won nineteen, lost eight and drawn two; he was now twenty-five years of age.

Jim won two of his next three bouts before tangling with Buddy Baer at Harringay Arena on 6th May 1937. Baer from Denver, Colorado, was the younger but bigger brother of former World heavyweight champion Max Baer. He stood six feet six and a half inches tall. The American won by knockout in the fourth round – eighteen days later Baer outpointed Jack London over ten rounds at the Vetch Field in Swansea.

Jim Wilde floors Tommy Farr at the Vetch Field on 18th May 1936.

Recognise the two shaking hands outside the Duke Hotel in Wind Street, Swansea, in 1936? Preparing for their fight for the heavyweight championship of Wales are Jimmy Wilde of Swansea and Tommy Farr. The contest at Vetch Field was won in the seventh round when Wilde sank to his knees and was counted out, floored by a heavy body blow. Also pictured, on Wilde's left, is brother Brinley, while the moustached gentleman on the right is Jimmy's father Dick.

The ex-Welsh heavyweight champion lost by a third round knock-out against Jack London at St Helen's Rugby Ground two months after the loss to Buddy Baer who made two unsuccessful challenges for the World heavyweight crown against Joe Louis. The Swansea boxer won three, lost one and drew one before challenging for the vacant Welsh title against George James. His bid to regain the title failed when he was disqualified in the fifteenth and last round in Mountain Ash.

Six months later Jim did well to take South African Ben Foord the distance of twelve rounds at Harringay Arena. Foord had won the Commonwealth title by knocking out Jack Petersen in three rounds and lost it to Tommy Farr.

The Swansea boxer challenged George James for the Welsh title in Swansea on 24th July 1939, but was stopped in round eleven. He didn't box again until 1941 when he lost by a third round knockout against Freddie Mills who went on to become World light heavyweight champion.

Over the next six years Jim boxed eleven times. Clearly past his best, he won only one, drew one and lost nine times, twice against Jack London, who won the British heavyweight title in the following year. Jim's final contest was on 21st January 1948 when he was knocked out in four rounds against Freddie Hicks in Islington. His final tally in a sixteen-year career stood at twenty-eight wins, twenty-six losses, many of them in the latter part of his career, and four draws.

Jim Wilde passed away on St David's Day 1991, six months short of his eightieth birthday, but is still remembered and often mentioned among Swansea's boxing fraternity. He was also well known in social circles as mine host of the Alexandra Social Club, 'Jimmy Wilde's', in Alexandra Road.

In only his second recorded contest, Swansea boxer **Jack Kiley** was matched with Rufus Enoch from Tonyrefail for the vacant Welsh fly-weight title on 7th November 1938.

Jack began his professional career in Swansea the previous January when he outpointed fellow debutant and Swansea boxer Len 'Davo'

Davies. On the same bill Len Beynon halted George Williams in the seventh of a scheduled fifteen round contest. Jack was crowned flyweight champion of Wales after stopping Enoch in the seventh round.

His next outing, and only his third recorded contest, the following February Jack travelled to Glasgow to do battle with Jackie Paterson in a ten round contest. Paterson had already knocked out Rinty Monaghan in Belfast and following his encounter with the Swansea boxer he went on to become flyweight champion of Scotland, Britain, British Empire and the World. He also won the British, British Empire and European bantamweight titles. The Scotsman defeated Jack Kiley by knockout in the first round.

Jack lost the Welsh title when he was outpointed over fifteen rounds by Ronnie Bishop from Markham in Gwent. Jack travelled to Bishop's backyard to regain the title in Crumlin on 13th May 1940, winning a points decision after fifteen rounds.

The Swansea boxer's next bout was in Belfast where he beat experienced Irishman Bunty Doran on points over ten rounds in front of the Irishman's own supporters.

Just over a year later Jack was stopped in five rounds by Ronnie Clayton, who later became British, British Empire and European featherweight champion. Clayton, from Blackpool, boxed professionally from 1941 until 1954 participating in one hundred and fifteen contests of which he won eighty-one, lost twenty-six and drew on eight occasions.

Ronnie also beat Swansea boxer Willie Grey on two occasions and defeated Manuel Ortiz from California, who was at the time the reigning World bantamweight champion in a ten round non title contest. Jack's next recorded fight was almost eighteen months after the Clayton bout in July 1943. He was halted in five rounds by Norman Lewis from Nantymoel, who boxed from 1939 until 1950, chalking up eighty-three wins and five draws in one hundred and thirteen contests.

It was almost three years to the day before the Swansea boxer fought again – he outpointed Billy Hazelgrove from Brighton over eight rounds at St Helen's Rugby Ground where he'd boxed in his previous contest against Norman Lewis. Hazelgrove had fought boxing commentator, the late Harry Carpenter, on three occasions.

Three former Welsh champions – Len Beynon, Big Jim Wilde and Jack Kiley.

Jack's last professional contest was on 18th April 1947 when he lost on points over eight rounds against Haydn Jones from Tiryberth, who later in his career won the Welsh featherweight title. According to the records of *boxrec.com* Jack boxed only ten times as a professional with lengthy periods of time between each contest, although *www.pre-warboxing* have recorded forty-seven fights in Jack's professional career without further detail.

Taffy Williams was born William McVeigh in Swansea on New Year's Day 1920. He was eighteen years of age when he made his professional debut in Portobello, Scotland, on 1st October 1938. He knocked out Glaswegian Pat Logue in the sixth round. Pat never boxed again.

In 1939 Taffy crammed in twenty-three bouts, winning twenty-two, thirteen inside the distance and drawing the other against Johnny Clements who was making his one and only ring appearance. In this year Taffy boxed fifteen times in Scotland, usually in Portobello, and in Swansea on just three occasions. In his last contest of the year, which happened to be the twenty-fifth of his career, he outpointed Swansea born George Reynolds, who boxed out of Wolverhampton, to win the vacant Welsh middleweight title over fifteen rounds in Swansea.

In the ensuing year, 1940, the Swansea boxer was beaten three times amidst six victories. His first defeat was against Bob McKluckie from Cambuslang who knocked him out in the ninth round, avenging a previous loss on points over twelve rounds. Taffy beat Bob on two other occasions in this year, both times by decision over ten rounds. He beat Harry Brooks twice on the same night in Edinburgh, winning by disqualification in each bout. In the first encounter Brooks was ruled out in the fifth round for punching low. To ensure the crowd had their money's worth Taffy agreed to a rematch. In the second contest Brooks was thrown out in the first round for the same offence. In his final contest of the year the Swansea boxer clashed with twenty-five-year-old Ernie Roderick at the Liverpool Stadium in what would be Ernie's one hundred and second contest.

His career was to span over nineteen years, he had already won the British and European welterweight titles and taken the great Henry Armstrong the distance in a fifteen rounds World title clash. Roderick beat Taffy by knockout in the second round.

Taffy's ring career was interrupted by the war and he didn't box again until 1945. At this time he was Welsh middleweight champion, had boxed thirty-four times and held a respectable record of thirty wins, one draw and three losses in just over two years as a professional boxer.

He drew with Tommy Davies from Ammanford in a ten round contest in Swansea, marking his return to the ring in 1945. In his only other contest of the year he stopped fellow Swansea boxer Willie Piper in the ninth round at the Vetch Field in Swansea.

In 1946 Taffy's successes were limited to two against four defeats including the loss of his Welsh title against Tommy Davies – the fight was stopped in round four when Taffy sustained a badly cut eye.

Tommy had fought in good company, losing twice against Dick Turpin, three times against Ernie Roderick and twice against Vince

Hawkins with one draw but was no match for Marcel Cerdan and Randolph Turpin, losing in one round and two rounds respectively. The Swansea boxer was stopped in eight rounds by Vince Hawkins who two months later took the British welterweight title from Ernie Roderick.

Taffy was inactive in 1947 and boxed a draw with Billy Stevens the following year, and in 1951 just a shadow of the Taffy Williams of 1939, the thirty-one-year-old was stopped in three rounds by George Riding from Lancaster.

Taffy retired with a career record of thirty-three wins, ten losses and three draws, a career that started with so much promise, but his absence from the ring during the war years clearly took its toll.

Taffy passed away on St David's Day 1992, he was seventy-two years old.

Chapter Four

WELSH CHAMPIONS, 1952-1983

On 29th March 1976 Swansea boxer **Neville Meade** stopped twenty-year-old Tony Blackburn from Tonyrefail in four rounds in Swansea to be crowned the heavyweight champion of Wales. Neville had become the first and only Swansea boxer since Jim Wilde beat Charlie Bundy in 1935 to win the Welsh heavyweight title and was also the first Swansea boxer since Taffy Williams beat George Reynolds in 1939 to win a Welsh title at any weight. Blackburn had been a professional since 1973, when he was just seventeen years of age, his finest achievement to date was going the full distance with John L. Gardner – only a few fighters managed that.

Neville Meade floors challenger Winston Allen in Welsh heavyweight title fight in Swansea.
(Courtesy of *South Wales Evening Post*).

After beating Blackburn to become Welsh heavyweight champion he made his first defence of the title in 1980, after teaming up with the Colin Breen stable. He was trained by Jimmy Bromfield, and the new training regime brought about a change in form and fortune for the Swansea boxer. He successfully defended his Welsh title in two successive fights, stopping Newport's David Pearce in three rounds and in October scored another quick win, halting fellow Swansea boxer Winston Allen in the second round at the Swansea Leisure Centre.

He lost the Welsh title along with the British title against David Pearce in Cardiff in September 1983 in his third defence in seven years as champion.

Ken Jones, the eldest of boxing brothers Colin and Peter, challenged Chris Lawson from Cardigan for the Welsh light heavyweight title in Haverfordwest on 19th March 1979 – he was adjudged the loser after ten hard fought bruising rounds. The Swansea boxer avenged that defeat and became Welsh light heavyweight champion in what turned out to be the penultimate contest of a professional career that had began on 2nd November 1977, when he outpointed Chris Lawson the defending champion at the Eisteddfod Ground in Gowerton on 12th August 1980.

After a distinguished amateur career in which he won the Welsh ABA title and numerous international honours, Ken made his debut as a professional boxer outpointing Dai Woods from Cardiff over six rounds in the Welsh capital city.

In 1978 the Swansea boxer turned out five times, beating Billy Lauder from Edinburgh, who had been unbeaten in four previous contests and later won the Scottish middleweight title, on points over six rounds. Ken outpointed Trevor Cattouse from Stoke Newington, Bonny McKenzie from Cardiff, both over eight rounds, and Shaun Chalcroft from Crawley in a scheduled six-rounder at Mayfair.

He returned to Mayfair in September where he suffered his first defeat against Denis Andries who was born in Guyana and based in Hackney. In his most recent contest Denis had lost on points to Bonny McKenzie, and had beaten his first two opponents in the second and

Ken Jones captures Welsh title from Chris Lawson.
(Courtesy of *South Wales Evening Post*).

first rounds respectively. Six years later Andries won the British light heavyweight title and won a Lonsdale belt outright in just nine months. He won the WBC light heavyweight title in 1986 and successfully defended the title by stopping Tony Sibson before losing the title on a ten round TKO against Thomas 'The Hitman' Hearns. Denis regained the vacant title by stopping Tony Willis in Tucson, Arizona, in 1989. He lost the title to Australian Jeff Harding in Atlantic City, New Jersey, four months later, but won the title for a third time when he knocked Harding out in seven rounds in Melbourne in July 1990. He finally lost the title on a majority decision against Harding in Hammersmith in September 1991.

Ken's next contest after the Andries fight and the first of 1979 was his unsuccessful challenge for the Welsh light heavyweight title against Chris Lawson, after which he suffered his third successive defeat, losing on points over eight rounds to Hackney-based Dominican, Carlton Benoit, who in his next bout knocked out Welsh champion Chris Lawson in two rounds.

Welsh Amateur Boxing Association
v
Midland Counties Amateur Boxing Association

	LIGHT FLYWEIGHT	
K. OWENS	v	J. DAWSON
	FEATHERWEIGHT	
P. COLEMAN	v	P. COWDELL (1976 Olympic Boxer)
	LIGHT WELTERWEIGHT	
C. BROWN	v	G. ALLEN
	WELTERWEIGHT	
C. JONES (1976 Olympic Boxer)	v	J. McINTOSH
	LIGHT MIDDLEWEIGHT	
D. SAUNDERS	v	G. AJNY
T. GRIFFITHS	v	J. KENNEDY
	LIGHT HEAVYWEIGHT	
K. JONES	v	G. McLEAN

also supporting bouts

Match Trophy kindly donated by WELSH BREWERS
Prizes for Best Winner and Loser presented by
MUNDAYS OFF-LICENCES

Official in charge of Tournament   Mr. T. T. BURGESS
Official in charge of Officials   Mr. B. J. DAVEY

Referees and Judges   GENTLEMEN OF THE W. A. B. A.
M.C.   Mr. R. C. ALLEN
Time-keeper   Mr. A. D. UZZEL
Doctors   Dr. I. PUGH & Dr. T. CROOKS
Welsh Team Manager   Mr. G. BEVAN
Midland Counties Team Manager   Mr. W. MEDDINGS

A SPORTING EVENING
Gower Round Table 907
Welsh Amateur Boxing Association
v
Midland Counties Amateur Boxing Association

Monday, 1st. November, 1976
Top Rank, Swansea Suite.

An Amateur Boxing Tournament Programme, Top Rank, Swansea Suit, 1st November 1976, featuring Colin Jones, Ken Jones, Pip Coleman and Pat Cowdell.

The Swansea boxer returned to the path of victory when he out-pointed Alex Thompkins from West Ham over eight rounds at the Double Diamond Club in Caerphilly.

In his next contest the Swansea boxer suffered his first and only inside the distance defeat when he was stopped in five rounds by Eddie Fenton from Leicester at the De Montford Hall in Leicester. Eddie had fought and been beaten by three British heavyweight champions. Swansea boxer Neville Meade had stopped him in five rounds in 1974, 'Dangerous' Danny McCalinden stopped Eddie in the fourth in 1976 and Gordon Ferris won by knockout in the first round in 1978.

Ken returned to the ring in November, losing a decision after six rounds against Steve Hill from Blackpool over eight rounds. In January of 1980 the Swansea boxer notched up a welcome win, outpointing Trevor Cattouse at the World Sporting Club – repeating his earlier triumph over the same opponent.

An eight rounds defeat on points against Shaun Chalcraft from Crawley preceded his second and successful Welsh title challenge against Chris Lawson in what turned out to be the penultimate contest of his career.

On 6th October 1980 Ken Jones entered the ring for the last time as a professional boxer at the Elephant & Castle Centre in London, where he drew a lively eight round contest against Londoner Steve Lewin. After almost three years as a professional, and a victor eight times with six losses and a draw, Ken retired undefeated light heavy-weight champion of Wales.

On 1st October 1980 the Swansea Leisure Centre was packed for a boxing extravaganza. Local entrepreneur, Pat Matthias, was staging a double header Welsh championship bill. Welsh heavyweight champion Neville Meade would be defending the heavyweight title against Winston Allen and Welsh bantamweight champion, thirty-five-year-old veteran Glyn Davies, would be defending his title against Swansea boxer **Pip Coleman**.

Pip was born in Neath on 16th April 1958, boxed as an amateur for Neath Amateur Boxing Club, before turning professional in 1978 shortly before his twentieth birthday. He made his debut against another debutant in the paid ranks – his opponent was Steve Cleak from Porthcawl. Pip displayed plenty of raw aggression and energy to win on points over six rounds in Barry.

He was beaten on points in his next two engagements against Bobby Breen in Birmingham and Terry McKeown in London. A return fight with Steve Cleak in Merthyr Tydfil ended in victory for the Swansea boxer, the referee stopped the fight in round two.

Pip made his Swansea debut next time out, outpointed Paddington's Mick Whelan over six rounds. In his last contest of the year he lost the decision after six rounds against unbeaten Gary Nickels from Paddington at the Royal Albert Hall. On the same bill Swansea boxer Frank McCord beat Sid Smith. Nickels lost a final eliminator for the British flyweight title later in his career against Swansea boxer David George.

Pip, who was now managed by Colin Breen and trained by Jimmy Bromfield at their gym in Treboeth, was a coalminer living in Morriston. 1979 began well for Pip, he won by TKO in the eighth round against Ian Murray from Manchester, followed by a six rounds points win over Jimmy Bott from St Helens, but was then beaten on points after four rounds by Alan Storey.

Pip suffered a setback in his next confrontation as he was knocked out in the sixth round by Neil McLaughlin in Belfast. His confidence was restored after his next engagement when he boxed Bermondsey prospect, highly regarded Gary Davidson on a Wembley bill glittering with stars: Dave 'Boy' Green, Charlie Magri and Jimmy Batten. Pip was given little and even no chance of beating the Londoner but he certainly did by everyone's opinion with the exception of the referee. Davidson, with a record of fourteen wins, one defeat and one draw had been battered from pillar to post by the relentless assault of the Swansea boxer. Even Davidson's mother acknowledged that her son had been well beaten. Despite all his promise Gary never boxed again.

Pip repeated his earlier victory over Ian Murray, this time on points over eight rounds, before challenging Glyn Davies from Llanelli for the

Pip Coleman wins the Welsh bantamweight title.

vacant Welsh bantamweight title in Ebbw Vale. Glyn had retired from boxing in 1971 and became trainer-manager to Mike McCluskie, Chuck Jones, Jeff 'Bulldog' Burns, Bobby Ruffe, Dai 'Muscles' Davies and a host of other fighters, before lacing up his own gloves again in August 1975. The meeting with Pip would be thirty-five-year-old Glyn's fifty-eighth professional bout in a career that began in 1962 when Pip was just four years old. The contest scheduled for ten rounds swung to and fro, Glyn using all his experience to avoid Pip's flailing attacks. The referee called a halt in round seven when Pip sustained a badly cut eye. Glyn was declared the bantamweight champion of Wales. In the return fight Pip kept the pressure on the champion, with Glyn's age beginning to tell in the later rounds. There was no let up from the Swansea boxer who worked hard to win the decision and become the bantamweight champion of Wales.

Soon after the championship contest Pip announced his retirement recording seven wins and six losses in a career of two and a half years.

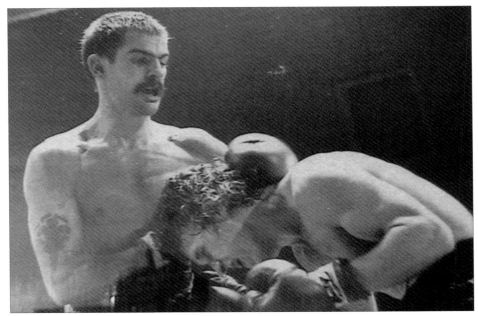

Don George winning the Welsh featherweight title from Mervyn Bennett.

Donald George, the eldest of three boxing brothers, had been a professional boxer for just over two years when he was matched with Mervyn Bennett from Cardiff, who was unbeaten in five contests, for the vacant Welsh featherweight championship. The Swansea boxer had boxed eleven times as a professional, winning six, with four losses and one draw before getting his title chance.

Don had started boxing with his younger brothers under the watchful eye of their father, the late Eric Sr., and Swansea Dockers ABC trainer Cliff Teasdale. He turned professional and made his debut on 12th September 1979. He was approaching his twenty-second birthday when he lost on points in a six round contest against Peter Keers in Liverpool.

The Swansea boxer had boxed eight times by the end of 1980, his first complete year as a professional. He had won five, lost two with one draw. In his final bout of the year he accomplished a notable triumph, outpointing compatriot Steve Sims at the Civic Hall in Nantwich. Sims became British featherweight champion and unsuccessfully challenged for the European title. This was a win of some considerable merit.

In the following year Don added to his tally of victories by outscoring Alan Cooper in Southend on St Patrick's Night. His next mission was in Ghana – he was presented with the unenviable task of boxing the unbeaten, hard-hitting Ghanaian prospect Azumah Nelson who had won all seven contests. The word **DANGER** was emblazoned all over his credentials – this was not a good match for young Donald. The bout took place in Accra on 2nd May, the Swansea boxer being knocked out in the fifth round. Nelson had captured the featherweight championship of Ghana and four months after beating Don he was crowned Commonwealth champion. In December 1984 the Ghanaian knocked out Wilfredo Gomez to become WBC featherweight champion. Losing to Nelson, even by knockout, as most of his opponents did, was no disgrace – it was to his credit that he went to round five.

The Swansea boxer returned to the ring in September dropping an eight round decision to unbeaten Scotsman Ian McLeod in Glasgow. On the back of two defeats Don deservedly won the Welsh title marring the unbeaten record of Mervyn Bennett by winning on points over ten rounds.

Don and Dave George.

159

The Welsh champion didn't box again for more than eighteen months, coming out on top after eight rounds against Mark West at the National Sporting Club on 21st April 1983.

Donald's swan song was on 1st November 1983. Approaching his twenty-sixth birthday, he took on the Belgian and Benelux champion Marc Renard, who had won sixteen of his eighteen starts. His two defeats were against Barry McGuigan and Steve Sims. Renard won by knockout in the fourth round, and he went on to win the European featherweight and super featherweight titles. Boxing against such a formidable opponent, having only boxed once in two years, was probably not the best match Don could have taken at that particular time. The same can be said of many other Swansea boxers, particularly when in the twilight of their careers.

In such a short career, Donald George boxed opponents of very high calibre and certainly never let anyone down. He had won eight, lost five and drawn one in four years as a professional.

Ray 'Peanut' Price was seventeen when he drew with Portsmouth's Gerry Howland in his first professional fight on 30th April 1979. He boxed eleven times in the year, winning on four occasions, losing three times and drawing the other four. He beat Barnet Bryan from Halifax on points over four rounds, Kid Curtis from Whitestone by KO in the second round, Neil Brown on points over six rounds at Stafford and again at Evesham. He failed to get the nod in a four rounder against Brighton's Tim Moloney, lost on points over six rounds against John Daly from Northampton and Moloney made it five wins in five again winning on points, this time over six rounds in London. Along with the drawn bout in his debut he also shared decisions with Bill Smith from Newcastle, Phillip Morris from Cefn Hengoed in the Double Diamond in Caerphilly and Shaun Durkin from Bradford.

In 1980 the Swansea boxer only boxed twice. He beat Terry Parkinson on points over eight rounds at the World Sporting Club in Mayfair, but was on the wrong end of a six rounds points decision against Colin Wake at the National Sporting Club.

1981 began and ended with disappointment. 'Peanut' lost on points against Merthyr's Billy Vivian and ended with a crushing defeat against Liverpool prospect Robbie Robinson who won by knockout in the first round. Sandwiched between these two losses were points victories over Tyrrel Wilson in Newport, Barry Price in Copthorne and a second round knockout win against John Lindo in Bradford. Ironically, after the loss to Robinson, Ray became the light welterweight champion of Wales in his next bout after outpointing fellow Swansea boxer Geoff Pegler in a ten round contest in Swansea on 22nd March 1982, four months before his twentieth birthday.

Following his title success, Ray lost on points against former Scottish lightweight and light welterweight champion Willie Booth in Glasgow and was stopped in the first round by Brixton's Tony Adams at the Royal Albert Hall on a bill featuring Frank Bruno. Later in his career Adams halted Swansea boxer Frank McCord.

Amidst a growing clamour for a return Welsh championship contest, Ray outpointed Lee Halford over six rounds in Evesham, but nineteen days later was stopped in the first round by hard-hitting Gunther Roomes from Lambeth. The rematch with Geoff Pegler, which took place at the Dolphin Hotel in Swansea, turned out to be an anticlimax as the referee halted the bout in the first round due to the hostilities between rival supporters of the two boxers. The fight was declared a 'no contest' which meant that Ray retained his title.

His next outing was in Bethnal Green where he lost the decision after eight rounds against Mo Hussein from West Ham, who was registering his seventh win in as many contests and later won the Commonwealth lightweight title. In his final bout of 1983 Ray lost his Welsh title in Swansea to Geoff Pegler who stopped him in round eight and became champion in his third attempt to wrest the title.

Ray was no longer Welsh champion but tasted victory in his first contest of 1984, outpointing Steve Tempro over eight rounds in Birmingham, but lost against Ken Foreman in Mayfair and Tony McKenzie in front of his own supporters in Leicester.

When Geoff Pegler vacated the Welsh light welterweight title, Swansea boxer Michael Harries was nominated to box Ray for the vacant title over ten rounds at the Afan Lido. Michael had won thirteen out of fourteen when he outpointed 'Peanut' to be crowned Welsh champion two months before his twentieth birthday.

Following his title fight defeat, Ray was stopped in four rounds by Irishman David Irving in Belfast and lost on points over eight rounds against Ghanaian Frankie Moro in Swansea. In 1985 Ray fought twice in London, losing the decision after four rounds against rising star George Collins who three months later knocked out Geoff Pegler in the first round. The Swansea boxer was stopped in five rounds by Londoner Steve Elwood in London. Ray would not box again until 1992.

It had been thirteen years since Ray Price made his debut in a professional boxing ring and seven years since his last appearance. Now thirty-one years of age and weighing close on twelve stone he won the decision after six rounds against Steve Thomas from Merthyr Tydfil in Barry, in October 1992. He was stopped in four rounds by Swansea boxer Russell Washer in Swansea the following October and in six rounds by Darren Dorrington in Bristol in March 1994, after which he finally hung up his gloves.

The Swansea boxer can claim to have boxed in three decades. He was a seventeen-year-old light welterweight when he began his career and a thirty-two-year-old super middleweight when he finally retired.

Doug James was approaching his twenty-fifth birthday when he stopped Cardiff-based Jamaican Horace McKenzie in the ninth round on 28th January 1983 to win the Welsh middleweight title left vacant by Caerau's Mike McCluskie.

Doug had been a professional for three and a half years, making his debut in Mayfair on 17th September 1979 when he outpointed fellow debutant Earl Edwards over six rounds. Edwards, a Jamaican based in Clapham, went on to win the Southern Area middleweight title.

In the next two months to the end of 1979 the Swansea boxer crammed in four more contests, scoring inside the distance wins against Joe Hannaford from Shrewsbury and Keith Roberts from Liverpool. He was awarded points decisions against Joe Jackson from Leicester and Clifton Wallace from Wolverhampton. Doug had boxed five times in less than four months as a professional, winning three by decision and two inside the distance.

The New Year began well. Doncaster middleweight Harry Watson was knocked out in the first round at the National Sporting Club in Piccadilly. In his next encounter the Swansea boxer experienced defeat for the first time when he was stopped in the sixth round by George Danahar from Bethnal Green at Mayfair on St Patrick's night. Doug then boxed an eight rounds draw with Peter Bassey

Doug James with stablemate Alan Minter, World middleweight champion.

from Manchester, who had recently lost an eight rounder against Swansea boxer Terry Matthews.

Doug returned to winning ways with a triumph over Dave Owens from Castleford, who was to become the Central Area middleweight champion. This bout took place at the Eisteddfod Grounds in Gowerton – the bill was headed by Colin Jones, who was defending his British title.

The Swansea boxer ended 1980 as he began with an inside the distance win, halting Carl Daley from Peckham in the second round in Merthyr Tydfil, despite sustaining a badly cut eye.

Doug James was inactive in 1981. His record stood at eight wins, one defeat and one draw, four of his victims weren't around for the final bell. Following his break from the ring, the Swansea boxer was elevated in class and as a consequence suffered two consecutive defeats, losing on a decision after eight rounds in Glasgow against Billy Lauder from Edinburgh, who later won the Scottish title, and Sheffield's Brian Anderson. He boxed Anderson, who went on to become Central Area and British middleweight champion, in Piccadilly in March.

Doug James wins the Welsh middleweight title
with cornermen Jimmy Bromfield, Colin Breen and John Parry.

Doug notched up his ninth and tenth wins when knocking out Kenny Feehan from Tonypandy in the fifth round in Swansea and gained sweet revenge over Billy Lauder, winning in four rounds in Piccadilly in May 1982. His last bout of the year was not an enviable task – he was matched against London prospect and former amateur star Mark Kaylor who had won sixteen straight as a professional. The bout took place at Bethnal Green on 26th October and ended in the second round with Kaylor having his arm raised in victory.

Doug commenced his 1983 campaign in Swansea, winning the Welsh title in his sixteenth professional bout. He'd won ten, lost four and drawn one before taking the scalp of Horace McKenzie.

In his first match as Welsh champion, the Swansea boxer stopped Swindon's Cameron Lithgoe in four rounds at Aberavon, it was Lithgoe's first professional defeat after four straight wins. Doug didn't fare so well in a return fight with Brian Anderson, losing by TKO in the first round in Mayfair in September. The Sheffield boxer possessed an impressive record of seventeen wins with four defeats and three draws – he was on the march toward the British title.

There was another tough assignment ahead against Coventry boxer with high expectations, Errol Christie, unbeaten in eight contests including a stoppage victory over Swansea boxer Terry Matthews. Doug boxed Christie in Coventry and was stopped in the fourth round having sustained a cut eye. On 6th December he shared the verdict after eight hard fought rounds against Tony TP Jenkins from Chiswick at the Royal Albert Hall on a bill that featured Lloyd Honeyghan and Frank Bruno. A return fight with Jenkins was scheduled for 3rd February 1984 in Mayfair, and on this occasion Jenkins was declared the winner when the bout was stopped in round seven.

Doug returned to Mayfair for his next bout in which he knocked out Johnny Elliot from Wellington in the fourth. He was then off to Toulouse to fight Pierre Joly, a Frenchman, who possessed a respectable tariff of twenty-three wins, two draws and three losses and was later to become French and European middleweight champion. Doug lost on points after eight rounds.

The Swansea boxer didn't box again until February of the following year when he lost on points after eight rounds against Conrad Oscar from the Dominican Republic and based in London. The Swansea boxer's next encounter, which was to be his last, was held in Grenoble against Frenchman Pierre-Frank Winterstein who had recorded thirty-three wins, one draw and one loss when he challenged Italian Lou Acaries for the European title. Doug was knocked out in the third round.

The defeat convinced the Swansea boxer that at twenty-seven years of age, after six years as a professional and a career record of thirteen wins, ten defeats, with one draw, it was time to call time on his boxing career. Six of those defeats were suffered in his last eight contests and against quality opposition.

In his very last professional contest, which was on 14th March 1986, Swansea boxer, twenty-seven-year-old **Geoff Pegler**, won his second Welsh title, when he had his opponent – the highly regarded Rocky Feliciello from Rhyl – on the canvas in the third and referee Adrian Morgan stopped the contest in the seventh round. The north Walian

Geoff Pegler signs up with Colin Breen (right) and Jimmy Bromfield (left).
(Courtesy of *South Wales Evening Post*).

had been beaten only five times in twenty professional bouts. He'd stopped Swansea boxer John McGlynn and lost on points over eight rounds to another Swansea boxer, Michael Harries. Against all the odds Geoff was crowned the welterweight champion of Wales. Trainer Jimmy Bromfield described the contest as 'Geoff's finest battle'.

Geoff had began his professional career losing a points decision after six rounds against fellow debutant Mick Rowley, an Australian, living in Merthyr Tydfil. He recorded his first victory in his next contest, out-pointing Winston Ho Shing from Sheffield over six rounds in Bradford. He outpointed Tommy Thomas from Tottenham over four rounds in Plymouth and stopped Wolverhampton-based Jamaican Errol Dennis in Nottingham. He lost on points over six rounds to Kostas Petrou in Evesham. Petrou later became Midlands and British welterweight champion. Geoff concluded a very busy opening three months of his professional career by winning decisions on points over six rounds against Tottenham-based Jamaican Delroy Pearce in Pembroke and Brummie Kevin Johnson in Bristol.

The Swansea boxer commenced 1982 with a draw against Gay Petty and then outpointed Jamaican Winston McKenzie over eight rounds in Lewisham. After only six months as a professional, with six wins, a draw and two losses, Geoff was to challenge the younger but more experienced fellow Swansea boxer, Ray Price, for the vacant Welsh light welterweight title on a Swansea bill promoted by local businessman Alan Davies, that also featured Swansea boxers Terry Matthews, Doug James, Dai 'Muscles' Davies and Steve Babbs. Referee Jim Brimmel awarded Ray the decision and the title by a margin of three rounds.

Back to business after his title defeat, Geoff halted Scotsman Colin Harrison in four rounds and lost a points decision over eight rounds against West Ham's Gary Knight to complete his 1982 campaign.

Next contest, his first of 1983, was at the Top Rank Suite in Swansea where he outpointed Ian Chantler from Merseyside. Swansea boxers Doug James, Frank McCord and Michael Harries were also in action on this bill.

Geoff was unsuccessful in attempting to avenge an earlier defeat against Kostas Petrou in Birmingham, losing on points after eight rounds. Petrou also beat Swansea boxer Frank McCord on points later in the year, but lost against Michael Harries in 1987.

In his fifteenth contest, of which he'd won eight and drawn one, Geoff lost on points after eight rounds against Mancunian Wayne Crolla in Rhyl, which was to be the venue of his greatest victory.

On May 27th Geoff tried in vain to wrest the Welsh title from Ray Price, referee Ivor Bassett declared the fight a 'no contest' in the first round due to crowd hostilities. At this time the Swansea boxer, as determined as he was, couldn't buy a win – he lost his next three contests against Tommy McCallum from Edinburgh at the National Sporting Club, Chris Sanigar from Bristol in London and Scotsman Ian McCleod, again in Glasgow.

After this dismal run the taste of success could not have been sweeter when he halted Ray Price in the eighth round at the Dolphin Hotel in Swansea to annexe the Welsh light welterweight title at the third attempt. Being Welsh champion didn't change the Swansea boxer's fortunes – he lost four successive points decisions against Jim Kelly, Tommy McCallum and John McCalister, all in Glasgow, and was defeated by Gary Knight in Port Talbot. However, beating Tony Smith on points over eight rounds in Swansea and a seventh round knockout win over David Irving in Belfast provided a welcome return to winning ways.

Geoff, now twenty-six years of age, was off to South Africa to fight Joseph Lala from the Bloemfonstein Free State, who boasted a record of twenty-four wins with just six losses. The Swansea boxer lost on points after ten keenly contested rounds.

Geoff was on the losing end of his next four contests in 1985 against very respectable opposition, he was beaten by Dave Dent from Camden Town (unbeaten in five fights), Scotsman Tommy Campbell (just one defeat in ten contests), Steve Ellwood from Camberwell (again only beaten once in ten bouts), and George Collins from Yately (unbeaten in eight contests). Collins continued on a winning run of thirty-five contests before losing to Gary Jacobs for the Common-wealth title and Kirkland Laing for the British title.

Geoff's next contest was the successful Welsh welterweight title challenge against Feliciello, after which Geoff retired undefeated welter-weight champion of Wales at twenty-seven years of age with twelve wins, eighteen losses, one draw and one no decision. He can claim to be among the elite in Welsh boxing, having been Welsh champion at two different weights.

Chapter Five

WELSH CHAMPIONS, 1984-2010

Michael Harries was approaching his twentieth birthday when he won an impressive but hard earned ten rounds decision over former Welsh light welterweight champion Ray Price at the Afan Lido on 13th June 1984 for the title that had been vacated by Geoff Pegler. Only six months previously, Michael had boxed in the chief supporting bout at the Dolphin Hotel when Pegler beat Price to win the title.

The title win was Michael's fifteenth contest, he had won fourteen, with just the one blemish – a six rounds points defeat against Dave Savage in Aberdeen in his seventh contest.

The Swansea boxer joined the paid ranks under manager Colin Breen and trainer Jimmy Bromfield on 18th November 1982. He was eighteen years old when he outpointed Frankie Lake from Plymouth, who had won his only other contest, the bout taking place at the National Sporting Club in Piccadilly.

Michael had been a professional for just over eighteen months when he won the Welsh title and had boxed in Swansea on three occasions – outpointing Stan Atherton at the Top Rank Suite, Bobby Welburn at the same venue and Gary Williams on the Pegler-Price Welsh championship bill. He had also beaten Kevin Pritchard, who later became British super featherweight champion, in the lead up to winning the Welsh title.

The new Welsh champion then boxed at the Midlands Sporting Club in Solihull, outpointing Tony McKenzie over eight rounds and losing on points over ten rounds against the experienced Dave McCabe, who had previously challenged for the British and Commonwealth titles and became Scottish welterweight champion.

Michael Harries.

Michael Harries was proving to be a big favourite at the Solihull venue, after halting Gary Williams in Cork, his next three contests were at the Midlands Sporting Club where he outscored Rocky Feliciello, lost on a four rounds TKO against Scottish welterweight champion Dave Douglas and then stopped Tommy McCallum in the sixth round.

The Swansea boxer kept busy winning the decision after eight rounds against Mickey Bird in Porthcawl, beating Joe Teteli on points over ten rounds in South Africa but losing the decision after eight rounds against Mohammed Kawaya in Denmark.

Harries didn't commence his 1986 campaign until May when he lost a close ten rounds contest against Tony McKenzie, who was avenging his loss to Michael in 1984. In his next contest McKenzie won the British light welterweight title, stopping Clinton McKenzie in three rounds. The Swansea boxer challenged the Leicestershire man for his newly-won title, but was knocked out in the tenth round in Stevenage.

Michael returned to the ring in May 1987 and made an impressive comeback, outpointing Kostas Petrou, who was the former British and Commonwealth champion and had beaten Swansea boxers Geoff Pegler and Frank McCord over eight rounds.

Six weeks later he outpointed Frankie Moro over eight rounds and then did extremely well in drawing with former European welterweight champion, Spaniard Alfonso Redondo, in Madrid. In his

Michael Harries after a sparring session with the legendary Roberto Durán.

Roberto Durán with Michael Harries and his team.

A triumphant Michael Harries.

next contest the Swansea boxer challenged Gary Cooper for the British light middleweight title, losing a twelve round contest on points at Wembley on 3rd February 1988.

Michael was now campaigning as a light middleweight and boxed in South Africa the following month where he lost on points over eight rounds against unbeaten South African Mbulelo Mxokiswa. He was outpointed in a return contest with Alfonso Redondo in Madrid and suffered his fourth defeat in succession against French middleweight champion Pierre-Frank Winterstein on points over ten rounds. The Frenchman had previously knocked out Swansea boxer Doug James and had won forty-four of forty-six contests with one draw when he faced Michael.

In his penultimate ring engagement Michael Harries, in his thirty-fourth professional contest, won his second Welsh title when he outpointed Kevin Hayde over ten rounds to become the light middleweight champion of Wales.

His final ring outing took him to New South Wales, Australia, when on 26th May 1989 he challenged champion Troy Waters for the Commonwealth light middleweight title and was stopped in the eighth round. Waters made three unsuccessful World title challenges against WBC champions Terry Norris, Simon Brown and Felix Trinidad.

Following the Waters fight, Michael – approaching twenty-five years of age and after seven years as a professional – announced his retirement. He had boxed thirty-five times against quality opposition, winning twenty-three, with eleven losses and one draw, had held the Welsh light welterweight and light middleweight titles and had challenged for the British light welterweight and light middleweight titles.

Although born the other side of the Loughor Bridge, **Chris Jacobs** lived, trained and boxed out of Swansea – thus qualifying as a Swansea boxer. Conversely, Swansea-born Dean Phillips, a useful lightweight, who boxed between 1994 and 2007, lived, trained and boxed in Llanelli – thus not recognised as a Swansea boxer.

Chris made his first entrance into a professional boxing ring on 13th June 1984 – he was twenty-three years old, and outpointed another debutant, Tony Tricker from Brixton, over six rounds at the Afan Lido in Port Talbot.

In only his fourth contest and still very much a novice heavyweight, Chris – who had notched up two wins and a draw – was matched against Andrew Gerrard from Risca in Gwent for the Welsh heavyweight title vacated by British heavyweight champion David 'Bomber' Pearce. The Swansea boxer was crowned the heavyweight champion of Wales, decisively outpointing Gerrard over ten rounds in Newport.

In the following year, 1986, the Swansea boxer was on his travels. He boxed in Italy, France and Germany against three very good opponents. He knocked out the Argentine champion Walter Falconi, who had won seventeen, lost one and drawn one of his previous nineteen contests, in six rounds in Calabria, Italy. He lost on points over eight rounds against French-based Congolese Anaclet Wamba, who had won fifteen of his previous sixteen bouts (Swansea boxer

Welsh heavyweight champion Chris Jacobs.
(Courtesy of *South Wales Evening Post*).

Winston Allen was among his victims), and became European and WBC cruiserweight champion. Chris then boxed in Hessa, Germany, losing on points over eight rounds against Zambian Michael Simuwelu, who was unbeaten in eleven contests and became African heavyweight champion later in his career. The Swansea boxer had earned a lot of respect on his travels.

The Welsh heavyweight champion continued his globetrotting, venturing to South Africa to fight the highly regarded Pretorian, Pierre Coetzee, who knocked out Chris in the second round in Johannesburg. The South African's record read thirty-nine wins, twenty-seven by knockout, and five defeats, three of which were against George

174

Foreman, Riddick Bowe and Frank Bruno. Chris continued his losing run against Paul Lister and Hughroy Currie, ex-British and Commonwealth heavyweight champion. He was glad to see the back of 1987.

In the ensuing year, the Swansea boxer notched up two very welcome consecutive wins, followed by defeats against Jess Harding and Jean Chanet, who later became European champion before losing his laurels to Lennox Lewis. Chris lost to unbeaten Manny Burgo on points over eight rounds and successfully defended his Welsh title with another victory on points over Andrew Gerrard in Cardiff to conclude his 1989 campaign.

Gerrard's next fight would be his last, as he was offered up as the sacrificial lamb for Lennox Lewis, who was making his professional debut and was keen to impress – he did!

1990 began on a high for the Swansea boxer, gaining revenge over Jess Harding by knockout in round four, but was followed by a shattering fifth round knockout defeat against ex-British cruiserweight champion, Ghanaian Tee Jay.

Herbie Hide, unbeaten in thirteen contests, then knocked Chris out in the first round. Hide became WBO heavyweight champion less than two and a half years later. The defeat against Hide convinced the Swansea boxer that approaching the age of thirty, having won eight, lost ten and drawn one in a career that began more than six years before, he should retire undefeated heavyweight champion of Wales.

It was 28th October 1987 – **Keith Parry**, who had quietly celebrated his twenty-fourth birthday the preceding day – was about to make his second assault on the lightweight championship of Wales. The Swansea boxer had been a professional since making his debut in Blaenavon on 12th September 1985, where he outpointed John Mudd from Liverpool over six rounds. By April of the following year Keith had reeled off six wins in as many bouts, four of which ended inside the distance, after only ten months in the paid ranks.

He'd beaten Tony Graham from Paddington, stopped Brian Wareing from Southport in the first round and Willie Wilson from Nottingham in the fourth. In his next outing he made his Swansea debut at the Dillwyn Llewellyn Leisure Centre, and he didn't disappoint his home supporters when he halted Denzil Goddard of Llanelli in the third round and followed up with a four round demolition of Marvin P. Gray from County Durham in Leeds.

Keith made his first assault on the Welsh title held by Andy Williams from Garndiffaith at the Ebbw Vale Leisure Centre, the decision going against him over ten keenly contested rounds. Suffering no ill effects from his first defeat, the Swansea boxer returned to the Ebbw Vale Leisure Centre to halt Cardiff boxer Mervyn Bennett in three rounds. Keith ended 1986 with an impressive tally of eight wins and just one defeat when he outpointed Edward Lloyd from Rhyl over eight rounds in Cardiff.

By March of the ensuing year, 1987, Keith had suffered two successive defeats, against Tony Willis in the St David's Hall in Cardiff and the other against South African debutant Elijah Sele in Johannesburg, both on points over eight rounds. Twenty-six-year-old Willis from Liverpool was the reigning British lightweight champion and had been the victor in twenty-one of twenty-three contests.

Seven months after the South African adventure Keith was ready to make a second attempt to lift the Welsh lightweight title against Andy Williams, who was still the titleholder. The Swansea boxer, refreshed from his break, performed well to stop the defending champion in the eighth round at the Mayfair Suite in Swansea.

The victory over Williams earned Keith a fight with Carl Crook from Bolton in a final eliminator for the British lightweight title. He lost on points over ten rounds in Bradford. Crook went on to become the British and Commonwealth champion.

The Welsh champion returned to the ring eight months later to stop Mohammed Lovelock from Manchester in four rounds. In his next contest, which turned out to be his last, Keith suffered the only stoppage defeat of his career when he was halted by London-based Ugandan Patrick Kamy in six rounds in Solihull.

Twenty-five-year-old Keith, a victor in ten of fifteen contests, seven inside the distance in three and a half years, retired from the ring as undefeated Welsh champion.

John Davies, a tall rangy welterweight, had teamed up with the Colin Breen stable at the Treboeth gym in 1982 to prepare for his first professional contest under the training regime prepared by Jimmy Bromfield. Nearly eight years later, still only twenty-six years old, John was working out in the same gym under the same team preparing for a crack at the vacant Welsh welterweight title.

He was to vie for the title against Kelvin Mortimer from Trebanog who was no match for the Swansea boxer and was stopped in round two at the Merthyr Leisure Centre. John Davies had probably taken a lot longer to win a Welsh title than his ability could have enabled him to achieve – the title had been vacated by Swansea boxer Geoff Pegler after he defeated Rocky Feliciello in 1986.

John had began his career in impressive style, knocking out Dalton Jordan a middleweight from Barbados in the fourth round, but suffered a minor setback when losing on points over six rounds against Rocky Feliciello in Liverpool. John was over the defeat very quickly and very emphatically when just ten days after the loss against Rocky he stopped Bert Myrie, a Jamaican based in Wolverhampton, in the first round at the Evesham Sporting Club. The Swansea boxer crammed in three more fights in the next two weeks to conclude his 1982 campaign. He outpointed Clifton Wallace an experienced middleweight who had previously been outpointed by Swansea boxers Terry Matthews and Doug James, drew and stopped Ian 'Kid' Murray within six days. Six fights, four wins, one loss and one draw in his first year, but John wasn't seen in the ring again until 1986 – according to his manager, he went 'walk about' in India!

He returned with a flourish, knocking out Paul Burton in the sixth round in Coventry and stopping Peter Reid from Derby in the second round. Two good wins in 1987 – outpointing Johnny Stone from Gloucester over six rounds, followed by a stoppage win over Ghanaian Frankie Moro, who had previously beaten Swansea boxer Ray Price. Frankie's career record was lined with big names like Chris Pyatt, Kirkland Laing, Michael Watson, Chris Eubank, Vicente Nardiello and Nicky Piper. He never beat any of them, but he would always put a good fighter to the test.

John had won eight and drawn one of ten contests over five years, and fight fans were beginning to recognise John as a rising star. Lo and behold he was gone again! – not even Colin Breen could keep tracks on John.

He graced us with his next ring appearance two years later when he outpointed John Smith over eight rounds in Solihull in March 1989, three months later he stopped Dave Andrews in three rounds in Cardiff.

The Swansea boxer scored an excellent win in Cape Town, South Africa, winning a unanimous decision over ten rounds against Linda Nondzaba – don't be fooled by the name – this guy had won fifteen with two losses and a draw when he fought John. Five months later John Davies was the welterweight champion of Wales and there were a number of doors opening for the Swansea boxer.

His first engagement as Welsh champion was another excursion to Cape Town where he stopped Phumzile Madikane in the tenth and last round – he was a popular attraction in South Africa.

John was then out of the ring for eleven months before challenging Londoner Andy Till for the WBC International light middleweight title, losing on points after twelve rounds. On the 11th March 1992 the Swansea boxer stopped Trevor Ambrose in five rounds in Cardiff and at the age of twenty-seven with a record of fourteen wins, two losses and a draw, walked away from boxing for good.

His manager, who was left confused and frustrated by his fighter's departure, swears that John Davies had all the ability to become a World champion, but lacked the application and dedication.

Peter Harries was in the twilight of his professional career when he boxed Llanelli's Nigel Haddock for the vacant Welsh featherweight title at the Glyn Clydach Hotel in Neath on 20th May 1994.

Peter was approaching his thirty-second birthday – this was his twenty-eighth contest – and six years had passed since he had lost his British title to Paul Hodkinson, and three years since he'd unsuccessfully challenged Steve Robinson for the Welsh featherweight title. Peter put the years behind him winning the decision and the title by three clear rounds on referee Ivor Bassett's scorecard.

The Swansea boxer fought on for another two years, winning one of five contests before retiring after losing on points against unbeaten South African Cassius Baloyi who became IBF and IBO super featherweight champion later in his career.

When Swansea boxer **Jason Williams** challenged veteran campaigner Keith Jones from Aberystwyth for the Welsh welterweight title in February 2003 he will probably be the first to admit that his best days in the paid ranks were behind him.

Jason was approaching his twenty-third birthday when he lost on points over six rounds against Jon Harrison in Plymouth on 19th April 1997 in his first professional contest. The Swansea boxer quickly shook off the disappointment by halting Dewi Roberts of Blaenau in Cardiff two months later. He then beat Darren Covill from London and Sheffield's Peter Federenko to end 1997 with three wins out of four bouts.

The 1998 campaign was a great success for Jason. He won all six bouts, three inside the distance. He won points decisions over Danny Quacoe from Crawley in Cardiff, Adrian Chase from St Albans in Windsor and Mark Ramsey, a southpaw from Birmingham, who had only recently lost a points decision over six rounds against Manchester prospect – a certain Ricky Hatton. Jason stopped Rob Pitters from Gateshead in Tenerife in the third round, Kasi Kaihu from Doncaster in Bristol in the second and he avenged his sole defeat by halting Jon Harrison in Reading. The Swansea boxer had won nine out of ten contests in twenty months as a professional boxer.

The ensuing year, 1999, got off to a good start with three impressive victories. He stopped Harry Butler from Worcester in the seventh at the Manor Park in Clydach, Essex man Paul Miles only managed two rounds in Cardiff and Brixton domiciled Jamaican Delroy Mellis was outpointed over six rounds in Bristol. Jason's next fight was probably the turning point in a career that to date was showing a lot of promise.

He challenged the 'Barry Bomber', hard-hitting Michael Smyth, for the vacant Welsh welterweight title at the Rhydycar Leisure Centre in Merthyr Tydfil. Jason was stopped in three rounds and although he won his next bout on points over six rounds against David Baptiste from Luton the following April, the Swansea boxer was probably never quite 'up to the mark' throughout the rest of his career. He was stopped in the fifth round by Frenchman Karim Bouald in Bristol and was knocked out in six rounds by Mark Ramsey, whom he had beaten the previous December.

With his batteries recharged, Jason returned to the ring in September 2001 and outpointed Mark Richards from Wednesbury over six rounds at Swansea Leisure Centre. He lost on points over ten rounds against Jimmy Vincent in Birmingham – later in his career Vincent challenged Irishman Eamon Magee for the World Boxing Union welterweight title.

In 2002 Jason fought just once, losing by a knockout in the fifth round against Las Vegas-based Congolese Charlie Ansoila in Northampton. Despite his indifferent form and relative inactivity Jason defeated Keith Jones to win the Welsh welterweight title the following February. Jones had won the vacant title by beating Swansea boxer Ross McCord the previous September at the Swansea Leisure Centre.

Winning the Welsh title didn't change the fortunes of the Swansea boxer for in May he was stopped by Leeds-based Irishman, ex-British welterweight champion Derek Roche, in Huddersfield. Four months later he lost on points over six rounds in Shrewsbury against Marcus Portman of West Bromwich, who two years previously had drawn with Ross McCord. In the following February the Swansea boxer lost on points over six rounds against former British light middleweight champion Michael Jones from Liverpool, who had only lost once in nineteen fights, that was against British and Commonwealth champion Jamie Moore. Six weeks later Jason was stopped in two rounds by former World Boxing Federation champion James Hare who came into the fight boasting a record of twenty-eight wins, one loss and one draw.

The Swansea boxer had lost eight of eleven contests since the Welsh title defeat against Michael Smyth. Prior to that contest Jason had won twelve with just one defeat. At the time he boxed Hare he was two months short of his thirtieth birthday and had been boxing as a professional for seven years. Jason realised his best days were behind him, he retired the undefeated champion of Wales.

Lightweight **Damian Owen** had been a professional less than two years, was approaching his twenty-second birthday, had won seven of eight professional bouts when he knocked out Swansea-born Dean Phillips in the fourth round to become the lightweight champion of Wales. Phillips lived and boxed out of Llanelli and had previously fought for the Commonwealth lightweight title.

The new Welsh champion had made his professional debut in Bristol in October 2004 when he knocked out Bristolian Darren Payne in the fourth round of a welterweight contest. After this bout Darren realised that there were easier ways to make a living and duly terminated his career in the ring.

Damian turned out at the Hereford Leisure Centre for his next engagement, where he stopped journeyman Peter Allen from Birkenhead in the first round. Victories over London-based boxers, Sri Lankan Jus Wallie and South African Bheki Mayo, made it four straight wins before running into his first defeat, dropping a six rounds decision against Kevin O'Hara in Belfast. The Irishman had only lost twice in twelve contests and later in his career lost a twelve round decision against Ricky Burns when challenging for the Commonwealth super featherweight title. Wolverhampton's Carl Allen was outpointed by the Swansea boxer in Bristol, who recorded a sixth round stoppage win over Liverpudlian Stephen Mullen in Belfast, and concluded his 2006 campaign by outscoring the well travelled Yauhen Kruhlik from Belarus at the Afan Lido in Port Talbot.

Damian began 2007 with the Welsh title victory over Dean Phillips. In his first fight as Welsh champion the Swansea boxer tasted defeat for the second time in ten contests when he was stopped in the third round by Venezuelan import Pedro Verdu, but returned to the ring on October 21st to win the decision after four rounds against Chris Long from Wiltshire at the Brangwyn Hall in Swansea.

Damian was inactive in 2008, resuming his career on 13th June 2009, outpointing veteran Jason Nesbitt from Birmingham over six rounds in Bristol. The following month he improved on an earlier success by knocking out Chris Long in the fourth round at Newport Leisure Centre, achieving his eleventh triumph in thirteen contests.

Light welterweight **Ceri Hall** never boxed for a Welsh title – however, he is included in this chapter as the only Swansea boxer to have held a British Boxing Board of Control Celtic championship. He won the title at the Neath Sports Centre on 2nd March 2007 in his penultimate professional contest, when he stopped Scotsman Stuart Green in the ninth round on a programme promoted by his manager, Paul Boyce.

Ceri made his professional debut at the Swansea Leisure Centre on 15th September 2002 – he was twenty-two years old when he stopped Martin Turner from Poole in the first round. Over the ensuing two years the Swansea boxer had shown encouraging signs of promise and by the end of 2004 had won five contests, drawing one, and his only loss was a four rounds points defeat against Dean Hickman from West Bromwich who was unbeaten in eleven contests when he touched gloves with Ceri.

Commencing his 2005 campaign the Swansea boxer suffered a successive defeat, an eight rounds loss on points against Robert Murray from Dublin in the fair city. However, he returned to winning ways in emphatic style, stopping trial horse Jason Nesbitt from Birmingham in two rounds at the Manor Park in Clydach on a Paul Boyce promotion. This was Nesbitt's fifty-seventh contest and by the end of 2010 Jason was still active, having participated in one hundred and thirty-one contests. Ceri rounded off the year with two victories, before travelling to Italy in March 2006 to box the unbeaten Italian, Giorgio Marinelli, for the vacant European title in Rome. Ceri justified his nomination for the challenge by forcing the Italian to rely on the decision after ten hard fought rounds. The Swansea boxer won, drew and lost in his three other bouts in 2006.

Ceri Hall, now approaching his twenty-seventh birthday, captured the BBB of C Celtic title which he held for three months, losing the title by way of a narrow points decision against Stuart Phillips from Port Talbot, again at the Neath Sports Centre – he was floored in the eighth round, probably costing him the decision and the title.

After losing his title the Swansea boxer called time on his career of nearly five years in which he'd boxed seventeen times, winning ten, with five defeats and two draws.

Chapter Six

SO NEAR AND YET SO FAR

Ten Swansea boxers have challenged for British titles and only two were unsuccessful. **Michael Harries**, whose career is chronicled under Welsh champions 1984-2009 and in chapter five, boxed for the vacant British light welterweight title, losing by knockout in round ten against defending champion Tony McKenzie in 1986 in Stevenage and for the vacant British light middleweight title at Wembley, losing on points over twelve rounds against Gary Cooper. The Swansea boxer also challenged Australian Troy Waters in New South Wales for the Commonwealth light middleweight title in 1989, losing by knockout in the eighth round.

Swansea boxer **David George** was knocked out in six rounds when he challenged compatriot Kelvin Smart at the Empire Pool, Wembley, for the British flyweight title, vacated by Charlie Magri on 14th September 1982. He was now approaching his twenty-third birthday and had been a professional boxer for a month short of three years. He had started boxing at the Swansea Dockers ABC along with his two brothers, Eric and Donald, encouraged by their father Eric and trained by Cliff Teasdale.

David turned professional in 1979 just before his twentieth birthday. He made an impressive start to his professional career winning his first nine contests between his debut in October 1979, when he knocked out Iggy Jano in the fourth round in Reading, and his first round victory over Gary Nickels at Ebbw Vale in November 1991 in a final eliminator for the British flyweight title. He had beaten Alan Storey from Sunderland, who had recently outpointed Swansea

David George, making his professional debut, stops Iggy Jano in 4 rounds.

boxer Pip Coleman, veteran campaigners Steve Enwright from Bradford and Selvin Bell, who had previously been beaten by Swansea boxer Dai Davies. Two decision victories over Jimmy Bott from Liverpool and an eight rounds decision win over Neil McLaughlin from Derry rounded off the 1980 campaign with a career record of seven straight wins.

In April of 1981 David won every round when outpointing George Bailey from Bradford at the Yorkshire Executive Sportsmen's Club in Bradford, setting up the British title final eliminator with Gary Nickels from Paddington, who had won twelve of fourteen contests, with one loss and one draw. The Swansea boxer inflicted a crushing defeat on the Londoner to earn a shot at the vacant British title against Caerphilly's Kelvin Smart.

Prior to his British title challenge, David lost his unbeaten record in an ambitious venture to Landes in France, where he was outpointed by the unbeaten Frenchman, Antoine Montero, who was to become European flyweight champion. The loss to Montero marked a sequence of five successive defeats, including the unsuccessful British title challenge.

After the British title defeat David's career seemed to be going off the rails – he lost on a six-round TKO in Belfast against Davy Larmour, followed by an eight rounds points defeat against Steve Cleak from Porthcawl in Glasgow. He suffered another defeat, losing the decision in Milan when he boxed Italian Franco Cerchi.

The Swansea boxer, now twenty-three years of age, returned to winning ways when in April 1983 he outpointed Scotsman Danny Flynn in Glasgow, drew and then won over eight rounds against Johnny Doran, before losing in two rounds against Ray Gilbody in a final eliminator for the British bantamweight title. At this time Gilbody was unbeaten as a professional and went on to capture the British bantamweight title.

After the loss to Gilbody, David was matched up with another formidable opponent, the up-and-coming Irish prospect, Dave McCauley. The bout would take place at the Ulster Hall in Belfast. At this time the Irishman was unbeaten in six contests – winning four with two draws – he went on to become British and IBF champion. He stopped David in the sixth round.

David was then inactive for three years before returning to the ring in October 1987 when, approaching his twenty-eighth birthday, he outpointed Keith Downes in Piccadilly. David was unable to recapture the sparkling form of the early part of his career. After his eight-fight winning streak he had won five, lost five and drawn one of the next eleven contests. Many boxers would have been quite happy with that tally, but David had set higher standards. He brought his career to an end after losing on a technical knockout against Peter Grabbitus in Doncaster in October 1989.

*   *   *

Sixteen Swansea boxers had between them made twenty-one unsuccessful attempts to win a Welsh professional boxing title. These statistics exclude Swansea boxers who had made or were to fail in title challenges either before or after winning a Welsh title.

In 1936 Swansea boxer **Willie Piper** challenged Ivor Pickens from Caerau for the Welsh welterweight title at the Vetch Field in Swansea, losing on points over fifteen rounds. On the same bill Swansea boxer Len Beynon beat Cuban Rafael Valdez. According to *www.boxrec.com* Willie had made his professional debut just five months earlier, drawing after twelve rounds with Ginger Dawkins from Gelligaer at the Mannesman Hall in Swansea, although Tony Lee records a six rounds points defeat at Ammanford in November 1931 against Handel Richards.

After his Welsh title opportunity, Willie returned to the ring on 14th December when he tangled with veteran Len Wickwar from Leicester, who was in his ninth year as a professional and was participating in his three hundred and sixty-ninth contest. The bout, which took place at the Vetch Field, ended in a ten round draw. Swansea boxers Jim Wilde and Ronnie James both triumphed on this bill.

A return bout was arranged for St David's Day 1937, and on this occasion the visitor earned the nod after ten rounds. In a third encounter at the Drill Hall on 5th June the Englishman again took the decision after twelve rounds.

Willie travelled down the A40 sometime in 1948 to outpoint Don Chiswell from Ammanford over ten rounds in Haverfordwest. The Swansea boxer's next recorded contest was over six years later when, in November 1944, he outpointed Des Jones of Birmingham over six rounds. Willie fought fellow Swansea boxer Taffy Williams in an eliminator for the Welsh middleweight title at the Vetch Field in September 1945 and was stopped in the ninth round. An up-and-coming prospect known as Cliff Curvis outpointed Tommy Plowright on this bill.

The bout with Taffy Williams was Willie's last professional contest. According to *www.boxrec.com* he had won one, lost four and drawn one of six bouts, although *www.prewarboxing* have recorded forty-eight contests.

Len (Davo) Davies was born in Swansea and turned professional in 1938, boxing against fellow Swansea boxer Jack Kiley in his first bout – he lost on points over six rounds in his home town. He won his next seven contests, five on points and two inside the distance, all these fights taking place in London. Len then lost a six rounds decision against Londoner Alex Lyons at Holborn – this was to be Lyons last contest, having won seven contests and drawing the other, he retired undefeated.

After outpointing Charlie Howser over ten rounds in London, Davo outpointed Dudley Lewis from Brecon and triumphed over Teddy Locke from Aberdare and Jack Llewellyn from Bargoed, both on points over six rounds. Len suffered his third defeat in fourteen starts when he was disqualified against Richie 'Kid' Tanner from Guyana in the seventh. Tanner had previously lost on points to Swansea boxer Len Beynon over twelve rounds in front of Len's home crowd.

Davo boxed his next five bouts in London between August 1939 and January 1940. He beat Wally Smith from Weighbridge on points over ten rounds, stopped debutant Jack Lewis in five rounds and outpointed Johnny Sage from Bethnal Green over six rounds. He then lost a decision over six rounds against Londoner Freddy Dixon and was disqualified in the second round against Poplar's Teddy Softley.

Len didn't box again until February 1942, two years after his last contest. He returned to Wales, beating Harry Thomas in Maesteg on points over eight rounds in what was Harry's final contest. Six days later Davo boxed a twelve round draw against Rhondda boy Warren Kendall, whose career spanned from 1936 to 1949; he had captured the Welsh lightweight title by beating Vernon Ball and lost it in his last contest to Reg Quinlan of Ammanford.

Len boxed six more times in 1942, winning four decisions and losing twice over ten rounds against the renowned 'Aldgate Tiger' Al Phillips and Fleetwood's Bert Jackson.

1943 was a very busy year for the Swansea boxer. He fought fifteen times, losing four, twice to Al Phillips and twice to Bert Jackson. Since January of 1942 Len had fought twenty-three times, losing six, three times to Al Phillips and three times to Bert Jackson! He beat Bobby Hinds from Barnsley three times in thirty-four days at the Blackpool

Tower, outpointed Scotsman Jim Brady in Cardiff, knocked out Londoner Wally Davies, again in Blackpool. He then outpointed veteran Nel Tarleton over eight rounds, who was engaging in his one hundred and fortieth contest. Tarleton from Liverpool was thirty-seven years old when he boxed Len and had been a pro since 1926, in which time he had annexed the British and Empire featherweight title and had twice fought Freddie Miller for the World featherweight title, losing close fifteen rounds decisions on both occasions. Tarleton, in spite of his age, was by no means a spent force when he fought Davo – he later beat Johnny King and successfully defended his British and Empire titles against Al Phillips in his final contest.

Len also beat the reigning British, British Empire and World flyweight champion, Scotsman Jackie Paterson, who held the World title until 1948 when he was knocked out by Irishman Rinty Monaghan in an epic battle in the King's Hall, Belfast. Davo also scored two victories over old adversary Bert Jackson on points over ten rounds and on a second round disqualification. He won an eliminator for the British featherweight title outscoring Ben Duffy of Jarrow over ten rounds and beat Billy Williams on points over ten rounds. He recorded a ten rounds victory over Scotsman Danny Woods at the Stadium in Liverpool.

In his last contest of 1944 Len came up against Al Phillips once again, this time in an eliminator for the British featherweight title, still held by Nel Tarleton. The contest took place in August 1944 – the Swansea boxer was disqualified in round six.

Davo had now been a professional for six years, had participated in forty-six bouts, of which he won thirty-four, losing twelve with one draw and despite the fact he'd beaten a number of champions he'd still not fought for a championship belt.

In 1945 Len fought just twice, losing on points to former British lightweight champion Dave Crowley, he also lost to Jim Brady.

The following year, 1946, Davo Davies fought twice and lost twice and in 1947 he lost and drew in two encounters. In January 1948 he outpointed Ben Duffy in London, his first victory since June 1944. He lost four of his remaining five contests in 1948.

It appeared that Len's pro career was now in rapid decline. Ironically, he gained his first shot at a title after losing on points to Selwyn Evans from Newbridge – he challenged Jackie Hughes from Pontypridd for the Welsh featherweight title at the Drill Hall, Abergavenny – losing on points over fifteen rounds. He won his next two contests in that year, outpointing Ivor Davies from Neath over ten rounds at the Drill Hall, Swansea, after outscoring Ben Duffy.

In 1950 he beat Bobby Anderson from Shepherd's Bush but was then halted in ten rounds by Jackie Hughes in a second attempt to wrest the Welsh featherweight title from him. This bout took place at Coney Beach, Porthcawl.

Davo didn't appear in the ring throughout 1951, but even after nineteen months out of the ring he challenged Selwyn Evans for the Welsh lightweight title in Carmarthen, losing on points over twelve rounds. In the penultimate contest of his career he was defeated by Johnny Mann in Walsall.

He then took his final bow in St Austell in Cornwall when he was unceremoniously stopped in five rounds by Cornishman Roy Coote. For Len 'Davo' Davies, after sixty-eight professional contests, of which he had won thirty-nine, drawn two and lost twenty-seven, sixteen of those defeats coming in his last twenty-two contests, it was the end of the road. After such an illustrious career in which he had fought and beaten some of the best around, it was astonishing that the Swansea boxer was never hailed a champion.

Swansea boxer **Doug Richards** challenged Dennis 'Nosher' Powell for the Welsh light heavyweight title, at the Drill Hall, Newtown, on 26th November 1949, losing by a knockout in the fifth round.

In 1951 Powell was stopped in six rounds by the ageing legend of Welsh boxing history, Tommy Farr, who was still battling fourteen years after his gallant attempt to win the World heavyweight title from Joe Louis.

Doug Richards was twenty-four years old when he made his professional debut in London on 21st April 1947 against Londoner Reg Spring, who had won eight and lost two of fourteen bouts. Reg stopped the Swansea boxer in round seven. A return match was arranged for May 15th in Watford – this time Doug won on points after ten rounds.

In only his third bout Doug took on the formidable north Wales boxer Johnny Williams, who had lost only once in twenty-two contests and later in his career became British and Commonwealth heavyweight champion. Doug took Williams the full distance, losing on points after eight rounds.

In 1948 the Swansea boxer won three out of six contests, beating Les Pam from Stepney by knockout in three rounds, Freddie Evans from Cymmer on points over ten rounds and Canadian Gene Fowler on points over eight rounds. He suffered a five round knockout defeat against Londoner Don Cockell, who had won thirty-six out of forty-three contests, became British and European light heavyweight champion, British and Commonwealth heavyweight champion and unsuccessfully challenged Rocky Marciano for the World heavyweight title.

In this year Doug was also beaten by TKO in seven by Elfryn Morris from West Bromwich, who had in days gone by beaten Freddie Mills. Doug was then knocked out in the first round by Matt Hardy from Doncaster in Kentish Town.

In 1949 and prior to his Welsh title challenge the Swansea boxer suffered a knockout by the fists of Charles Patrick Henry from County Mayo in Shepherd's Bush. He then beat Peter Gravon from Brighton and Don Trapnell from Weston-Super-Mare, both on points over eight rounds, and then repeated the points victory over Trapnell in a six round contest. He outpointed Derek Alexander from Willenhall in the West Midlands to make it four successive wins. He was stopped by Tony Lord from Liverpool in four rounds and scored a hat-trick over Don Trapnell, winning their third encounter on points over six rounds before outpointing debutant Jack Walker from Manchester over eight rounds.

In a non title affair Doug was knocked out in three rounds by Dennis Powell in Trealaw. His journey toward the title shot proved to be a bumpy ride – after the knockout defeat against Powell the Swansea boxer was beaten by Tony Lord on points over eight rounds and knocked out by Jock Taylor from Sidcup, who had earlier knocked out Don Cockell. Forty-five days after the defeat against Taylor and following three successive defeats, two by knockout, Doug challenged Dennis Powell for the Welsh title. In 1950 Doug was knocked out by Irishman Denny Garnett and Dave Williams from Barry, who later in his career became Welsh light heavyweight champion.

The Swansea boxer was twenty-seven years of age, had won ten out of twenty-four contests and had lost seven 'on the bounce', when he called it a day after the Williams bout which took place in Worcester.

Ken Curvis boxed Alan Wilkins from Ystradgynlais for the vacant Welsh welterweight title in Porthcawl on 21st June 1950 and lost on a disqualification in round eight. Brother Cliff and Eddie Thomas also fought on the Porthcawl bill against continental opponents.

Ken had been inactive for nearly two years before this fight. Alan Wilkins had kept himself busy, having boxed eleven times since their previous encounter which had ended in a draw at the Drill Hall in Neath.

Ken, brother of Cliff and Brian, boxed professionally between April 1947 and June 1950 and like his brothers he boxed at welterweight, winning his first four contests, he drew the fifth and lost by disqualification in the Welsh championship bout. His first professional contest took place in Cirencester where he stopped fellow debutant Ray Summers in the fourth round. He then outpointed Danny Jones from Ammanford in Llanelli – Jones had previously stopped Swansea boxer Ken Morgan. Ken rounded off the year with two good wins beating West African Johnny Tarone and Birmingham-based Scotsman Johnny McClaren on points over eight rounds in Llanelli and West Brom respectively. Ken retired after the second contest with Alan Wilkins.

Dave Lloyd lost on points after twelve rounds of boxing when he fought Haydn Jones for the vacant Welsh featherweight title in Cardiff on 16th February 1953. Six years earlier Haydn, who was from Tiryberth, had beaten Swansea boxer Jack Kiley in Merthyr Tydfil. The fight for the vacant title warranted a return match, which took place in

Rhyl three months later, Haydn was once again adjudged the victor retaining the title after twelve closely contested rounds.

Dave Lloyd made his professional debut in Aberystwyth on Boxing Day 1946 winning on points after eight rounds against Wally Prendergast from Blaina followed by a six rounds points defeat against Johnny Morgan from Treherbert, who was unbeaten in three contests.

Dave boxed six times in 1948. In his first bout of the year he drew with Danny Nagle from Cork in Weston-Super-Mare, he followed up with an eight rounds points victory over Peter Gaskell from Wigan and then lost on points over eight rounds against the very experienced Richie Kid Tanner from Guyana who was making his one hundred and eighth ring appearance. Six months later in November Dave reversed the decision again over eight rounds in Morecambe. Twelve days on the Swansea boxer drew with Ivor Davies from Neath who had previously drawn with another Swansea boxer, Curly Roberts, before ending his campaign for the year losing by TKO in five rounds against Tommy Bailey from Merseyside, who won the Central area featherweight title later in his career.

In 1949 Dave boxed just once according to *www.boxrec.com*, losing a ten round decision to Dai Davies from Skewen at the Drill Hall in Neath.

In 1950 the Swansea boxer is recorded as having four bouts without a success, losing on points over eight rounds in Edinburgh against Jock Bonas, he was then knocked out in the first round in Bedford against hard-hitting Lincolnshire man Badge Johnson, but recovered quickly to draw with Tony Llanelly from Doncaster over eight rounds in Grimsby. The year ended with another knockout defeat in the second round against Irishman Eddie Magee in Belfast.

There was no change of fortune in the ensuing year. He lost twice on points in eight round contests before drawing over six rounds with debutant Ivor David from Neath at the Sophia Gardens in Cardiff.

There are no matches recorded for 1952, although it is likely that Dave may have boxed several times as his first contest of 1953 was his Welsh title challenge. After the two title defeats he was knocked out for the third time in his professional career by old adversary Dai Davies, who delivered the *coup de grâce* in the first round.

After suffering another one round knockout defeat in Weston-Super-Mare against knockout specialist Roy Coles, Dave decided it was time to call it a day. There may well be seven fights missing off his record – according to Miles Templeton, Dave had twenty-seven professional contests.

Teddy Barrow challenged Freddie Cross from Abertillery for the vacant Welsh middleweight title in Cardiff on 16th January 1957. Freddie repeated an earlier triumph, this time stopping the Swansea boxer in round eleven. Teddy, the elder brother of Swansea boxer Len, was born nearly three years earlier on 28th April 1934, also in the Sandfields area of Swansea.

Teddy was a promising amateur, winning two ABA youth titles, two British army cadet finals and reached the semi-finals of the ABA Championships where he lost on points to Trinidadian Percy Lewis, who went on to win the British Empire featherweight title after earlier taking World featherweight champion, Hogan 'Kid' Bassey, to a fifteen rounds decision. Teddy was also recorded as having inflicted the first amateur defeat on the legendary Dai Dower from Abercynon.

The Swansea boxer turned professional in 1954 at twenty years of age, signing up with Tony Vairo in Liverpool, but did most of his training at the Empire Boxing Club in Swansea. Unlike brother Len, he boxed in Wales eight times but never managed to fight in his home town where at that time professional boxing tournaments were few and far between.

He won his professional debut by outscoring fellow debutant Bob Simmonds over six rounds in what turned out to be Bob's only professional contest held in his home city of Leicester on 11th August 1954.

Teddy remained unbeaten in his first thirteen contests, including wins over George Harrison, who had won and lost against Mickey Duff, who later became a top matchmaker and promoter. He beat Ken Ashwood who had lost a six round decision to Welsh middleweight champion and British title challenger, Cardiff's Phil Edwards. The Swansea boxer also beat Ron Richardson, before losing on a technical knockout to Andy Andrews in Abergavenny. Teddy's next fight was to be his last victory with an eight round decision win over Ron Richardson in the Blackpool Tower in November 1955.

He then lost to Tommy Molloy, who went on to become British welterweight champion, Rees Moore who was Welsh welterweight champion and the Scottish welterweight champion Jimmy Croll in successive fights between February and April 1956.

Teddy fought fellow Welshman Freddy Cross in London, losing on points over eight rounds, just two months before they clashed for the vacant Welsh middleweight championship. His last two fights were against Eddie Bee, a Trinidadian boxer based in Cardiff, who knocked Teddy out in the fourth round in Cross Keys on 21st November 1957, and thirteen months later Eddie won on a second round technical knockout – apparently Teddy broke his leg during the course of the bout on 3rd September 1958 in The Coney Beach Arena, Porthcawl.

Teddy was just twenty-four years of age and according to younger brother Len had lost heart in the game. "To be perfectly honest," said Len, "Teddy's heart was never really in boxing, he was just such a nice man to be a boxer, he didn't like conflict of any kind, he preferred playing football and cricket."

At the end of his boxing career in which he had won fourteen of his twenty-three bouts Teddy continued to work as a gas fitter at Trostre steelworks until his sudden death in 1988 at just fifty-four years of age.

Jeff 'Bulldog' Burns reached the pinnacle of his ring career when he challenged his old adversary Mike McCluskie for the Welsh middleweight title on a sold out Eddie Richards promotion at the Top Rank Suite in Swansea on 27th June 1973. Ahead on points going into the eighth round of a ten round contest super fit Jeff went for a knockout win against his tiring opponent only to walk onto a terrific left hook counter and, although on his feet at seven, he was counted out by referee Joe Morgan. After the fight the referee visited the Swansea boxer's changing room, offering some consolation, informing him that he was ahead at the time of the stoppage.

Jeff Burns was born on 16th May 1948 in Waun Wen. He took up boxing training at the Swansea Youth Amateur Boxing Club in Penlan School gym run by Jack Kiley. In 1963 he joined the Royal Navy where he took up amateur boxing competitively, winning the Royal Navy Junior Championships twice and the Naval Air Command Senior Championships before being discharged from the service in 1967.

After several months in 'Civvy Street', Jeff rejoined Swansea Youth ABC and boxed under his old coach Jack Kiley. He later boxed for Gwent ABC under coaches Bill Pitson and Terry Grey, then the Swansea Dockers Club under Cliff Teasdale. Jeff represented Wales in one full international against Ireland and a number of representative matches, including the Home Counties, Western Counties, Midland Counties, the Army and the RAF.

Jeff turned professional with Llanelli manager, ex-Welsh bantam-weight champion Glyn Davies, making his professional debut at the National Sporting Club in Piccadilly on 8th May 1972, just eight days before his twenty-fourth birthday. Although he was only five feet five inches tall Jeff boxed at middleweight and was always conceding height and reach to his opponents. He boxed very aggressively and always tried to keep his taller opponents on the back foot.

His debut fight ended perfectly – his opponent, Brixton's Danny Barrett, was on the canvas three times in the first round; he didn't answer the bell for the second. After this fight Burns' manager nick-named him 'Bulldog', complementing his tenacious and aggressive style of boxing.

Under the management of Glyn Davies, Jeff fought seven times between May and September 1972, winning six with one loss. After his win over Barrett he boxed in Reading six days later, winning a hard fought six rounder on points against Peter Blake from Southend. The Swansea boxer's next bout was at the Top Rank Suite in Swansea in June where he gained revenge for a defeat as an amateur against Clive Collins from Llantwit Major, winning comfortably on points over six rounds. A month later Jeff ventured into the Black Country, where he stopped Dave Nelson in four rounds in Dave's home town of Wolver-hampton.

On July 24th his next fight ended in a shock defeat, knocked out in the sixth and last round of a contest he was winning by a mile against London Irishman Billy Brooks at the Top Rank Suite in Swansea. Burns avenged the defeat three weeks later when he convincingly outpointed an opponent brimming with confidence, over six rounds at the Glen Ballroom in Llanelli. The Swansea boxer won this contest virtually one handed, having injured his right hand in training for the fight – so determined was he to gain revenge he told no one about the injury for fear of being withdrawn from the bill. He was receiving good advice, for in his corner that night was that master exponent of the left jab, former World featherweight champion, Howard Winstone.

On September 18th Jeff was again appearing on an Eddie Richards promotion at the Top Rank Suite, Swansea, and despite being troubled by his hand injury he outpointed experienced Cardiff boxer Les Avoth from the fighting Avoth family, brother of Eddie and Dennis. The hand injury forced Jeff into a six-month period of inactivity during which time he severed his ties with Glyn Davies and joined up with the Brian Curvis stable, training at the old fire station in Mumbles.

Jeff returned to the ring on 5th February 1973 with the aid of regular cortizone injections in his right hand, and lost a close decision over eight rounds to Mike McCluskie from Caerau on an Eddie Richards promotion at the Top Rank Suite in Swansea. Mike, who was managed by Glyn Davies, had held an equally close points decision over the Swansea boxer during their amateur careers; the contest with the Swansea boxer was Mike's twentieth professional bout.

In spite of his continuing hand problem, Burns battled on – winning two of his next three bouts. The first of these was again held at the Top Rank Suite promoted by Eddie Richards an eight rounder against the ring-wise Liverpudlian, Ronnie Hough. Jeff did well to win this fight as the Scouser, a former Central Area middleweight champion, was ranked as number two contender for the British title and had fought and beaten some of the best middleweights on the British circuit. The win over Ronnie Hough elevated Burns to number four in the British middleweight rankings after only nine professional bouts.

He was unlucky to lose his next fight, a return against Clive Collins. Even though he sustained a bad cut over his right eye in the second round, due to a clash of heads, the 'Bulldog' dominated the first four rounds, but referee Ivor Bassett decided to halt the bout in round five due to the cut eye. On May 15th Jeff comfortably outscored Crewe's six-feet-two-inch Pat Brogan over eight rounds in Swansea. The 'Bulldog' was ready for his assault on the Welsh middleweight title that had been vacated by Cardiff's Carl Thomas.

Jeff Burns on his way to outpointing Pat Brogan in May 1973.
(Courtesy of *South Wales Evening Post*).

Jeff fought on six more times after his title defeat, winning just twice, stopping Granville Lloyd in the fifth round and outpointing Mike Manley, both contests taking place at the Sophia Gardens, Cardiff. The Swansea boxer again took on Welsh champion McCluskie at the National Sporting Club, Piccadilly, at just twenty-four hours notice and was stopped in four rounds. Next time out he was stopped in four rounds by Liverpool prospect Tony Byrne, again taking the fight at a day's notice.

After this bout Jeff ended his partnership with Brian Curvis and returned to the stable of former manager Glyn Davies. His fortunes didn't change, losing a controversial eight rounds decision to Oscar Angus and then being knocked out in seven rounds by Mick Hussey when well ahead on points, both fights taking place at the National Sporting Club.

'Bulldog' Burns decided to call it a day in November of 1974, still struggling with the recurring hand problem. He returned to the ring in August 1976 with Eddie Richards acting as his agent and Jimmy Bromfield as his trainer. He beat Caerphilly boxer Tony Burnett on an Eddie Richards promotion in the Sophia Gardens, Cardiff, before losing to future British Champion Jimmy Batten at the Royal Albert Hall, where Alan Minter successfully defended his British and Commonwealth crown against former champion, the late Kevin Finnegan.

After the Batten contest Jeff give his wounds time to heal before returning to the gym in preparation for his next contest, a return bout with Tony Burnett. Two weeks into his training schedule the Swansea boxer, in a steady job as the Bars Manager in Swansea's Dolphin Hotel, realised he was just 'going through the motions', the dogged determination to get into tip top shape, the great desire to win, had really left him before the Batten fight, Jeff knew his time in the ring was up. Although only twenty-eight years of age, his 'do or die' approach to each contest meant that every bout was a war, these wars weren't made any easier by his injured hand, the injury still visible today.

On 10th October 1978 twenty-two-year-old Swansea boxer **Mike Copp** lost on points over ten rounds against Horace McKenzie at the Afan Lido, Aberavon, in an attempt to win the Welsh welterweight title that had been vacated by Terry Phillips of Cardiff in 1967.

Mike started boxing in 1968 at the Gwent Amateur Boxing Club. After a distinguished amateur career he turned professional under the management of Eddie Richards and made his debut on 9th February 1976, six months short of his twentieth birthday. His first opponent was Mick Minter from Crawley, the brother of future world middleweight champion Alan. Minter beat Mike on points over six rounds in Croydon, pretty much on Minter's home turf. Mike also lost his second fight a six round points decision to Peter Neal from Abingdon, who later unsuccessfully challenged Colin Jones for his British title.

He chalked up his first win on 29th March 1976 with an impressive knockout victory over Russ Shaw in Swansea, where Mike only made three appearances in his thirty-one fight career. Top of this bill was

Swansea boxer Neville Meade who halted Rhondda boy Tony Black-burn in four rounds.

Mike won his next four contests, knocking out Yorkshireman Chester Coburn, outpointing Terry Schofield in Cardiff, Mick Baker from Portsmouth and a repeat win again on points over Schofield. Baker was later a KO victim of Swansea boxer Frank McCord. Cardiff's promising Chris Davies brought Mike's winning run to an end, earning a six round points decision in Treorchy, on a bill topped by rising star, one Johnny Owen. Mike then travelled to Manchester to outscore Jimmy King, who had previously beaten Swansea boxer Yotham Kunda. In his last performance of 1976 Mike Copp accompanied fellow Swansea boxer Neville Meade to Belgium, where he was disqualified in the fourth round against Belgian favourite Dirk Declerq. Neville lost on points over ten rounds against Jean-Pierre Coopman, who earlier in the year had unsuccessfully challenged Muhammad Ali for the heavy-weight championship of the world.

Mike got off to a bad start in 1977, losing by knockout in round three against Manchester's Roysie Francis in Swansea on a bill where fellow Swansea boxers, brother Alan and Colin Breen, both recorded victories. His next encounter was at the National Sporting Club in Piccadilly, where he lost on points to Londoner Mickey Morse before being offered up to highly fancied former amateur star, Swansea boxer Colin Jones. The contest took place at the Afan Lido in Aberavon on 3rd October 1977 and ended in Colin's favour in round five. Mike's year ended in triumph when he outpointed the very experienced Tommy Joyce who was boxing for the forty-ninth time as a professional. Mike had completed two busy years as a professional and had won seven and lost seven of fourteen contests. He fought four times in 1978, losing the decision after six rounds against Johnny Elliott at Hove, drawing with Terry Peterson in Doncaster, outpointing Steve Goodwin from Bootle in Aberavon before his Welsh title challenge.

In 1979 the Swansea boxer, now boxing at middleweight, beat Terry Knight from Brighton on points, lost to Wolverhampton-based Jamaican Mick Morris and outpointed Liverpool's Jimmy Roberts over eight rounds in Bangor. In his next bout eight days later Mike retired with an injured hand at the end of round three against Central Area light middleweight champion, Prince Rodney, who went on to become British champion at the same weight.

After a three month break, the Swansea boxer won his next two contests, outpointing Trevor Kerr from Belfast and Richard Kenyon from Halifax. Between September of 1979 when he lost on points to Torben Anderson in Denmark and July 1980 when he lost another eight rounds decision against Doncaster's Leo Mulhearn, Mike lost each of his next five contests.

At the age of twenty-four, four years as a professional and thirty-one contests under his belt, Mike decided it was time to call it a day on his professional career. He later opened his own gym in Swansea and became a professional boxing manager/trainer.

Frank McCord made his first Welsh title challenge against Billy Waith from Cardiff, who was engaging in his eighty-eighth pro contest, for the vacant Welsh welterweight title at the Top Rank Suite in Swansea on 7th June 1982. He lost on points over ten rounds.

Frank engaged in his first professional contest at Ebbw Vale Leisure Centre on 29th March 1977 when only eighteen years of age. He boxed fellow debutant Phillip Morris of Cefn Hengoed and won on points over six rounds. Morris went on to fight three other Swansea boxers – he drew with Dai 'Muscles' Davies, Ray 'Peanut' Price and lost to Nigel Thomas.

The Swansea boxer won his next two bouts, outpointing Roger Doyle of Bedford and George Daines from Doncaster over four rounds. Next time out Frank experienced defeat for the first time in the pro ranks when he was halted in three rounds by London-based Jamaican Winston Spencer, who went on to win the Southern Area lightweight title. After losing to Spencer, Frank suffered three consecutive defeats – against Eric Purkis from Battersea on points over six rounds, Dillwyn Collins from Llantwit Major by disqualification in round six and he was stopped in five rounds by Martin Bridge from Bradford, who went on to win the Central Area light welterweight. Frank completed his first year in professional boxing with two knockout wins. Eddie Porter from

Luton was knocked in round four and Doncaster's Ian Pickersgill was counted out in the first round in Swansea.

In 1978 Frank entered the ring thirteen times and recorded five wins, six losses and two draws. He knocked out Mick Barker from Portsmouth in two rounds at Ebbw Vale, stopped Irishman Benny Purdy in round four at Derry, outpointed Scotsman Harry Watson in London over six rounds, stopped Al Stewart in three rounds in Liverpool and outpointed previously unbeaten Londoner Sid Smith at the Royal Albert Hall. Swansea boxer Pip Coleman was also on that bill.

Frank McCord.

Among Frank's defeats in that year was a six rounds decision against Allan Burrows from Cardiff, who had previously beaten Swansea boxer Dai Davies. He lost to Lloyd Lee of Nottingham and was on the wrong side of a six round verdict against Norwegian-based Moroccan, Omar Salhi, in Oslo.

1979 was a bleak year for the Swansea boxer, losing all of his six contests, firstly against Stan Atherton from Liverpool, losing the decision after six rounds in Manchester. He was then knocked out in the first by Coventry's Steve Early, who at that time was unbeaten in twelve contests and later became Midlands Area light welterweight champion. Frank lost an eight rounds points decision against Irishman Hugh Kelly in Belfast and another decision over the same distance against Gary Pearce from Newport in Pontypool. Pearce later beat Swansea boxer Terry Matthews for the vacant Welsh light middle-weight title. He lost points decisions against Roy Varden from Nuneaton and Tony Martey from Ghana, who had previously been beaten by Swansea boxer Colin Jones.

Frank McCord, just twenty-one years of age, had boxed twenty-eight times as a professional, winning ten, with sixteen losses and two draws. After a discouraging run of defeats Frank won a comfortable eight rounds decision over John Mount at the National Sporting Club followed by an eight rounds points defeat against Jeff Pritchard from Merthyr Tydfil. The Swansea boxer lost another on points over eight rounds against Chris Christiansen from Stoke Newington at the Anglo American Sporting Club in Mayfair in March 1980. Christiansen went on to make an unsuccessful challenge for the British and Commonwealth light middleweight title against Herol Graham. Frank then lost to Allan Lamb, who later became Central Area light welterweight champion at the Tower Circus in Blackpool, and completed the year by dropping an eight rounds decision against unbeaten Mickey Durkin from Bradford.

In 1981 the Swansea boxer drew with Alan Burrows, who had previously beaten Frank, he stopped Stan Atherton from Liverpool in two rounds in Blackpool, reversing an earlier points defeat, and lost on points over eight rounds against the experienced Wolverhampton-based Jamaican, Dennis Pryce, who had previously lost to John 'The Beast' Mugabe.

In November 1981 the Swansea boxer was triumphant in his last fight of the year, outpointing Gary Buckle from the West Midlands over eight rounds. Buckle lost an eight rounder against Swansea boxer John McGlynn, also at Evesham, the following November.

In February 1982 Frank stopped Alan Cable from Croydon in the first round. Cable never boxed again. He then lost against Yorkshireman Mick Mills in Sheffield, prior to his first Welsh title challenge. Frank went on his travels to Belfast for his next encounter with Irishman Charlie Nash, who had been British and European lightweight champion and had challenged Jim Watt for the WBC title; the Swansea boxer lost on points over eight rounds. He then beat Dave Sullivan from Plymouth and knocked out Gunther Roomes from Lambeth in the first round. The knockout of Roomes was no mean achievement, the Londoner went on to stop Swansea boxer Ray Price in one round and ended his career with a respectable record of twelve wins with only three defeats.

Frank's last fight of the year ended in defeat against Lloyd Honeyghan, a Jamaican boxing out of Bermondsey, who was undefeated in twelve contests – he went on to become the WBC, WBA and IBF welterweight champion by stopping 'The Lone Star Cobra', Don Curry, in six rounds.

In 1983, Frank's seventh year as a pro, he boxed three times, losing on points over eight rounds against Ian 'Kid' Murray in Swansea and Kostas Petrou in Solihull before challenging Billy Waith for his Welsh welterweight title. Like their first fight, the champion outpointed the gallant Swansea boxer over ten rounds at the Top Rank Suite on 12th December.

The Swansea boxer fought twice in 1984, losing over eight rounds against Tony Adams from Brixton at the Royal Albert Hall and was stopped in five rounds due to a cut eye by Martin McGough from Coventry in Birmingham.

In 1985, the Swansea boxer – still only twenty-six years of age and had boxed fifty times as a professional – stopped Granville Allen, a Midlands-based Jamaican, in three rounds on the Isle of Man. He then travelled to Copenhagen to test Danish prospect John Mortensen, losing on points over six rounds.

In the following year, Frank dropped Liverpool-based Ghanaian Junaidom Mussah in round seven, before the referee stopped the contest. He next fought Steve Davies from Pembroke for the vacant Welsh light middleweight title – he lost by TKO in round four.

The Swansea boxer didn't box again until October 1987 when he stopped Plymouth's Glyn Mitchell in two rounds in Swansea, on a bill that featured fellow Swansea boxer Keith Parry.

On 12th January 1988 Frank boxed in Cardiff in what was to be his final professional contest – he was halted in round six by Kevin Thompson from Birmingham who had won all five of his previous contests. Frank had been a professional boxer for eleven years, in which time he'd boxed fifty-six times. He was a boxer who would not shy away from any opponent and always give of his best.

Although born in Cardiff on 12th November 1957, **Winston Allen** for part of his professional boxing career resided in and boxed out of Swansea and did have support from the Swansea boxing fraternity thus qualifying Winston as a Swansea boxer.

Winston will be best remembered in Swansea for his challenge for the Welsh heavyweight title against Neville Meade, who was later to become the British heavyweight champion. According to *www.boxrec.com* the fight took place at the Top Rank in Swansea, but actually took place at the Swansea Leisure Centre, as recalled by the promoter of the show – Swansea entrepreneur and promoter of the confrontation, Pat Matthias. There was much ballyhoo in the pre-flight build up, a lot of money was wagered on the outcome of the contest, which was a genuine grudge match – Swansea's version of Ali v. Frazier. Winston, the challenger, was determined to take the title from Neville, but it was not to be.

He made his professional debut on 20th April 1978, losing a six rounds decision to Terry Chard at the National Sporting Club in Piccadilly, but avenged the defeat by stopping Chard in three rounds in Newport the following month. The six-foot-one-inch heavyweight fought in a heavyweight competition in Merthyr Tydfil beating Jon Depledge and knocking out Londoner David Collins who was participating in his first and only professional contest.

In January 1979 Winston lost on points after eight rounds to Terry Connor in Solihull. He then suffered a second round knockout to Londoner Bobby Hennessey, who was to lose the final against Newport's David Pearce – the Welshman went on to become British heavyweight champion.

On March 4th 1980 the Swansea boxer scored a stunning first round knockout win over Stan McDermott, who later lost a British title eliminator to Swansea boxer Neville Meade. Winston knocked out Jean-Pierre Coopman in one round – the Belgian had previously challenged Muhammad Ali for his heavyweight crown, losing on a five round stoppage and had knocked out the Spaniard Jose Urtain for the vacant European title.

The Swansea boxer lost his next eleven bouts before hanging up his gloves following his last fight, which was in Copenhagen, when he lost an eight round decision to the well respected John Odhiambo who had only lost once in nineteen professional bouts.

Winston took on some of the best British fighters around at that time including Joe Bugner, lost by KO in the third, and Frank Bruno, lost by a TKO in the second. He also went the scheduled eight rounds with Argentine strongman Alfredo Evangelista, who notably went the full fifteen rounds with a waning Muhammad Ali.

Terry Matthews boxed fellow debutant Ronald Pearce from Newport at Pontypool on 10th May 1979 – he lost on points after six rounds in his first professional contest. He was back in the ring two weeks later when he halted Joey Sanders from Nottingham in the third round.

The Swansea boxer boxed six more times in 1979, beating Tony Britton from Lewisham, Owen Stafford from Herne, Mickey Kidd from Nuneaton, and Curtis Marsh from Islington all on points over six rounds. He lost on points in a return bout with Britton and also failed to get the nod against Tommy Williams from Kirby.

Terry commenced his 1980 campaign by sharing the verdict with Wayne Barker from Manchester, who in his professional debut outpointed Swansea boxer Jeff Aspel, also a debutant. The Swansea boxer then won five successive decisions against Gary Newell from Wolverhampton, Peter Bassey from Manchester, Clifton Wallace from Wolverhampton, who had beaten Swansea boxer Mike Copp, and lost to another Doug James, John Smith from Glasgow, who had lost to Swansea boxer Chuck Jones and Peter Simon from Battersea. Terry ended the year with two defeats, losing against George Walker, a Tottenham-based Jamaican, at the National Sporting Club and Kenny Webber, who was Central Area light middleweight title holder.

The Swansea boxer, approaching his twenty-second birthday, boxing most of the time at middleweight, remained active in 1981, firstly losing to Nigerian Billy Savage in Birmingham. On 7th April he was stopped in round nine by Newport's Gary Pearce for the Welsh light middleweight title vacated by British champion Pat Thomas. He then lost the decision in an eight round middleweight contest in Black-pool against home town boy Billy Hill. Terry concluded 1981 with two knockout wins against Neville Wilson from Wolverhampton and Kenny Feehan from Tonypandy at the Ebbw Vale Leisure Centre. Feehan was also KO'd by Swansea boxer Doug James at the Top Rank Suite, Swansea, the following March.

In 1982, Terry stopped Steve Davies from Pembroke in the first round at the Top Rank in March, his first and only appearance in front of his home supporters. The Pembroke fighter later beat Swansea boxer Frank McCord for the vacant Welsh light middleweight title and successfully defended the title against another Swansea boxer, John McGlynn.

On 24th May Terry, participating in his twenty-third bout, lost on points against John Humphreys, unbeaten in thirteen contests, from Shrewsbury, at the Civic Hall, Wolverhampton. A month later the Swansea boxer was stopped in five rounds by another unbeaten boxer, Sammy Brennan, from Liverpool, at the Kirkby Sports Centre.

On 18th November Terry entered the ring for the last time to take on amateur star, highly regarded prospect Errol Christie from Leicester at the Sports Centre Coventry. The Midlands boxer was declared the victor when referee Paul Thomas halted proceedings in the third round. Terry retired from the ring, nearly twenty-four years of age, he'd been a pro three and a half years, had boxed twenty-five times, winning thirteen, with eleven losses and one draw.

Andy Thomas's biggest fight was most probably his challenge for the vacant Welsh lightweight title on 4th March 1983 against Ray Hood, a Crawley-based Welshman, who beat the Swansea boxer on points over ten rounds, repeating an earlier eight rounds victory on points.

Andy Thomas was born Andrew Bruton in Swansea on 5th March 1962. He was eighteen years old when he made his professional debut at Aylesbury against Clyde Ruan from Slough on 30th April 1980 – he lost on points after four rounds. Ruan went on to become Southern area featherweight champion and also challenged Barry McGuigan for the British and European featherweight titles – he was knocked out in round four. Andy's professional career spanned a few days short of three years, ending in defeat by technical knockout in the second round against Irishman Seamus McGuiness, who retired undefeated in seven fights after his next contest, the bout taking place in the Ulster Hall, Belfast.

The biggest name on Andy's record was undoubtedly that of Terry Marsh, who stopped the Swansea boxer in four rounds at Cheltenham Town Hall on 16th March 1983. Marsh had won ten fights and drawn once before meeting Andy. The Basildon fireman went on to become British, European and IBF light welterweight champion before retiring undefeated with twenty-six wins and one draw.

Andy's only bout in Swansea was at the Top Rank Suite on 7th June 1982 when he outpointed Tyrell Wilson, a Jamaican based in Newport, over eight rounds. Tyrell had outpointed Swansea boxer Dai 'Muscles' Davies two months earlier, in Dai's final contest.

Andy outpointed debutant Denny Garrison from Wolverhampton at Evesham over six rounds in October 1982, but won only once in his next seven contests, when he beat Roy Burke from Ipswich, four losses inside the distance culminating in his retirement after the McGuiness fight on 12th April 1983 at the age of twenty-one.

On 17th February 1984, **John McGlynn** challenged Rocky Feliciello from Rhyl for the vacant Welsh light middleweight title in Rocky's home town. John's challenge for the title ended in defeat, the north Walian halted his opponent in round eight. The following January, Felliciello was outpointed over eight rounds by Swansea boxer Michael Harris and on 14th March 1986 lost his Welsh title on a seventh round TKO against another Swansea boxer, Geoff Pegler.

John made his professional debut on 7th June 1982 four months before his twentieth birthday. He knocked out fellow debutant Colin Neagle from Merthyr Tydfil in the third round at the Top Rank Suite, Swansea. Later in his career Neagle was defeated twice by Swansea boxer Michael Harries. John outpointed Irishman Ray Ross over eight rounds in Derry, he lost on points over eight rounds against Mick

Courtney from Chorleywood in London, outpointed Gary Buckle from Wednesbury over eight rounds in Evesham and lost on an eighth round TKO to Julian Boustead from Plymouth in Piccadilly.

The following year, 1983, the Swansea boxer outpointed Steve Tempro from Leicester over eight rounds at Evesham; ten months later Tempro dropped another eight round decision against Swansea boxer Ray Price. John knocked out Peckham-based Jamaican, Sylvester Gordon, in round six at Ebbw Vale. He lost on points over eight rounds against Richard Wilson from Nuneaton in Dudley, who had won ten of thirteen contests but never boxed again after beating McGlynn. On 19th December the Swansea boxer concluded his 1983 campaign by halting Wolverhampton-based Jamaican, Bert Myrie in round four at the Dolphin Hotel in Swansea.

John McGlynn was now twenty-two years of age, a pro for eighteen months and a winner in six of nine contests, three of those winning bouts ending inside the scheduled distance. John ran into more trouble in his next contest against Martin McGough from Coventry, who halted the Swansea boxer in six rounds in Birmingham. In his next contest McGough stopped Swansea boxer Frank McCord on a cut eye. In the following April McGough failed in an attempt to wrest the British Commonwealth title from Sylvester Mittee, losing the decision after twelve rounds.

After two consecutive stoppage defeats John embarked on a five-fight winning run – he outpointed Phil O'Hare from Manchester over six rounds in Southend. He travelled across the water to the Isle of Man where he outpointed six feet three inches tall Theo Morris from Hackney over six rounds. Cyril Jackson from Wrexham, unbeaten in three previous contests, was knocked out by John in round one in December 1985. Jackson later stopped Swansea boxer Rocky Reynolds at the Afan Lido. John halted Claude Rossi from Derby in the sixth round in Stoke and Dean Turner from Southampton in four rounds at Southend.

He made a second assault on the Welsh title against Steve Davies from Pembroke, but was once again unsuccessful when referee Adrian

Morgan stopped the contest in favour of the champion in round four. John didn't box again for nearly five years, returning to the ring on 27th August 1991 when he outpointed Micky Lerwell from Telford over six rounds.

A month later the Swansea boxer ventured to the Royal Albert Hall for an ill-fated clash with the promising debutant Kevin Lueshing from Beckenham who later became British and International Boxing Organisation welterweight champion – he unsuccessfully challenged the legendary Felix Trinidad for the International Boxing Federation title. Lueshing halted John in the second round in this bout that took place on 30th September 1991.

The Swansea boxer's career had spanned over nine years, he'd won twelve of nineteen contests, six of those triumphant bouts ending inside the scheduled distance. Three days short of his twenty-ninth birthday John unlaced his gloves in the professional ring for the last time.

On 12th April 1989 **Dean Lynch** fought for the vacant Welsh super featherweight title in Swansea and was stopped in the fourth round by James Hunter, who lived in Middlesborough, but was born in Port Talbot.

Dean made his professional debut on 18th September 1986, just two months short of his twenty-second birthday. He lost on points to Billy Barton from Blaengarw, who was to draw with another Swansea boxer, Dave George, the following December. Dean won his next two contests, beating Paddy Maguire from Birmingham and Phil Lashley from the same city. The bout with Lashley, in which Dean won every round, took place in Swansea where fellow Swansea boxers Peter Harries, Carl Parry, Rocky Reynolds, and Kevin Roper were also victorious.

He was inactive in 1987, but fought six times in 1988, winning twice with four defeats. The highlight of the year was a trip to France, where he lost on points over ten rounds against Frenchman Raymond Armand, who in his next fight challenged the European champion, Piero

Moriello, for his title, losing a majority decision in Italy, before his tilt at the Welsh title. One month later the Swansea boxer boxed in Lombardia, Italy, against the very experienced Valeno Nati, who was participating in his fifty-first contest having won forty-two, lost four and drawn four. He had held the European bantam and featherweight titles and just seven months after boxing Dean won the WBO super bantamweight title. The Swansea boxer was stopped in round six.

In 1990 Dean entered the ring on three occasions and was defeated each time, but against good quality opposition. He boxed Donnie Hood from Glasgow, Regilio Tuur – a Dutch-based boxer from Surinam – and Freddie Cruz from the Dominican Republic. He lost on points to Hood, who was the Scottish bantamweight champion, and also lost by unanimous decision against Tuur who went on to win the WBO super featherweight title. He was stopped in the sixth round by Cruz, who in 1994 was himself stopped in six rounds by Naseem Ahmed.

In 1992 the Swansea boxer notched up two wins in three contests followed by two defeats in 1993. He beat Lee Fox from Chesterfield, lost to Henry Armstrong from Manchester, and stopped Karl Norling in four rounds. In 1993 he lost on points over eight rounds against unbeaten Tony Silkstone from Leeds and Francisco Arroyo from Panama in Belfast.

An inside the distance defeat at the hands of the promising Mark Bowers, who had won all of his eight previous contests, convinced Dean it was time to throw the towel in on his ring career. Dean's record of only six wins in twenty professional contests doesn't appear too impressive, but he did mix it with boxers of a very good standard, most of whom were at the top of their game when Dean fought them.

Twenty-seven-year-old **Russell Washer** lost a close points decision over six rounds in his first professional contest against fellow debutant Dean Cooper at the Thornbury Leisure Centre on 15th September 1990. Cooper was a decent fighter who became Western area light middleweight champion, losing only three out of eighteen contests, against Kirkland Laing, Robert McCracken and in his final contest against Swansea boxer Paul Lynch at the Dillwyn Llewelyn Leisure Centre. Russell boxed another four times in 1990, winning three inside the distance.

The Swansea boxer commenced 1991 in fine style, stopping Wayne Panayioutiou from Llanelli in four rounds in Gorseinon and drawing with Marvin O'Brien from Leeds. Russell's next victory was in December 1992, after fifteen consecutive defeats, which included a six rounds points defeat against Swansea boxer Lee Crocker and an unsuccessful shot at the Welsh light middleweight title, losing on a five rounds TKO against Llanelli's Carlo Calarusso. His sole victory in 1992 was at the expense of Abel Asinamali, an American-based in Tooting. Russell won a six round points decision at the York Hall, Bethnal Green.

In 1993 the Swansea boxer won two and lost thirteen, but most of his defeats were against a good standard of opposition and often the fights were arranged with very little notice. His two victories were against Swansea boxer Ray 'Peanut' Price, who was stopped in four rounds, and Darren Blackford from Brixton, whom he beat on points over six rounds. Despite the succession of defeats the Swansea boxer battled on, beating Jamie Robinson on points in Cardiff, a very good win – his opponent from West Ham had only been beaten once in eleven previous contests. He had previously beaten Russell and fellow Swansea boxer Lee Crocker.

The Swansea boxer outpointed Robert Harper in Bloomsbury in April 1985 over six rounds, sandwiched between points defeats against Andy Ewen from Ipswich and Sven Hamer from Margate. On 27th October 1995 Russell was knocked out by Jason Matthews from Hackney in the fifth round at Brighton. Matthews had won all six previous bouts, four of the wins coming inside the distance. Jason later became WBO Interim champion when he knocked out Ryan Rhodes in two rounds.

Russell Washer was thirty-five years old, he had won nine, drawn one out of forty-six contests against some very tough opposition; he decided it was now time to call time on his boxing career. He had shown a lot of courage, an abundance of determination and resilience throughout his time in the ring.

Carl Hook, alias the 'Karaoke Kid', made his professional debut at the National Sports Centre Cardiff on 18th July 1991 when he lost on points over six rounds against Jason Matthews from Bargoed, who was also making his first start as a pro. Carl won his next two fights, winning both on points over six rounds, against Wayne Taylor from Birmingham at Dudley and Nicky Lucas from Waltham Abbey, who was participating in his seventeenth contest. Carl rounded off 1991 losing an eight rounds decision against experienced Ron Shinkwin from Watford and beating John 'O' Johnson from Nottingham, both fights taking place in Dunstable.

Carl lost five in a row in 1992 before avenging an earlier defeat by stopping Derrick Daniel from Bethnal Green. In his last fight of the year he dropped a six rounds decision against Edward Lloyd from Rhyl at Cardiff.

On 27th January 1993 Carl challenged Mervyn Bennett for the Welsh lightweight title, losing on points over ten rounds. At the age of twenty-three and having won four of thirteen contests, this was to be Carl's last professional fight.

Twenty-year-old **Ross McCord** was stopped by Harry Butler from Worcester in his professional debut in Swansea on 2nd December 1997. In his next contest the following May at the York Hall, Bethnal Green, the Swansea boxer stopped Sonny Thind from Bedford in round three. Thind had won his two previous contests, including a win over Harry Butler. Ross achieved his second consecutive inside the distance win when he halted Birmingham's Pedro Thompson in November at the Manor Park in Clydach. Two stoppage defeats ensued – he lost by TKO in five rounds against Sammy Smith from Bracknell, who was unbeaten in four bouts when entering the ring to box Ross at the Town Hall in Acton on December 7th. He was stopped in two rounds by Scott Garrett from Liverpool the following February at Thornaby in Yorkshire. On 23rd April at the Manor Park in Clydach the Swansea boxer stopped Darren Underwood from Blackwood in the first round and then outscored Arv Mittoo from Birmingham over six rounds in London. Mittoo's professional boxing

Ross McCord in action.

career commenced on 31st January 1996 and ended after his one hundredth contest on 3rd September 2005.

Ross went through a bad patch, losing four in a row, at the start of the new millennium – firstly to Woody Greenaway at Swansea Leisure Centre on points over four rounds. In March he was stopped in the first round by Karim Boulali, a London-based Frenchman, who in his next bout stopped another Swansea boxer, Jason Williams. Ross was beaten by Ian Eldridge at the Watford Leisure Centre in July before losing a return contest against Woody Greenaway at the Manor Park. The Swansea boxer outpointed Tony Smith from Sheffield at the Swansea Leisure Centre at the commencement of his 2001 campaign and in December he drew with Marcus Portman from West Bromwich at the Manor Park.

In April 2002 the Swansea boxer fought in the Burlington Hotel, Dublin, where he outpointed Paul McIlwaine from Belfast in his penultimate ring battle. On 15th September 2002 twenty-five-year-old Ross challenged Keith Jones for the vacant Welsh welterweight title at the Swansea Leisure Centre and was halted in four rounds in his final contest.

Chapter Seven

FIGHTING FAMILIES

In April 1986 Michael Spinks outpointed Larry Holmes in Las Vegas to win the World heavyweight championship, and in doing so he became the first boxer to defeat Holmes as a professional. Going into this fight Holmes record stood at forty-eight wins in as many fights, and had he beaten Spinks he would have equalled the record of Rocky Marciano who retired as undefeated heavyweight champion of the World having won all forty-nine professional contests. The victory over Holmes presented Spinks with another first, he became the first boxer to emulate his brother and win the World heavyweight title. Eight years earlier novice underdog Leon Spinks outpointed a thirty-six-year-old, overweight, out of condition World heavyweight champion, Muhammad Ali over fifteen rounds also in Las Vegas.

The Klitschko brothers, Vitaly and Vladimir, from the Ukraine, both lay claim to different versions of the heavyweight title.

In May 1941 and again in January 1942 Buddy Baer unsuccessfully challenged Joe Louis for the World heavyweight crown in an attempt to equal his brother Max's achievement in winning the title. Max beat Italian giant Primo Carnera in New York in June 1934 when the referee stopped the contest in the eleventh round. Marvis Frazier was stopped in the first round when he attempted to take the heavyweight crown from Larry Holmes in 1983, his father Smokin' Joe had held the title from 1968 until he was crushed in two rounds by George Foreman in Kingston, Jamaica, in January 1973.

The Clay brothers, Cassius and Rudolph, brothers Floyd and Ray Patterson, siblings Gene and Don Fullmer, the Mayweather family and the Dundee brothers – Johnny, Vince and Angelo – were just a few of the blood relatives who boxed with some distinction out of the United States. Boxing is never discussed in South Africa without mention of the Toweels, Willie and Vic. Frenchman Ray Famechon challenged Willie Pep for the World featherweight title; his nephew Johnny, who had migrated to Australia, succeeded where his uncle had failed when he outpointed Jose Legra in London in January 1969 to become featherweight champion of the World. Legra had won the title by beating Howard Winstone.

Fighting families have also achieved success in British boxing circles – father and son Jack and Brian London both held the British heavyweight title. Jim Cooper never quite matched British Commonwealth European heavyweight champion and World title challenger twin brother Henry in boxing achievements. A good scrap was guaranteed when either of the late Finnegan brothers, Chris and Kevin, were boxing, whilst Cardiff brothers Eddie, Dennis and Les always attracted a good following wherever they fought.

When **Ken Curvis**, family name Nancurvis, entered the ring on 21st April 1947 to stop fellow debutant Ray Summers in the fourth round in Cirencester, he became the first Swansea boxer to follow a family member into professional boxing. Seventeen-year-old brother **Cliff** had been a professional boxer since 26th August 1944, when he beat Bryn Collins in Brynamman. Only once did Ken and Cliff box on the same bill together when Ken challenged Alan Wilkins for the Welsh welterweight title in Porthcawl on 21st June 1950. Ken retired after that fight while Cliff went on to become British and Commonwealth champion before retiring after unsuccessfully challenging for the European title in Paris in March 1953 at the age of twenty-five. Six years later younger brother **Brian**, managed by elder brother Cliff, made his professional debut at the Empire Pool, Wembley, where he stopped Harry Haydock in two rounds. Brian became British and Commonwealth champion and challenged for the European and World titles in a seven-year career in which he had won two Lonsdale belts.

Len and Teddy Barrow.

Brothers **Teddy and Len Barrow** were both keen and talented footballers who had caught the eye of scouts from some big clubs, but according to younger brother Len their dad had decided that boxing would be their chosen sport. Teddy, the elder of the two brothers, made his professional debut in August 1954 when he was twenty years old and later in his career, which is highlighted in chapter six, challenged unsuccessfully for the Welsh middleweight championship.

Both brothers were born in the Sandfields area of Swansea. They started boxing together at the Empire Boxing Club under the watchful eye of ex-Welsh flyweight champion, Jack Kiley. Len won schoolboy, youth ABA titles and the Welsh ABA light middleweight title, he was the youngest ever Welsh ABA team captain when he led the Principality against the Army when only seventeen years of age in 1954. He boxed for Wales six times before being called up for national service. In 1957 he won the RAF and Inter Services titles. In the same year Len

216

turned professional with manager Ted Walker, but was later managed by Sam Burns – in the same stable as former World middleweight champion Terry Downes, with whom he had engaged in some hostile sparring sessions. Len claimed that he usually came out on top. The Swansea boxer also sparred regularly with the British, British Empire and European lightweight champion, Dave Charnley, and South African Willie Toweel, who had held Robert Cohen to a draw in a World bantamweight title fight; he also held the British Empire light-weight title.

Len made his professional debut on 21st November 1957, when he knocked out Tony Masebo in the third round at the National Sporting Club, Piccadilly. Masebo, from Cymmer, was previously unbeaten in four professional outings. The Swansea boxer followed his debut success by stopping Peter Anderson of Cricklewood at Epsom and a week later he was boxing at the National Sporting Club where he outpointed the experienced Dudley Cox, who was participating in his forty-eighth contest and had gone the eight rounds distance with unbeaten Pat McCateer, who later became British and Commonwealth champion. The Swansea boxer beat Ted Buck at Shoreditch Town Hall and then outpointed debutant Al Bereti at Earls Court over six rounds. In his next contest he won an impressive six rounds decision against Derek Liversidge, who had only lost to Freddie Cross and Terry Downes in sixteen contests. Len's seventh straight win was on points over eight rounds against George Happe from Bethnal Green, who was engaging in his forty-first and last contest which took place at the Empire Pool Wembley on the undercard of the Henry Cooper versus Zora Folley first encounter, when the Londoner won on points over ten rounds.

Len Barrow's next contest took place on 2nd June 1959, when he outscored Paddy Graham, a veteran of forty fights, again at the Empire Pool. Six months later Graham was stopped by Swansea boxer Brian Curvis in five rounds. His unbeaten record was tarnished in his ninth professional fight when he lost on points over eight rounds to Liver-pudlian Tony Smith at the National Sporting Club. Smith was unbeaten in fourteen fights before his tussle with Len and went on to win the

Central area welterweight title and later unsuccessfully challenged Brian Curvis for the British and British Empire titles. Len's recollection of the Smith fight is that it was so close it could have gone either way.

After the Smith fight Len Barrow had just three more fights, beating Johnny Berry on points over eight rounds before dropping eight rounds decisions to Albert Carroll from Bethnal Green and Brian Husband from Hull in a 'nobbins' bout at the National Sporting Club on 12th May 1960.

He retired due to hand injuries that had troubled him throughout his professional career at the age of twenty-three with a professional record of nine wins and three defeats – which were conceded in his last four fights. Len recalls his hardest pro fight was his last with Brian Husband, but remembers his toughest experience was the pain in his hands. Boxing was never Len's number one sport – he was also a promising footballer, and at sixteen years of age he was on the books of Arsenal. He recalls that he received offers from Leeds, Huddersfield and Hull City. He chose boxing because at that time you could earn more money throwing punches than kicking footballs.

Interestingly, both the Barrow brothers boxed for English managers – Teddy in Liverpool and Len in London. They were both highly regarded in British boxing circles, but neither of the Barrow boys won a professional boxing title.

Len passed away on 15th August 2010.

The **Copp** brothers, **Alan and Mike**, from Mayhill, started boxing at the Gwent Amateur Boxing Club and between them won a host of schoolboy and junior titles. Twenty-three-year-old Alan turned professional under the management of Eddie Richards, and made his debut on the Eddie Richards promotion in the Sophia Gardens, Cardiff, on 11th August 1976, when he stopped Graham Laybourn from Barnsley in three rounds. Younger brother Mike was on the same bill – his career is featured in Chapter Six. He had made his professional debut six months earlier. Alan's next engagement was in February 1977 when he outpointed the previously unbeaten Chris Glover from Liverpool on points over eight rounds in Swansea. Alan didn't box

Brothers Michael and Alan in a friendly sparring session.
(Courtesy of *South Wales Evening Post*).

again until November when he took the decision after four rounds from Kendrick Edwards at Hemel Hempstead. The following April, and not yet twenty-five years of age and unbeaten in three professional starts, Alan Copp participated in what was to be his last professional contest when he drew after eight rounds with Johnny Elliot at the Top Rank Suite in Reading. Elliot had previously beaten Alan's brother Michael on points over six rounds. Alan sadly passed away in 1994 just forty-one years old.

Brothers **Ken**, **Colin** and **Peter Jones** all learned the tricks of the trade at the Penyrheol Amateur Boxing Club, where their father was the Secretary and the coach was Gus Bevan. Mrs. Jones had to buy an extra cabinet to house her offspring's many amateur trophies. The professional careers of Colin and Ken are covered in Chapters One and Four respectively.

Peter, the younger brother of Colin and Ken, was born in Gorseinon, Swansea, on 16th June 1961. He made his professional debut on 3rd September 1981 when he stopped Mike Wilkes from Merthyr Tydfil in round four in Cardiff. The clash with the Swansea boxer was Wilkes's second contest, having emerged victorious from his professional debut.

Peter travelled to Marton in North Yorkshire for his second contest where he outpointed Ray Plant from South Shields. The Swansea boxer suffered defeat in his first bout of 1982, losing a close decision to Pat Doherty of Croydon over eight rounds in Solihull. His opponent went on to become the Commonwealth lightweight champion. Nine days later Peter enjoyed victory once again when he outpointed Nottingham's Stuart Shaw in front of his home crowd over eight rounds. After beating Shaw he was off to the Empire Pool, Wembley, where he outpointed Robert Hepburn from Norwich over eight rounds; his opponent had twenty-two skirmishes under his belt. This bout took place on September 14th on a star-studded bill featuring brother Colin who successfully defended his Commonwealth title with a second round knockout – also on the programme were Frank Bruno and Tony Sibson, who both notched up victories.

In the following March 1983 the Swansea boxer outpointed experienced Dutchman Ray Somer in an eight round contest in Rotterdam. Peter lost his seventh, and what was to be his last contest, losing on points after eight rounds against Danish-based Kenyan Mike Urungu in London on 20th April 1983. Urungu had won ten out of eleven before the Jones bout and went on to become the bantamweight champion of Kenya.

Frank and **Ross McCord** – father and son – both challenged unsuccessfully for the Welsh welterweight title, Frank losing twice to Cardiff's Billy Waith, both times on points over ten rounds, and Ross was halted in the fourth round against Keith Jones. Frank turned professional in 1977 and son Ross joined the paid ranks of boxing twenty years later.

The **George** brothers – **David, Donald and Eric** – were steered toward the Swansea Dockers Amateur Boxing Club by their late father, Eric Sr. All three progressed into the professional ranks – the careers of Donald and David are featured in chapters four and six respectively.

The George family – father Eric with sons Don, Eric, David and Terry.

Eric, the youngest of the three, was also a protégé of the Swansea Dockers ABC. He turned professional in 1989, making his debut on his 21st birthday boxing fellow debutant and future British and European flyweight champion, WBO bantamweight champion Robbie Regan, to a six round draw. Eric came through his 'baptism of fire' pretty well. His career spanned from August 1989 until 7th December 1991, retiring when just 23 years of age. In his short career Eric came up against some pretty tough opponents, including the Ghanaian 'pocket battleship' Francis Ampofo, whom he fought twice. Ampofo went on to become British and Commonwealth flyweight champion.

In his final contest on 7th December 1991, 23-year-old Eric earned a creditable draw against Italian Mercurio Ciaramatoro in Lazio. The Italian subsequently became the champion of Europe in both the flyweight and bantamweight divisions. A draw against any Italian in Italy is indeed a creditable draw.

Brothers **Peter** and **Michael Harries** were encouraged into boxing by their late father Gordon, who was not a bad exponent of the noble art himself, disadvantaged by brittle hands and a lifestyle that was not commensurate with the disciplines that professional boxers have to impose upon themselves. Elder brother Peter turned professional in 1983, his career spanned over thirteen years until he finally retired in 1996, having once held the British featherweight title. Michael had held the Welsh light welterweight and light middleweight titles in a career that had spanned over seven years from 1982 to 1989. He had challenged unsuccessfully for the British light welterweight and light middleweight titles.

Mario Maccarinelli, founder of and chief trainer at the Bonymaen Amateur Boxing Club, has nurtured and guided both his sons, **Enzo** and **Valo**, into the paid ranks. His grandson, **Tobias Webb**, has also benefitted from his mentoring and is now making his mark as a professional boxer.

Enzo won the WBU and WBO cruiserweight titles – details of his career are recorded in Chapter One.

Valentino, who was better known as Valo, the elder brother of Enzo, boxed as a professional at welter and light middleweight. His pro career commenced on 27th April 1982 and ended on 12th April 1983. Within those twelve months Valo kept busy, boxing eight times. He made his debut at Southend where he stopped Noel Blair from Slough in the third round. In June he outpointed Jimmy Ward from Paddington at the Top Rank Suite in Swansea, where Cardiff's Billy Waith defended his Welsh title against Swansea boxer Frank McCord. Ward had won five out of his previous six contests. The Swansea boxer then dropped a six rounds decision to Irishman Davy Campbell, the fight taking place in Derry, Northern Ireland. In October Valo was knocked out in two rounds by Danny Garrison from Wolverhampton at Evesham.

In the following February the Swansea boxer drew with debutant Mick Leachman from Dagenham at Walthamstow in London. Valo outpointed Johnny Burns from Birmingham at Edgbaston two weeks later and then lost on a four round TKO against Patsy Quinn at the King's Hall in Belfast. He suffered a second inside the distance loss on a return trip to the King's Hall on 12th April against unbeaten Damien Fryers, who like Quinn hailed from Belfast. After this contest the twenty-four-year-old Swansea boxer retired from professional boxing.

Tobias Webb.

Following a prolific amateur career Tobias Webb, the nephew of Valo and Enzo Maccarinelli, boxed as a professional for the first time in Manchester on 14th March 2009, five months short of his twenty-first birthday. He comfortably outpointed Reading-based Gambian, Patrick Mendy, in Manchester. In June he beat Staines-based Pole, Michael Gambala, on points over four rounds in Glasgow, followed by another four rounds points win against Tooting-based, Pawel Tebinski, in Liverpool. The Swansea boxer drew with Lee Duncan from Sheffield over four rounds in March 2010 on a star-studded Frank Warren promotion in Liverpool and concluded his 2010 campaign by outpointing experienced Dean Walker from Sheffield over four rounds in Glasgow on 4th December 2010.

Neil Crocker, elder brother of **Lee**, made his professional debut on 8th September 1983, when he was outpointed over six rounds by fellow debutant Danny Sullivan in London. He was twenty-two years old. The win over Neil was the first of six straight for Sullivan who was from Finchley. Neil boxed Joe Lynch from Plymouth at Basildon and was knocked out in the first round. He then scored two straight wins, halting debutant Stephen Hibbs at the Dolphin Hotel, Swansea, in the first round and then outpointed Carlo Giomo from Swindon in Bristol. On October 13th the Swansea boxer fought in the King's Hall, Belfast, on a bill topped by Barry McGuigan, Neil was stopped in three rounds by Irishman Rocky McGran. He lost on points to Terry Baker from Greenwich and fought Steve Davies from Pembroke at the Mayfair Suite in Swansea, losing on points over six rounds. Davies had fought three other Swansea boxers – he suffered a one round stoppage defeat at the fists of Terry Matthews but won the vacant light middleweight title by stopping Frank McCord and stopped John McGlynn in defence of that title. Neil retired after the Davies contest having won two of seven contests in fourteen months as a professional.

Lee Crocker also boxed at light middleweight. He took part in his first professional boxing contest when he was approaching his twenty-first birthday on 31st January 1991 – he lost on points against Colin Manners in Stockport. He boxed five times in 1991, with two victories, two defeats and one draw. In his sixth professional bout he took a points decision over six rounds from fellow Swansea boxer, Russell Washer, in Cardiff. Lee boxed three more times that year, stopping Winston May but getting stopped by Nick Manners in Leeds and James Robinson in London. He ended the year by losing to David Larkin in York.

Lee's losing run continued in 1994 – two outings in Cardiff and two defeats. In February 1995 he was stopped in two rounds at the National Ice Rink in Cardiff by debut making Ryan Rhodes, twice British light middleweight champion and holder of two Lonsdale belts. Following the Rhodes defeat Lee was victorious in his next three fights. Making his Swansea debut he outpointed Darren Dorrington at the Dillwyn Llewellyn Leisure Centre in March 1995 and knocked out

Carl Harney in four rounds at the Brangwyn Hall two months later. Lee was clearly on a roll. In his next engagement he went to London and stopped Andy Ewen in three rounds, but didn't fight again until the following April, when he took on the impressive prospect West countryman, Glen Cattley, who had won eighteen of his nineteen bouts. Cattley stopped Lee in two rounds in Cardiff in a fight that really was a big task for the Swansea boxer. Cattley went on to become British middleweight and WBC super middleweight champion.

In his last fight on 31st May 1996, the twenty-seven-year-old Swansea boxer bravely challenged the big punching Dane, Mads Larsen, who was later to become European, IBO and WBF super middleweight champion. Larsen knocked out Lee in round one, after which he decided to call time on his boxing career.

Keith Parry won the Welsh lightweight title on 28th October 1987 gaining revenge for an earlier title fight loss by stopping defending champion Andy Williams in round eight, the Swansea boxer was twenty-four years old. In the last bout of a career that had begun promisingly Keith retired undefeated Welsh champion after losing to Ugandan Patrick Karmy on 22nd March 1989, he was twenty-five years old.

Brother **Carl Parry**, who boxed at featherweight, outpointed Derek Amory of Birmingham over six rounds in his professional debut in Swansea on 18th November 1986. In 1987 Carl boxed six times, losing three bouts on points against Ginger Staples from Rhydfelin in Newport, Johnny Good from Croydon in London and in a return encounter with Derek Amory at Solihull. He stopped Charlie Brown from Glasgow in four rounds at Cumbernauld. Charlie had previously been halted by Swansea boxer Robert Dickie. Carl outpointed Jimmy Lee from Blackburn in Swansea and Alan McCullough from Belfast in his own backyard.

The Swansea boxer entered the square ring just once in 1988 when he outpointed John Knight from Bridgewater over six rounds in London. In the following year he drew with Andy Abreau from Cardiff in Swansea and was stopped in four rounds by Frenchman Henri Jacob in Calais – at the time Jacob was unbeaten in nineteen contests and in 1993 was crowned the European featherweight champion. After this fight, Carl – not yet twenty-two years of age – retired from professional boxing having won five, lost four and drawn one of his ten contests.

A third member of the Parry family, brother **Paul**, then twenty years old boxed twice at featherweight in 1986. In his debut at the Dillwyn Llewellyn Leisure Centre he lost on points after six rounds against Llanelli's Nigel Haddock. Paul ended his career on a winning note when he stopped fellow Swansea boxer, Geoff Sillitoe, at the Ebbw Vale Leisure Centre.

Dean Lynch made his professional debut on 18th September 1986, just two months short of his twenty-second birthday. On 12th April 1989 he fought for the vacant Welsh super featherweight title in Swansea and was stopped in the fourth round by James Hunter. Dean boxed on until 1993, retiring at the age of twenty-nine.

Paul Lynch, who was two years Dean's junior, boxed at light middleweight and made his professional debut in October 1989. He was two months short of his twenty-third birthday when he outpointed Darren Burford over six rounds at the World Sporting Club in Mayfair. The Swansea boxer won his next five contests, including a very impressive win over Ray Rowland from West Ham, who had won sixteen out of seventeen contests before mixing it with Paul.

After a promising start to his career with six wins, three inside the distance, the matchmaking became a little adventurous. His next contest in October 1991 was against up-and-coming Rhode Islander, Peter Manfredo, on his home territory. Paul was beaten on points over eight rounds.

In his next contest, just over a year later, the Swansea boxer boxed Robert McCracken from Birmingham who had won all ten of his previous contests inside the distance and later held the British light middleweight and the Commonwealth middleweight crown in a career that culminated in a record of thirty-three wins and two defeats. Both of McCracken's losses were in his last two contests against Keith Holmes for the WBC middleweight championship and Howard Eastman for the British, Commonwealth and European middleweight titles. Paul suffered the second defeat of his career against McCracken when he was stopped in round four.

Two months later he was beaten by Paul Jones from Sheffield who at the time was Central Area middleweight champion and later became WBO light middleweight champion, he also won the Common wealth middleweight championship.

The Swansea boxer returned to winning ways in 1993 in a middle-weight contest at the Tooting Leisure Centre, when he outpointed Tony Velinor from Stratford. He was then stopped by big punching Kevin Sheehan from Crawley who had boxed for two years building up a career record of fourteen wins, ten inside the distance, and two defeats: he was stopped in his first and last bouts.

The Swansea boxer fought three times in 1994, firstly losing to Robert Welin, a Swede born in Brazil, who did most of his boxing in the States racking up a career record of twenty-three wins with just four losses. Following that defeat, Paul stopped Sean Baker in three rounds, the Bristolian was previously unbeaten in twelve outings and only lost twice in a nineteen fight career. In his last fight of the year the Swansea boxer was beaten on points over eight rounds by the reigning British welterweight champion, Del Bryan.

Paul's swan song was on 25th March 1995 when the twenty-eight-year-old stopped Dean Cooper from Bristol in the sixth round. Cooper had previously beaten Swansea boxer Russell Washer but quit the ring after his clash with Paul, retiring with a respectable career record of seventeen wins and just three losses, against Kirkland Laing, Robert McCracken and the Swansea boxer.

Paul retired with a career record of nine wins and six defeats, a record that doesn't do justice to his true potential, which perhaps could have been realised had he been steered a little more carefully.

Neil Burder made his professional debut on 23rd June 1987 in the light heavyweight division, losing a six-round decision to Darren Hob-son who was chalking up his third win in as many fights. Darren's career spanned two years in which time he had thirteen contests, losing only twice, to Nigel Benn and Sam Storey. Neil's second fight ended in success when he stopped Steve Aqualina in four rounds in Dulwich after which he brought the curtain down on his pro career with one stoppage win and one points defeat. **Nigel Burder**, brother of Neil, fought Swansea boxer Chris Mylan in his professional debut at the Rhydycar Leisure Centre in Merthyr Tydfil on 11th April 1991 – he was knocked out in the third round. The Swansea boxer returned to the ring the following March at the same venue and was stopped in the first round by debutant Steve Edwards from Haverfordwest. Two months later, Nigel boxed Dewi Roberts from Blaenau in Llanelli and was knocked out in three rounds. Having been stopped in each of his three professional bouts Nigel decided not to continue with his boxing career.

Darren Williams outpointed John Smith of Liverpool, a veteran of ninety-one professional fights, at the Star Leisure Centre in Cardiff over six rounds on 21st June 1997 to mark his entrance into the paid ranks. The Swansea boxer won the decision after six rounds against Harry Butler at the Port Talbot Rugby Ground, but lost his next bout against Steve Tuckett from Wakefield in Swansea.

Darren Williams with trainer Jimmy Bromfield.

In 1998 Darren beat Paul Salmon from Plymouth in Cardiff, outpointed Danny Quacoe from Crawley in his first eight-rounder at the Glyn Clydach Hotel, Neath, and lost against Anthony Farnell from Manchester, who was unbeaten in nine contests and later won the World Boxing Union title.

Darren was inactive in 1999 and only boxed once in the first year of the new millennium, drawing with debutant Gareth Jones from Merthyr Tydfil.

Darren Williams takes advice from trainer Paul Boyce.

In 2001 the Swansea boxer won three out of three, beating Richard Inqueti from Nottingham in Dublin, Jon Harrison from Plymouth at Swansea Leisure Centre and James Lee from Portsmouth at the Manor Park Clydach, all by decision.

On 24th April 2002 Darren, not yet twenty-seven years of age, and a winner in seven out of nine contests with one drawn, laced up the gloves for the last time at the Burlington Hotel in Dublin, where he'd beaten Inqueti just over a year previously. The Swansea boxer stopped Archie Kirkbride from Carlisle in two rounds, both boxers retired after this bout.

Brother **Jason**, twelve months Darren's senior, also boxed at light middleweight and boxed between 1997 and 2004. He won the Welsh light middleweight title in 2003 and held it without making any defences until he retired.

Chapter Eight

THE VICTORS AND THE VANQUISHED

When World heavyweight champion Rocky Marciano successfully defended his title by knocking out World light heavyweight champion Archie Moore in the ninth round on 21st September 1955 at the Yankee Stadium, New York, he had boxed forty-nine times as a professional and had won every fight, forty-three of his victories were inside the distance. After this contest the 'Brockton Blockbuster', as he was nicknamed, retired without a blemish on his record undefeated heavyweight champion of the World. Joe Calzaghe from Newbridge in Gwent WBC, WBA and WBO super middleweight champion, retired undefeated in forty-six fights after outpointing Roy Jones over twelve rounds in the Madison Square Garden, New York, in November 2008.

Welterweight **Cush Allen**, like a number of other Swansea boxers, can claim to be among an elite group of boxers who retired undefeated. Unlike Marciano or Calzaghe, Cush never won a title. He is recorded as only having boxed once as a professional, that was in Swansea on 24th January 1938, against nineteen-year-old Benny Price from Ammanford, winning the decision after eight rounds. Several months later Price lost to another Swansea boxer, Taffy Williams. On the same bill Len Beynon stopped George Williams and Jack Kiley outpointed Davo Davies. Cush never appeared in the ring again, retiring undefeated, one fight and one win.

Alan Copp, brother of Swansea boxer Mike Copp, boxed in the welterweight division on four occasions as a professional between

August 1976 and April 1978. He won his first three bouts and drew the fourth. He never boxed again, retiring unbeaten.

Pat 'Young' Doherty joined the Colin Breen stable and made his professional debut on 31st July 1985 seven months after his nineteenth birthday – he boxed in Porthcawl, where he stopped Jess Rundon from Plymouth in the third round. Swansea boxers Michael Harries and Robert Dickie were also victorious on this bill. Pat halted Northampton super featherweight John Daly in Swansea in the second round, the following March. After two fights, two inside the distance wins, Pat ended his professional career with the perfect record.

Darren Liney from Morriston outpointed Julian Eavis over six rounds at the National Sports Centre, Cardiff, on 28th May 1991. Prior to boxing Darren, Julian – from Bourton on the Water in Gloucestershire – had boxed forty-one times, winning ten and drawing three. He was on a run of twenty-four bouts without a win and went another seven contests after losing to Darren before having his arm raised as a victor, a run of thirty-one fights without a victory. Despite showing lots of promise, Darren never boxed again, ending his one fight career with the solitary win.

Mark Verikios stopped Lee Farrell from Pontypool in five rounds in Swansea on 15th May 1991, to mark the twenty-five-year-old's entrance into the professional fight game. His appetite whetted, he was back in the ring at Barking in London on 6th June, when he knocked out Tim Harmey from Brighton in the fourth round. His next contest was in Liverpool on 9th September, where he won the verdict after six rounds against Liverpudlian Dave Maj. Despite his hat-trick of victories in four months Mark didn't fight again until May of the ensuing year, when he stopped Steve McNess from Bethnal Green at the Royal Albert Hall. On 12th November the Swansea boxer repeated his earlier success over Dave Maj, again on points over six rounds and again in Liverpool. Five fights, five wins, twenty-seven years of age Mark joined the immortals, Rocky Marciano and Joe Calzaghe, retiring undefeated.

Nineteen-year-old Swansea boxer **Darren Pullman** boxed only once as a professional, drawing with Steve Thomas from Merthyr Tydfil on 10th April 1993 in a six round middleweight contest. The bout was held in Swansea on a bill that featured Swansea boxers Julian Johnson, Rocky Reynolds and Russell Washer.

Mark Hughes was born in Swansea on 8th July 1971 and after boxing for the Gwent ABC, he turned professional in 1994 at the age of twenty-three. He made his professional debut against experienced campaigner Graham McGrath from Warley, who was participating in his thirty-first contest. Mark, boxing as a flyweight, won on points after four rounds on September 21st in Cardiff. McGrath had participated in one hundred and twelve contests throughout his career. Mark was back in the ring just ten days later when he outscored Anthony Hanna from Birmingham over four rounds, again in Cardiff. He repeated the victory over Hanna by way of a six rounds points win in London on 6th March 1995, the Birmingham boxer went on to win the Midlands flyweight title in his career total of one hundred and eleven fights. The Swansea boxer returned to London on 19th May to take a six-round decision from Shaun Norman from Coalville, and retired undefeated after drawing with Harry Woods from Bargoed in Cardiff on 25th October 1995.

Gareth Perkins made his professional debut at the Marriot Hotel in Bristol on 29th February 2004 when he outpointed Chris Long from Caine in Wiltshire over six rounds. In his only other professional encounter the Swansea boxer, who stood at just five feet three inches tall, drew with Paul Porter from Dunstable over four rounds at the York Hall in Bethnal Green on 17th January 2006, nearly two years after his previous contest. Gareth never boxed again and can claim to have retired undefeated after just two professional starts.

Ricky Owen was just nineteen years of age when he took his own fireworks to the Hereford Leisure Centre to stop Scotsman Sandy Bartlett from Inverness on 5th November 2004, marking his entry into the paid ranks.

He boxed just twice in 2005, winning four round decisions against Billy Smith from Kidderminster on 16th June and Ukrainian Rakhim Mingaleev in Carmarthen on 30th September. In 2006 he was even less active, boxing just once, coming through his first six rounder un-scathed, beating Bulgarian Alexander Vladimirov at Hartlepool. The Swansea boxer was adjudged to have won five rounds and tied the other. In March 2007 he boxed Hungarian Egon Szabo at the Neath Sports Centre, winning on points after six rounds and imposing the first defeat on his opponent in four outings. He stopped veteran Anthony Hanna, who was engaging in his ninety-eighth bout, in the fifth round at Wolverhampton. He travelled to Irvine in Scotland for his final contest of the year where he halted Robin Deakin in the second round in his seventh straight win as a professional.

Ricky had three contests in 2008, maintaining his unbeaten record by outpointing French journeyman Frederic Gossett over six rounds in Dagenham – the Frenchman never won too often, but very rarely was he beaten inside the distance. Dai Davies from Merthyr Tydfil was knocked out in five rounds at the Afan Lido, and Ghanaian Sumaila Badum was Ricky's next victim, losing by a wide margin over six rounds in Glasgow.

On 3rd April 2009 Ricky came close to experiencing defeat for the first time – although well ahead on points he sustained a bad cut over his left eye due to a clash of heads in round three of his bout with Jimmy Ancliff from Aberdeen at the York Hall in Bethnal Green – the Swansea boxer survived three separate inspections of the eye to win the contest decisively.

On 29th May 2010 Ricky was one of eight contestants in the Prize-fighter tournament, super bantamweight division, having to win three contests over three, three-minute rounds all in one night to collect the £32,000 cash prize. In his quarter final bout he outpointed Gavin Reid, a tough, hard-hitting Yorkshire-based Scotsman, only to be matched with another Scottish exile, Cwmbran-based Welsh super bantamweight champion Jamie Arthur in the semi-final in Ricky's thirteenth contest. It proved unlucky thirteen for the Swansea boxer.

He won the contest by decisively outpointing Arthur, but had to withdraw from the competition due to a badly cut eye he had sustained in the semi-final contest.

At the end of December 2010 light heavyweight **Tobias Webb**, who is featured with the Maccarinelli brothers in Chapter Seven, remains unbeaten in five professional contests.

*   *   *

For there to be boxers who win all their bouts some have to lose and unfortunately, some have embarked on a professional boxing career and have never savoured the sweet taste of victory, when after all the sacrifice and discipline and all the hard work, at the end of the combat the referee raises your hand as the winner.

Swansea boxer **Danny Thomas** boxed in the featherweight division and according to *www.boxrec.com* he made his professional debut at the Mannesmann Hall, Swansea, on 4th April 1935, losing by knockout in round eight of a twelve-round contest against Tommy Hyams from King's Cross. Tommy had been boxing professionally since 1930 and had participated in one hundred and twenty bouts of which seventy-three were victories and fifteen were drawn. Tony Lee in his book, *All in my Corner*, refers to an eight rounds drawn contest against Ginger Jones in Milford Haven on 31st October 1931. Just fifteen days after the bout with Hyams, Danny did well to box the scheduled ten rounds against Londoner Dave Finn in London who had also been a professional for five years and had boxed eighty-three times. Four months later he was sharing a ring with Dick Corbett, who by this time had been a professional for nine years and had won, lost and regained the British and Commonwealth bantamweight titles and had beaten Swansea boxer Len Beynon. Danny ended his career where it began at the Mannesmann Hall where he was stopped by eighteen-year-old rising star Ronnie James. Danny could never be accused of carefully selecting 'soft touches' as opponents.

Curly Roberts made his professional debut at the Drill Hall in Swansea on 20th March 1945. His first contest proved to be a 'baptism of fire' when he took on the promising Swansea boxer, seventeen-year-old Cliff Curvis, at bantamweight, and was stopped in the third round. Curly didn't box again until January of the following year when he was stopped in five rounds by Ronnie Taylor from Horwich at the Stadium in Liverpool. On 24th June he boxed Ivor Davies of Neath to a six-round draw at the Gwyn Hall, the nearest he came to success in the ring. In his final contest, which was in 1952, Ivor fought Nigerian Hogan 'Kid' Bassey, who became World feather-weight champion when he beat Cherif Hamia for the vacant title in Paris in 1957. The Swansea boxer's career came to an end after losing a six rounds decision against Joe Hughes from Gilfach Goch, in the Judges Hall, Trealaw, on 13th September. He never won a profes-sional fight, but at least he could boast that he boxed a future British and Commonwealth titleholder.

The only recorded professional bout involving Swansea welter-weight **Willie James** was an eight rounds points defeat at the Drill Hall, Swansea, on 20th March 1945 against Dennis Chadwick from Bridlington, who was participating in his one hundred and fifty-fourth contest, one of which was a twelve round points defeat against Swansea boxer Ronnie James in 1939, also at the Drill Hall.

Albert Govier boxed at the St Helen's Rugby Ground, Swansea, on 29th July 1946, when he lost on points to Doug Thomas of Ystrad-gynlais in his only recorded professional contest. Also boxing on that programme were Swansea boxers Cliff Curvis and Ken Morgan.

The first recorded contest for **Billy Jones** was on 17th February 1949 when he was stopped in two rounds by Dick Langley from Peckham in Poplar. Langley was very experienced, having won twenty-two out of twenty-three contests when he touched gloves with Billy. In November the Swansea boxer lost on points to Billy Wagner from Gloucester in Gloucester over six rounds. These are the only recorded professional contests for Billy Jones.

Alan Couch with two of his many amateur trophies.

Alan Couch started boxing in 1960 and after a brilliant amateur career in which he boxed for Wales against Czechoslovakia, South Africa, England, Holland and France and was Welsh ABA Champion and ABA finalist in 1965, he turned professional with Eddie Thomas in 1967, turning his back on a career as a professional footballer – he was at one time on the ground staff of Leeds United. His professional debut was at the Afan Lido, Port Talbot, on 28th November 1967 in a bill studded with Eddie Thomas protégés, including heavyweight hope Carl Gizzi, light heavyweight Eddie Avoth, and former amateur stars Alan Ball and Roy John. The Swansea boxer's opponent was the experienced, hard-hitting South African, Ronnie Van de Walt, who boasted a stoppage victory over Willie Ludick who went on to beat renowned Swansea boxer Brian Curvis. There were a few raised eyebrows when Alan's manager accepted the match, which appeared to be a severe test for Alan in his pro debut. Concerns were justified as the experienced South African stopped the Swansea debutant in the second round, Alan suffering permanent eye damage, and never boxed again. There can be little doubt that this bad match denied Alan of a promising professional career.

Richard White, better known in Swansea as Gerry Rich, was the resident singing artist at the Top Rank Suite in Swansea. He was a compatriot of fellow Swansea boxer Neville Meade, hailing from Montserrat, and decided to follow in his footsteps and swap his microphone for a pair of boxing gloves. He was managed by George Evans from Merthyr Tydfil but lived, trained and boxed out of Swansea. His first professional engagement was in the National Sporting Club in London on 3rd November 1980, when he was outpointed over six rounds by Bobby Welburn from Hull. Less than four weeks later the thirty-one-year-old Swansea boxer was back in the ring at Bloomsbury in London, where he lost on points against Londoner, Dave Finigan. After this bout Richard decided his future was on the stage and not in the ring.

Steve Kane, who is also a professional singer, was a protégé of the Gwent ABC. He boxed at lightweight, losing on points over four rounds against Alan Thomas in front of his opponent's home crowd in Bristol on 4th December 1981. This was eighteen-year-old Steve's one and only professional contest. He was managed by Colin Breen and trained by Jimmy Bromfield.

David Haycock was twenty-four years old when he made his professional debut in a cruiserweight bout at the Prince Regent Hotel in Chigwell on 15th November 1988. He boxed Terry Duffus from Gloucester and was knocked out in the sixth round. His next contest was in Battersea the following February when he was stopped in four rounds by Ali Forbes from Sydenham who in 1995 won the vacant British super middleweight title. In October he was stopped in two rounds by unbeaten Darren Westover from Ilford, who in his next contest stopped Swansea boxer Kevin Roper in the first round. Badly needing a win David was hardly likely to achieve that in his next fight – fourteen months later he was matched against Phil Soundy, who was unbeaten in eight bouts. He stopped the Swansea boxer in three rounds at the Royal Albert Hall. In March 1991 David was up against it once again when he fought Michael Gale, who was born in Cardiff but resided in Leeds, and had won all ten professional bouts, seven of those wins inside the distance. The contest was held in Dewsbury where David was stopped in two rounds in what turned out to be his last fight. Statistically, his record wasn't very impressive, but the match-making didn't offer him any favours.

Super middleweight **Mick Morgan** was nearly twenty-seven years old when he made his professional debut in Swansea on 12th April 1989. He was stopped in four rounds by Dario DeAbreu from Guyana but based in Cardiff. The Swansea boxer fought next in September, again in Swansea, and was stopped in round four by Spencer Alton from Derby. At the age of twenty-four, Mick was convinced that a career in boxing was not for him.

Nigel Burder, brother of Neil referred to in Chapter Seven, boxed three times at welterweight in 1991-92 and lost inside the distance on each occasion.

Phil Cullen boxed just once as a lightweight in 1992, when he boxed at the Royal Albert Hall in London on a bill headed by Duke McKenzie, who successfully defended his WBO flyweight title against Puerto Rican, Wilfredo Vargas. The Swansea boxer was stopped in three rounds by Londoner Roger Hunte.

Paul Davies boxed in Cardiff on 30th March 1993 in a light welter-weight contest – his opponent was Phil Found from Hereford, who was also making his professional debut. Eight months after this bout Found fought and beat another Swansea boxer, the waning Robert Dickie. Paul Davies was no more successful than his fellow Swansea boxer, losing to his opponent over six rounds. He never boxed again.

Craig Dyer made his professional debut on 21st September 2007 against Jamie Spence from Northampton, losing on points over six rounds at Peterborough. He was twenty-one years of age. Craig has yet to gain a victory in fourteen professional contests, but to his credit he has only been stopped once, he lost by technical knockout against the promising Lee Pundy from Dagenham, who at the time they met was unbeaten in five starts. Craig fought on 4th October 2009 when he lost on points over four rounds against unbeaten Ben Wakeham from Torquay, who had beaten Swansea boxer Adam Farrell in his most previous encounter. Craig lost his fifteenth successive bout as a professional losing on points over four rounds against Dan Carr from Trowbridge in Bath on 20th November 2010. He continues in pursuit of his initial success in a professional boxing ring.

Twenty-year-old **Adam Farrell** was stopped in three rounds in his first professional contest at Newport Leisure Centre by Ben Wakeham from Torquay, who had entered the ring on 13th March 2009 with a record of three straight wins. Adam returned to Newport Leisure Centre on 5th June to do battle with fellow Swansea boxer James Todd, who won every round, to take his tally to two wins and one draw, leaving Adam searching for his first win.

Chapter Nine

THE REVIVAL

Following the retirement of British and Commonwealth Welterweight champion Brian Curvis in 1966, only one Swansea boxer climbed through the ropes of a professional boxing ring during the remainder of the decade, when Alan Couch took on experienced South African Ronnie van de Walt in 1967.

Hereford-born Swansea boxer Bobbie Ruffe marked the revival of Swansea boxers when he boxed Kenny Webber from Merthyr Tydfil at the Cwmfelin Club, Swansea, in April 1972. Promoting the show was Swansea businessman and cousin of soccer legends John and Mel Charles, Eddie Richards, who had previously been operating at the Afan Lido in Aberavon – but his ambition was to revive interest in professional boxing in Swansea. He was planning further events in the City and had pencilled in June 12th at the Top Rank Suite, having built a strong team around him, including his wife, the late Phyllis, friends Gwyn Powell and the late Billy Floyd, Board of Control representatives, the late Cliff Curvis, the late Billy Wilkins, John Lewis, timekeeper the late Ivor Campbell,

Cliff Curvis and Billy Wilkins, key members of the Welsh Area British Boxing Board of Control.

Eddie Richards promotion at the Top Rank, Swansea Suite,
12th June 1972.

boxing manager and trainer Glyn Davies and trainer, the late Dickie Dobbs. The bill at the Cwmfelin Club was headed by Welsh heavyweight champion Dennis Avoth from Cardiff, who outpointed Llanelli's Delme Phillips over ten rounds in a Welsh title affair. Caerau's Mike McCluskie also starred on the bill, losing a narrow points decision over eight rounds against Maurice Thomas from Bradford.

In a 'sold out' Dinner Show at the Top Rank Suite which took place on the intended date of 12th June 1972, for which Eddie Richards was again the promoter, engaging the main source of interest for the local boxing fraternity was the billing of two Swansea born boxers, debutant light heavyweight heavy hitting Chuck Jones and battling middleweight Jeff Burns, who had won his first two professional outings. Chuck flattened Glasgow's John Smith in just one round, whilst his stablemate battled hard to overwhelm Llantwit Major's Clive Collins over six rounds. Eddie, encouraged by the success of his first show at the Top Rank, featured Chuck and Jeff as joint bill toppers in a follow-up at the same venue on 24th July 1972. The two Swansea boxers supported former British light welterweight champion Des Rea in a three-fight bill on 18th September. Chuck outpointed Pat Thompson over eight two-minute rounds; Jeff won comfortably on points over six rounds against Les Avoth from Cardiff. Chuck, Jeff and Bobby Ruffe were managed by Glyn Davies from Llanelli. Glyn's stable, which was reinforced by the signing of another Swansea boxer Dai 'Muscles' Davies, who had made a successful debut at the National Sporting Club in Piccadilly, outpointing Cardiff's Joey Deriu over six rounds.

Over the next six months there was considerable turmoil on the Swansea boxing scene. Chuck Jones, winner of seven out of eight bouts and showing great promise, was forced to retire with rheumatoid arthritis. Jeff Burns had been forced to rest with an injury to his right hand. Eddie Richards and Glyn Davies had severed ties, the promoter forming a partnership with Brian Curvis and opening a gym at the old fire station in Mumbles. Bobby Ruffe had also retired, leaving only Burns, now managed by Curvis, and Dai 'Muscles' in the Glyn Davies camp as the only two active Swansea boxers.

Eddie resumed promoting in Swansea on 5th February 1973. Welsh heavyweight champion Dennis Avoth outpointing Guinea Roger in the main event, while Jeff Burns suffering his second defeat when he lost a narrow points decision after eight rounds against Mike McCluskie. The Swansea team of Eddie Richards and Brian Curvis promoted three more shows in Swansea between March and June 1973, all featuring Swansea boxer Jeff Burns, who had been elevated to fourth contender in the British middleweight rankings. Swansea's other active professional boxer, Dai Davies, was plying his trade out-side of Swansea and after four defeats in four bouts didn't box again until 1977. Three consecutive defeats and recurring hand problems forced Jeff Burns into retirement at the end of January 1974.

Swansea was once again without any active professional boxers. Eddie Richards promoted two tournaments in Swansea, the first in May featuring Llanelli light welterweight Glyn Watts, who outpointed Ray Fallone a veteran of eighty-eight fights over six rounds. On 14th October Eddie Richards introduced his two new charges who had settled in Swansea: 1974 ABA and Commonwealth Games heavy-weight champion, Neville Meade, and welterweight prospect from Zambia, Yotham Kunda, to the Top Rank Suite – both boxers were victorious on the night.

In 1975 Eddie Richards promoted just one show in Swansea. Meade stopped Lloyd Walford in the sixth round and Cardiff's Swansea-born middleweight, Terry Davies, outpointed Carlton Lyons over six rounds; this was to be Eddie's last promotion at the Top Rank. Yotham experienced mixed fortunes, winning four of thirteen contests, and by the middle of 1976 had returned to Zambia.

In February of 1976 Mike Copp had made his professional debut, amateur stars Alan Copp and Colin Breen were training at Eddie's Gym where Jeff Burns who was sparring with Neville Meade, Colin and the Copp brothers and was regaining his appetite for the fight game. Witnessing the increased and enthusiastic activity in the gym, Eddie Richards was planning a resumption of promotions at the Sophia Gardens in Cardiff, where he had staged two shows in 1973, with a team of five Swansea boxers on one side of the bill. Following his triumph on the Cardiff bill, Jeff Burns fought in the Royal Albert Hall in September after which he finally retired, leaving Neville Meade, the Copp brothers and Colin Breen to carry the flag for Swansea.

At this time the amateur gyms in Swansea were bubbling with activity, spearheaded by the Penyrheol Amateur Boxing Club, where Colin Jones had won an ABA title and was representing Great Britain at the 1976 Olympic Games in Montreal. Elder brother Ken had won a Welsh ABA title and younger brother Peter had won a schoolboy title, all under the guidance and mentoring of Gareth (Gus) Bevan. At the Gwent Amateur Boxing Club, Terry Grey, aided by Paddy Simons, was grooming the likes of Terry Matthews, Frank McCord and Jeff Aspel, who were assisted by useful amateurs, including veteran Charlie Leyshon, James Parry, Kevin Cullen, Cyril Johnston and others who maybe could have had some success in the professional game. Former Welsh flyweight champion Jack Kiley, who had nurtured the likes of brothers Wynford and Stuart Morgan, Alan and Donnie Couch, John Rees, ex-Army champion Richie Jones, Cliff Nancurvis (son of Ken Curvis) and Jeff Burns, was training Doug James for future stardom at Swansea Youth ABC. At the Swansea Dockers Club, Cliff Teasdale, aided by Eric George, was mentoring a useful crop of youngsters, including the three George Brothers, Nigel Page, Keri Wakeman, Bryan Dalling and Tony Brittle – who was always willing to offer his services in sparring to Swansea boxers.

Travelling showman George Linsey would provide lively sparring practise for the Swansea boxers at Eddie's Gym; he boxed for Trostre Amateur Boxing Club. In future years John Rees, Jake Mainwaring, Ray Sillitoe, Mario Maccarinelli, Billy Parry, Spud Brophy, Trevor Russell, Jimmy Bromfield, John Parry, Gordon Harries, Terry Tennant and many others would play an integral part in preparing Swansea boxers for the leap into the paid ranks. Gordon's boys, Peter and Michael, when still at schoolboy and junior level, were raising a few eyebrows.

Enthusiasm rekindled in Swansea boxing, Pat Matthias emerged as Eddie Richards's successor, promoting a number of shows at the Top Rank, including Frank McCord's two gallant but unsuccessful attempts to wrest the Welsh welterweight title from the clever Cardiff boxer, Billy Waith, and that much publicised grudge match for the

Welsh heavyweight title fight at the Swansea Leisure Centre between champion Neville Meade and challenger Winston Allen. Local businessman Alan 'Tighty' Davies picked up the torch, promoting professional tournaments in Swansea and managing Swansea boxers.

Swansea boxer Colin 'Honest Col' Breen had retired from boxing after drawing with Joe Jackson in May 1977, but didn't walk away from boxing – he teamed up with trainer Jimmy Bromfield and bought the lease of Eddie's Gym in Oystermouth Road. Colin, fulfilling his ambition, was granted a manager's license and signed up a number of Swansea boxers, including Frank McCord, Mike and Alan Copp, Dai Davies, Nigel Thomas, Doug James, Winston Allen, Pip Coleman, Neville Meade, Young Doherty, Keith, Paul and Carl Parry, Steve Crocker, Steve Kane, Paul and Dean Lynch, Ray Price, Geoff Pegler, Chris Jacobs, Jeff Aspel, Robert Dickie, John Davies, Lee and Neil Crocker, Mick Morgans, Floyd Havard, Michael and Peter Harries. Colin and Jimmy moved from Eddie's Gym to an annex at Colin's family home in Treboeth, which was previously a workshop for Lotts Furniture Company.

Neville Meade trained at the gym in preparation for his successful British title challenge against Gordon Ferris in October of 1981, sparring with Doug James, Steve Babbs, Delme Phillips, Dennis Avoth, Darren Pullman and Julian Johnson. Boxing managers Eddie Thomas, George Evans, Billy May and Chris Sanigar would bring their boxers to the Treboeth gym to mix with the wide range of sparring available.

Colin Jones was a regular visitor at the gym to spar with the likes of Doug James in preparation for his title challenges against Milton McCrory. There was always a good atmosphere at the gym, plenty of camaraderie, laughing and joking, but also a very strict training regime.

Colin and Jimmy had taken boxers all over the world to box in Australia, Bahamas, Belgium, Denmark, France, Germany, Holland, Italy and Spain and had managed and trained British champions: Neville Meade, Peter Harries, Robert Dickie and Floyd Havard, and also a host of Welsh champions: Pip Coleman, Keith Parry, Doug James, Ray Price, Geoff Pegler, Chris Jacobs, Michael Harries and John Davies.

Robert Dickie, Jimmy Bromfield, Colin Breen and Michael Harries.

Colin Breen with some of his stable, including Steve Babbs and Dai 'Muscles' Davies.
(Courtesy of South Wales Evening Post).

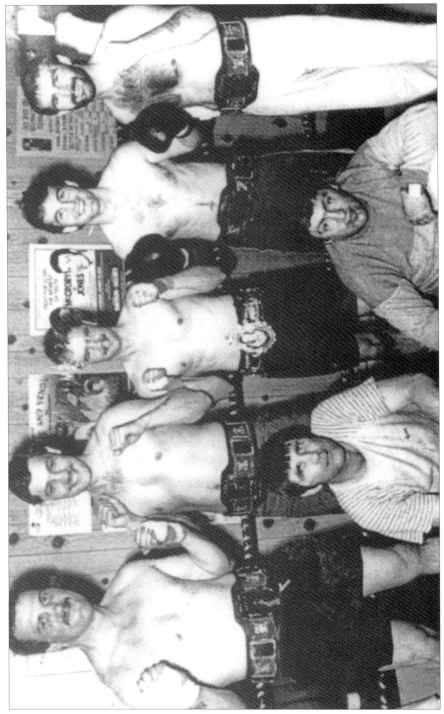

Champions Chris Jacobs, Doug James, Robert Dickie, Michael Harries and Geoff Pegler with trainer Jimmy Bromfield and manager Colin Breen.

Jimmy Bromfield (trainer), Dai 'Muscles' Davies, Pat Mathias, John Conteh, Billy Wilkins, Nigel Thomas, Richard White, John Parry and Colin Breen at Colin's boxing gym in Treboeth.

The Swansea boxing scene was becoming increasingly active. Just down the road in Gorseinon, Colin Jones had become British Commonwealth and European welterweight champion and oh so very nearly champion of the World. Brother, Ken, became Welsh light heavyweight champion.

Swansea businessman Alan Davies promoted a number of professional boxing tournaments in Swansea, including the controversial Welsh light welterweight title series between Geoff Pegler and Ray Price.

In the lower Swansea valley, Clydach's Floyd Havard was to become British featherweight and super featherweight champion and would set up his training base at Colin Breen's gym in Treboeth, while over at Bonymaen Mario Maccarinelli was training his son, Valo, and trimming the rough edges off his younger son, Enzo, in preparation for future ring stardom.

In the new century Paul Boyce became active as a busy fight promoter of professional boxing events at the Manor Park Hotel in Clydach, ensuring Swansea boxers are able to display their wares in the presence of their home supporters. Enzo Maccarinelli would emerge as WBU and WBO cruiserweight champion, Jason Williams and Damian Owen won Welsh titles. Unbeaten Tobias Webb leads the way as Swansea's hottest prospect to become the first Swansea boxer to win the ultimate prize in professional boxing and become the undisputed champion of the World.

In his wake there are some great memories of Swansea boxers on an uphill struggle to achieve ring stardom or quite simply just to earn a crust.

Promoter Paul Boyce with former British and Commonwealth light heavyweight champion Eddie Avoth (left).

INDEX